Praise for

Domestic Extremist

"Yesterday's soccer mom is today's domestic extremist. Raising your own family is becoming a radical act of rebellion—one well worth committing, as Peachy Keenan brilliantly describes."
—**Tucker Carlson**, host, *Tucker Carlson Tonight*

"Reading Peachy Keenan's jeremiad against feminists and other 'clowns hell-bent on shredding whatever's left of the delicate fabric of our society,' one is tempted to describe the book as irreverent, witty, biting, and many other adjectives so overused and misapplied they're practically meaningless. But make no mistake, Mrs. Keenan's wit is biting the same way that particular species of pit vipers are biting—it's aggressive, appears in places where you least expect it, and it's frequently deadly."
—**Mollie Hemingway**, editor-in-chief of The Federalist, Fox News contributor, and author of the bestseller *Rigged: How the Media, Big Tech, and the Democrats Seized Our Elections*

"Peachy Keenan cuts through the madness of modern feminism and provides a bold, funny, and radical plan for retaking domesticity in the twenty-first century. This book is a challenge to women—and men—to recapture their dignity and reestablish the possibility of family bliss. Essential reading."
—**Christopher F. Rufo**, senior fellow, Manhattan Institute, and author of *America's Cultural Revolution: How the Radical Left Conquered Everything*

"In an age of absurdity, jokesters are the best truth-tellers. No one proves this more definitively than Peachy Keenan, whose very online wit conveys some very real-life genius. This is one of the year's most

exciting books by one of the country's most original writers."
    —**Spencer Klavan,** editor of The American Mind and author
    of *How to Save the West: Ancient Wisdom for 5 Modern Crises*

"Peachy Keenan has written a book for the ages—especially our Current Stupid Age. Her poison-tipped truths come at you fast, so you better learn to duck. This is a must-read manifesto and blueprint for how women (women!!) can take back the culture, and God help us all if we don't heed her words. Hilarious and sharp, Peachy knows her medicine goes down better with a spoonful of sugar. Take your medicine, America! You need it!"
    —**Bridget Phetasy,** writer, comedian, and host of the podcasts *Dumpster Fire* and *Walk-Ins Welcome*

"Peachy Keenan is a wickedly funny island of uncompromising conservatism in the fanatical heart of West Coast woke monoculture. If anyone has a handle on how to keep yourself sane and your kids un-brainwashed, it's her."
    —**Mary Harrington,** author of *Feminism Against Progress*

"The internet's favorite pseudonymous Gen X suburban wine mom turned based domestic queen has written the manual to escaping the dreary girlboss life cycle of our times. Written in Peachy Keenan's characteristic witty, laugh-out-loud style, *Domestic Extremist* is a book that shakes the moss off once-preachy political arguments against feminism and the blurring of the sexes, giving them new urgency and life. Most importantly, this book lays out how younger generations can make practical countercultural choices and build better, happier families and lives. This is a book mothers—at least those with a sense of humor—will be bequeathing to their daughters for generations to come."
    —**Inez Stepman,** senior policy analyst, Independent Women's Forum, and host of the podcast *High Noon*

"Peachy Keenan is the voice of the mother you never knew you needed. Unapologetic, hilarious, and supremely practical, *Domestic Extremist* is a manual for avoiding the void at the heart of modernity."

—**Alex Kaschuta,** writer and host of the podcast *Subversive*

"With her characteristic charm and brilliance, Peachy Keenan takes down feminist ideology in a way that no one else can. *Domestic Extremist* is both a delightful read and a devastating critique, but also woven throughout with the heart that comes from having seen its ravages up close. How I wish every young (and not-so-young) adult would read this."

—**Noelle Mering,** author of *Awake, Not Woke: A Christian Response to the Cult of Progressive Ideology*

"Put this book down and report yourself to federal law enforcement. Peachy Keenan is a dangerous woman with dangerous doctrines."

—**Ryan P. Williams,** president of the Claremont Institute and publisher of The American Mind and the *Claremont Review of Books*

DOMESTIC EXTREMIST

Domestic Extremist

A Practical Guide to Winning the Culture War

Peachy Keenan

Regnery Publishing
WASHINGTON, D.C.

Regnery® is a registered trademark and its colophon is a trademark of Salem Communications Holding Corporation

Cataloging-in-Publication data on file with the Library of Congress

ISBN: 978-1-68451-352-9
eISBN: 978-1-68451-431-1

Library of Congress Control Number: 2022950381

Published in the United States by
Regnery Publishing
A Division of Salem Media Group
Washington, D.C.
www.Regnery.com

Manufactured in the United States of America

10 9 8 7 6 5 4 3 2 1

Books are available in quantity for promotional or premium use. For information on discounts and terms, please visit our website: www.Regnery.com.

*To my darling husband, who made me the
domestic extremist I am today*

*To my children, who taught me everything I know about
infinite love and give me everything I need—including just
enough time to write*

And to my mother, whose shoes I will never be able to fill

Land Acknowledgment

This book was written on unceded stolen lands first settled by my ancient California ancestors, who came to the coast seeking better lives, mostly by way of the 10 freeway and LAX.

*Push back against the age as hard as it
pushes against you.*

— *Flannery O'Connor*

*A dead thing goes with the stream, but only
a living thing goes against it.*

— *G. K. Chesterton*

IN THIS HOUSE WE BELIEVE:

Parents Are the Bosses of Their Kids

Babies Are Good, More Babies Are Better

Dating Is for Suckers

Two Genders Are Plenty

Your Career Is Overrated

Feminism Is a Cope for the Unpopular
and Undateable

Mainstream American Culture Destroys Families

We Are Going to Win

CONTENTS

PART ONE
WHAT THEY TOOK FROM YOU

About the Title

My name is Peachy Keenan, and I am a domestic extremist. Unless you feel violently threatened by monogamous breeding pairs or large families, my use of the term "domestic extremist" has exactly zero to do with violence. You can call off the no-knock raid. Tell the guys at the CIA black site they won't have to prep my gulag cell. My waterboarding will have to wait.

A note to my CIA readers: if you must waterboard me, I prefer Fiji. Do *not* attempt to waterboard me with tap water or—*shudder*—Aquafina.

When I say, "domestic extremist," I am referring to someone who is extremely domestic, literally. The dictionary defines "domestic" as "of or relating to the home, the household, household affairs, or the family, devoted to home life or household affairs."

My fellow domestic extremists and I choose peace, love, and the radical—yes, extreme—rejection of the bleak lifestyle promoted by mainstream culture that is leading entire generations to rack and ruin.

Instead, we pursue (and achieve!) true and lasting happiness by embracing natural, organic, inborn domesticity. By elevating family, parenthood, and (trigger warning!) tradition. The word "tradition" scares some people, but I'm not talking about returning to the Middle Ages or the Colonial Era. We don't have to search that far back to recall a time when American culture wasn't this depraved. Forget the 1780s. I'll take the 1980s!

By becoming just a bit more domestic, we can develop immunity from progressive social engineering—and pass this precious gift on to our (many) descendants. We will recklessly, even wantonly, flout societal scolds and community commissars. Once you experience the thrill of our quiet domestic rebellion (and see how much it enrages progressive harpies), you may be hooked for life.

At least, I hope so. Because America needs more domestic extremists, badly: men and women guided by forgotten ways and beliefs handed down over generations—or perhaps discovered anew in times of darkness.

Guess what? You already know what to do! To become a domestic extremist, all you must do is listen closely for the ancestral longings that lurk in the heart of every human being. As you listen, dormant instincts may rouse themselves from slumber. Pay attention to them—they will lead you out of the barren wasteland that stretches before us!

Good news: you don't need to own a ranch, live on a farm, or bake cookies wearing high heels and pearls to become domestically extreme. Instead, you will simply begin to make choices, large and small, that come not from without, but from deep within.

You will be able to construct impermeable, invisible defenses around your soul that protect it from our broken culture. You will happily reject the Current Era and all its poison. You will reclaim authority over your life—and your children. Too much of our parental authority has been handed over blindly to a culture that many of us don't recognize and most of us want little to do with. Let's kiss it goodbye for good.

You can become a domestic extremist in any setting: city, suburb, or countryside. You don't need any special equipment, clothing, or books (except this one, and . . . maybe one other).

Becoming a domestic extremist is so simple you can start this second! All you have to do is choose to live again in a way that, *within recent memory*, was considered "normal."

WE didn't become the extremists—THEY did.

Remember "normal"? Why did *being normal* get canceled? Becoming a domestic extremist requires reclaiming normalness as a way of life—as the only way of life that can ensure your family's survival through these dark times.

From the outside, I look extremely normal (well, for a writer). Looking and acting normal is my gender identity. Of course, being "normal" these days makes me a dangerous lunatic compared to most American women my age. Almost like I'm some sort of . . . domestic extremist!

In fact, if you compare me to my ultra-woke college classmates and former corporate colleagues (who were the only type of people I knew for the first few decades of my life), I am a *hardcore* domestic extremist.

Here is what makes me so normal—I mean, so extreme: I am in a monogamous marriage, and I intend to stick with it until death do us part. My husband and I had more than four children together. I stayed home to nurse and raise our babies. We rejected local Marxist public schools for a combination of homeschooling and classical parochial schools. Every person in our household remains the gender they were assigned at conception. The only flag we fly on our home has fifty stars and thirteen stripes. We are trying our best to instill normal (or what was considered normal a few years ago) American values in our kids. We hope they marry young and produce a lot of grandchildren for us to dandle on our arthritic knees one day.

Wake up, CIA reader! You might want to write this one down: we even . . . *believe in God.*

Frankly, I'm surprised I haven't been rounded up yet.

These simple lifestyle choices, and not who I vote for or what my grubby politics are, have forever set me apart from my former peers—and from mainstream American society. My husband and I ran off the edge of that cliff a while ago. We are still blinking into the camera like Wile E. Coyote, realizing we are no longer on solid ground.

There are no people like us on TV or in movies—unless they're getting mocked for their hopeless provincialism and backward mores. In my resolute normalness, I am a fringe weirdo upon whom the Regime's ideological brainwashing didn't quite take.

The social scientists who tried and failed to reeducate me must be big mad. They're smashing the beakers in the lab and pounding their fists on the Bunsen burners. "Vhy didn't ze indoctrination verk on her!? She vatched *Sesame Street*, she drank Coke, she liked her MTV, she even went to ze Ivy League! How did Frau Keenan escape ze mind virus?"

Folks, I don't know how I made it past their gauntlet. I have no idea how I *remained normal*, despite our culture's best efforts. Sorry, culture: you failed!

The funny thing is, I am not that classically "domestic." I don't love to cook, I bake with Duncan Hines, and I loathe doing laundry. I claim no special skill with the sewing needle, the knitting needle, or the glue gun. I have never crocheted anything, or darned a sock, or touched a loom. I don't skip through fields in gauzy prairie dresses. I have never practiced animal husbandry or interacted with a live cow. I prefer *not* to spend any time around barnyard animals, thank you very much. As Woody Allen said, "I'm two with nature."

I've spent my entire life in big cities where tending plants is something the gardener does. While I have the deepest respect for country life, and more than a little envy of those who enjoy that lifestyle, it's too late for me to learn how to milk goats. (You're welcome, goats.) I have accepted my limitations, and I hope you will, too.

For better or worse, I was raised as a fairly spoiled, totally secular, suburban American princess, and, outwardly at least, I haven't changed *that* much.

Nevertheless, my character arc is long—and it bends inexorably towards domestic extremism.

When I finally got around to having a family of my own, I took refuge among a legit community of authentic domestic extremists. These are people you might pass on the street—*just walking around like regular people.* You would never know how domestically extreme some of them are behind closed doors—unless you spot them driving around in their giant family vans. Because I have fewer than eight children, I am something of a lightweight. "How many kids do you have? You gotta get those numbers up—those are rookie numbers!"

A friend my age recently welcomed her twelfth baby. (That's a one followed by eleven more.) I mistakenly asked her if the new baby was number thirteen. "Thirteen! Come on, that's crazy!" she laughed.

Compared to these families, the ones who will end up ruling the world with billions of descendants, I am practically childless. It's not my fault; I spent way too long among the heathens and got started on my domestic extremist career a little late. I'm lucky I managed to squeeze out (so to speak) my own moderately large family!

I even went beyond the simple acts of getting married, staying married, and having lots of kids. I did some things you are *absolutely not* allowed to do in my former social circles. Trigger warning: I refused to hire strangers to raise my kids for me. We made hard sacrifices to avoid sending kids to toddler jailcare—an unforgivable transgression, and I regret nothing.

My final burn-the-ships, cross-the-Rubicon moment was the day I converted from secular atheism to Catholicism, officially reversing my long-held feminist positions on abortion, premarital sex, birth control, and more.

The old Peachy was dead. Long live the new, domestically extreme Peachy!

And to my CIA reader, whoever you are: call me. I can fix you.

Quiz:

Are You a Domestic Extremist?

Do you put the well-being of your family and household first, ahead of amorphous euphemisms like "society" and "your community"? Do you tend to make life choices that resist social trends, contagions, and pressures? Are you a little *too* comfortable with nonconformity?

Let's find out if you've got what it takes to join our noncompliance team! For each statement you agree with, give yourself 1 point:

- ❏ I am married or would like to be
- ❏ I want/have at least three children
- ❏ I want/have four or more children
- ❏ I/my wife stays home with our baby, or I wish I/she could
- ❏ I believe parents are a child's primary authority and educators
- ❏ Kids generally do best when raised by their married mother and father
- ❏ I wouldn't trust the average politician or "childcare expert" to walk my dog
- ❏ We try to attend religious services as a family
- ❏ Life begins at conception
- ❏ Children can't choose their gender
- ❏ "Sex education" should be left up to parents and not taught to elementary school–age kids

❏ Promiscuity, pornography, and abortion are not conducive to long-term human happiness

Score Yourself:

1–3: Yikes, you might be a domestic extremist.

4–7: Warning, you are *definitely* a domestic extremist.

8–10: Red alert: you are a dangerous domestic extremist and should expect a knock on your door by a government official shortly.

11–12: Buh-bye, have fun in the gulags!

Oh, you didn't check any boxes? Wipe that smug smile off your face, pal. Because you are not gonna make it.

Why This Book

In times of still greater danger the salvific power must be sought deeper, in the mothers. This contact liberates primal forces, to which the mere powers of time cannot stand up.

— *Ernst Jünger,* The Forest Passage

Reclaim Your Identity, Your Family, and Your Country—by Becoming More Domestic

The first step when fighting a culture war is to accept that you're in a culture war. Perhaps you've noticed. Or perhaps, like some, you pretend not to. Hate to be the bearer of bad news, but it's true: we are in a hot culture war, and it's only getting hotter. It's not a *real* war—at least not yet. Real war is hell, and I am anti-war. I have no interest in learning to fire a weapon; that's what my husband is for.

But a *culture* war? That's a little easier. There are no messy entrails to mop up, no blood splatters on your shoes, and victory tastes just as sweet.

But the only way to win is to get busy fighting back. And make no mistake: we're going to win, folks. However, our total, totally peaceful victory is only possible if all of you reject our present-day, literally pox-ridden excuse for a culture.

And by *all*, I'm looking at *you*, ladies.

I wrote this book as a rallying cry and a morale booster for normal people who find themselves stuck in foxholes, under attack from incoming cultural shrapnel, shocked and appalled by the status quo. Every time I open up Twitter, I feel like Charlton Heston at the end of *Planet of the Apes* when he realizes mankind has destroyed itself. "You finally, really did it. You maniacs!"

The good news is that the battle has finally been joined. The Normal People's Rebellion is on like Donkey Kong. It kicked off in the last few years with the explosive rise of parent activists: the Battle Moms of the Republic. These brave mothers—and fathers—are fighting to wrest back control of their children's schools from the imbecilic and authoritarian school boards that dominate their lives. Masks, vaccines, pornographic books in school libraries, boys in girls' locker rooms, and more: these parents said, "Enough!"

How do we know things are changing for the better? Because the United States government called those parents "domestic terrorists."[1] That means they are right over the target—and are a clear and present threat to the powers that be.

The tide is beginning to turn, and now is not the time to go wobbly. Now is the time for all good men and women to come to the aid of their country. How? By becoming ever so slightly more *domestic*—to become domestic extremists, if you will.

Mothers and fathers, regular American families, men and women, can win this battle together. But quite a lot of ground has been lost. For decades, we stood around and watched as feminism and progressive policies steamrolled through our institutions—formerly robust, now comically inept entities like our military, our government, our education system, and our economy—leading to profound national weakness at home and abroad, with life-and-death implications.

But our national weakness is not confined to just the big institutions. The rot has taken hold in all of us, in our families and our friends. Young men and women are unable to proceed to the next stage of adulthood. Women are choosing childlessness to "save the climate" or their career. Couples are unable to build families. Children are growing up confused and vulnerable to poisonous ideologies. An entire generation is failing to launch. "Adulting" is going extinct.

Many have simply surrendered to the faceless overlords who wish to control our destinies, the fates of our families, our children's minds, and our bodies—while offering nothing but the cultural, moral, and spiritual equivalent of abortifacients.

I wrote this book as an antidote to what ails us. In it, I will make the case that *only* domestic extremism can save you and your family—and the country, and indeed, our entire civilization—from our collective nosedive. Because America is in free fall, and everyone knows it. What is the root cause of this disaster? What has befallen us? The answer is clear. It's not mass immigration, unbridled wokeness, or disastrous foreign policy (though all of that sped our descent). The answer is: women have lost their way. The science is settled: feminism, and all its works, and all its empty promises, has nearly erased the God-given point and purpose of *being female*. And when you do that, things tend to go sideways.

This was the first domino to fall, and the shockwaves are now on the verge of toppling the greatest country on Earth. Girls have forgotten how to be fully female and have rejected "femininity." Genitals and reproductive organs no longer matter. Mothers have surrendered their children to degenerate cultural influences. Parents have been replaced by the State. "Equality" has emasculated our boys. Our institutions have been overthrown, slowly and then overnight, feminized into submission, and permanently, irreversibly sterilized. Our very survival as a nation—as a species even—hangs in the balance.

But fear not—there is hope!

Imagine if, instead of gleefully gorging on the moldy bread and grotesque circuses sold by our clownish elites, we began orienting ourselves around more "domestic" values. These are stronger bonds that cannot so easily be torn asunder by the miserable morons and spinster cat moms who nip at our ankles and eye our joy enviously.

With apologies to race hustler Ibram X. Kendi, author of bestselling hate books like *How to Be an Anti-Racist* and *Anti-Racist Baby*, it is not enough to *not* be a feminist. We must become anti-feminists. We must raise anti-feminist babies. How? By becoming—you guessed it—domestically extreme.

Practically, this means totally and completely rejecting mainstream culture's ideal version of being female. By choosing to keep your baby. By having another baby, and maybe a third for good measure. By staying home with your very young children. By rejecting the myth of "toxic masculinity" and celebrating men as heroes and protectors. By getting married young and staying married. And crucially: by avoiding emotional enslavement to destructive contemporary ideas and influences, in all their forms. "Hide your kids, hide your wife!"

The empty promises of "girl power" and "female empowerment" have led directly to the creation of today's oppressive dystopia, which deforms every aspect of our culture. This, in turn, has produced a soft, weak, shrill culture that is about to be flown straight into Mount Doom by the deranged eunuchs and unhinged harpies locked inside the cockpit.

Even worse: these maniacs had a fifty-year head start. We must, therefore, take the culture fight to them, this second, if we hope to reclaim our country, our children, and our latent, hidden power levels as American women.

We will claim victory peacefully. We will extinguish their ideas elegantly; we will dismantle their dictates with decorum. We will grind their gruesome ideologies to dust gracefully. We will take prisoners and claim scalps, but not a hair on their shrunken heads will be harmed.

Yes, we may enrage our enemies, and outnumber them, and outvote them, and condemn them to a life of abject contrition, but we will do so by simply and totally *rejecting* them—and every single thing they stand for.

Good news: I happen to have the antidote to the cultural poison you're choking on right here in my pocket—and so do you.

The solution to this existential crisis is right in front of you.

In fact, it IS you.

The cure to the American cultural malaise is not what you think—I'm not asking you to take up survivalism or homesteading. Not that there's anything wrong with that!

I'm not asking you to loom your own fabric or spin your own wool. We have people to do that for us these days!

Instead, all you must do is *remain authentically female*, as in, the timeless ways of being female: as a daughter, mother, and wife. To "lean in" to the very essence of your being by making sea changes in your mindset and approach to life. To become a little bit more "domestic," as females have been since the very dawn of time.

It also means turning away from the diseased offerings of the elites, the media, Hollywood, your child's school, and Big Tech, and towards a more human lifestyle. This is a lifestyle that will reorient you away from the broken culture and towards a family, your home, and your best chance at true, lasting happiness. The life-changing magic of domestic extremism will spark joy—and help you create a legacy that outlasts you.

Winning is not even going to be hard! We can *easily* win the culture war—by simply *exiting* their culture and creating our own. By becoming bulletproof. By immunizing ourselves and our children from dangerously dumb ideologies.

We can do this. We *must* do this.

The aim of this book is to help you build a firewall around your mind, your soul, and—if you manage to make one—your family. Because they want your children, and they're coming for them. For some of you, your children—or at least, their minds—have already been taken, and you may not even know it yet.

They want you childless, lonely, and dependent on them for love, support, and an income. They want to keep you comfortable and compliant as they extract and mine your valuable resources—your labor, your loyal votes, your eggs, your taxes, your blind obedience—and then euthanize you, drained, impoverished, and spent, as you succumb to a lifetime of broken promises and despair.

If you do manage to eke out a marriage and a kid or two, that's great, but it's not going to be enough of a buffer. Your unreinforced family is fragile; you're living in a house made of straw. The big bad wolves who run our lives are going to blow it down. You need to harden your perimeter immediately.

If they fail to keep you single and sterile, never fear. You will simply fall into the next Great Filter: public school indoctrination of your children, who will be taught to hate you, to love their other masters, and to become single and sterile themselves. If you and your children somehow manage to swim through all their nets, stubbornly resistant to these plans for you—well, they have ways of making you comply.

They may resort to calling you racist and sexist, a white supremacist, a conspiracy theorist, even a terrorist. You may risk cancellation or worse. You don't agree that aborting healthy, full-term babies is health care? You hate women and want them to die. You don't think schools should encourage eight-year-olds to change their genders in secret, without the parents' knowledge or consent? You are a bigot, a transphobe, and a conversion therapist. You have a problem with toddlers slipping dollar bills into the G-strings of nude men with large, exposed fake breasts at X-rated burlesque shows (yes, this really happens)?[2] Into the gulags you go!

The best part is, becoming a truly authentic female turns you into a deadly weapon against the Regime. Your very existence will become a sharpened dagger through the obsidian hearts of the wicked supervillains who wish to pervert your female identity, sever your bond with your children, emasculate your husband, sterilize your loins, and destroy your ability to experience joy.

Are you even *ready* for this superpower?

Other women got us into this mess. It's up to us to dig everyone out of it.

With help from a few good men, of course. We're going to need as many non-gelded, virile, intact American males as we can find.

I just hope there are enough of you left.

A final note: giving people recommendations and advice on how to live their lives is a little dangerous. It provokes some to shout, "People in glass houses shouldn't throw stones!"

I can assure you, my glass house was shattered into a thousand pieces long ago. I have since carefully rebuilt it out of much stronger stuff.

PART ONE

WHAT THEY TOOK FROM YOU

Answer: Almost Everything

Those who can make you believe absurdities can make you commit atrocities.

— *Voltaire*

Masculine republics give way to feminine democracies, and feminine democracies give way to tyranny.

— *Aristotle*

Aborting American Society

A better question might be: what haven't they taken from you? At least, that's what it feels like these days. American families have been strip-mined, plundered, and debrided of healthy tissue, that essential primordial ooze from which happy parents and children spring. Americans have been forced to soak in sterilizing solvent—liberal feminism, K–12 school indoctrination, toxic social media, and four years at woke finishing schools formerly known as "college." How could anyone escape with their morals, identity, and mind intact? Many don't.

Some manage to make it through the gauntlet intact, but their children aren't so lucky; their budding hopes and dreams are blown apart or mangled by landmines buried in the ground. These landmines

3

include infinite-horizon dating, the abortion industry complex, the failure to marry or stay married, unwanted childlessness, careerism, opioid addiction, pornography, "finding yourself," and the temptation to sell your eggs, your sexuality, your identity, and your soul to the highest bidder—among many others.

All that's left is a cohort of young people unable to form meaningful relationships, raise children, and otherwise perpetuate the species into the future. Loneliness, depression, drug abuse, infertility, and generalized despair have taken hold.

As of this writing, abortion is banned to various degrees in twenty-six states. But even if it was banned nationwide, this wouldn't magically transform young men and women into capable parents prepared to embrace the sacrificial love parenthood requires. For *that* to happen, we need more people to commit to a lifestyle that is not always the easiest choice: a lifestyle that will bear the most fruit *only after you are dead*. A lifestyle that may bring you little social media glory—and will make you a social pariah in certain zip codes.

The hour grows late. We are facing an extinction-level event as a species. The *Wall Street Journal* reported that "the total fertility rate—a snapshot of the average number of babies a woman would have over her lifetime—has fallen to 1.64. That is the lowest rate on record since the government began tracking it in the 1930s."[1] The replacement rate is 2.1, and that snapshot was taken before the 2020 pandemic and subsequent economic recession fully took hold.

Civilization, our greatest human achievement, has led us directly to sterilization. Our supply chain of newborns is caught in a tremendous bottleneck. Demand has dried up. We can no longer produce enough raw material to keep the cribs full. Alarms are going off on the ship. The loudspeaker is intoning, "T minus thirty seconds until self-destruction."

We have no time to lose!

But Wait: Who Is "They"?

It's easy to blame everything on our favorite supervillains, the ones we all love to loathe: child-hating feminists, spittle-flecked progressive politicians, and twisted college professors who invented "studies" departments (Women's Studies, Gender Studies, Transgender Indigenous Disabled Asexual Vegan Studies, and so forth).

But what if . . . they're simply the useful idiots who greased the skids for this all-out assault on our identities, our families, the American Dream, our traditions, and our children? Who else could be scheming to seduce young women and mothers into choices that do not lead to happiness, and only create more dysfunction and misery in the world? I have a few ideas.

Author Carrie Gress lays out one theory of who is behind the push to decadence in her book *The Anti-Mary Exposed*. In it, she makes the Catholic case that the power at work here is the female equivalent of the "anti-Christ," a malevolent demonic presence tempting women away from their most crucial job: keeping humanity going. I'm no theologian, and this is not a religious book, but the case could certainly be made that real evil has taken hold in some hearts in this barren modern age.

Here's a non-supernatural theory: when I say "they" in this book, I am referring to the pantsuited girlboss petty tyrants who do, in fact, run the world, as Beyoncé promised they would. That's what the modern female careerists are carefully groomed to do: run the world—and hire servants to run their households. They, along with their mentally castrated male enablers, are running it right into ruin. (Some of these petty tyrants are former men, but I digress.)

Certain factions on the right call this oppressive institutional ethos "the Longhouse," after the neolithic thatch dwellings in early human settlements that were controlled by overbearing matriarchs who crushed the men's warrior spirit and kept an iron grip on young women. But the enemies arrayed against us are not restricted to feminist career girls. We should be so lucky. We are up against a short bus full of scary clowns hell-bent on shredding what's left of the delicate fabric of our society. Whatever demonic forces may be at work, we are now left to contend with a truly toxic witch's brew of human foes that goes far beyond the wildest dreams of the early feminists.

They pretend their plan to destroy the family is a right-wing conspiracy theory, only they have been saying it—out loud—in academic circles for years.[2] In the last two decades, this "fringe" Marxist idea to quash the nuclear family, erase the middle class, and take control of children to form them into pure revolutionaries has been hijacked and swallowed whole by even more powerful, largely invisible villains.

These are the New World Order globalists, the "you'll own nothing and you'll be happy" sociopaths who control everything from the World Economic Forum to most Western governments, Big Tech, Big Media, the wine aunt hive mind, teachers' unions, the media, Hollywood, celebrity culture, think tanks, institutes, climate change radicals, NGOs, Planned Parenthood, the woke velvet mafia in charge of the Catholic Church, the global monetary system, Wall Street, Big Tech, Big Pharma, Big Gender (that is, the all-powerful LGBTQ+ lobby), D.C., and the entire American educational system from pre-K to grad school.

I haven't even gotten to our politicians. The forests would run out of trees if I tried to list on paper all the nasty women (and men) who hold public office.

What does this vibrant and diverse group want?

They want you, my dear. Alone, defenseless, huddled in the dark, unable to phone a friend or ask the audience for a lifeline, awaiting the salvation only they, with their infinite powers, can grant you.

Warning: if you are a mother, any children you managed to produce are their favorite delicacy. Children are their prey and their prize. But to get to them, first they had to bulldoze through a wall of masculine protectors, dismantle your God-given maternal authority, and strip you of your agency. Mission accomplished!

All that's left is a consumer data point to be mined and monetized, converted into votes when required, silenced at will, and euthanized when no longer of value. Sayonara, suckers!

Industrial-Scale Grooming

Our supervillains are not motivated by dusty, old-fashioned progressive ideas like radical feminism or racial "equity," although they claim to care about them. Instead, our elites realized a few decades ago that long-hairs, hippies, boomer feminists burning their bras, abortion activists throwing fake blood on politicians, shouting BLM race-baiters, Antifa skinnies, and other freakish militants, while annoying, would be *quite* helpful to their cause. Ideological fanatics make perfect mindless foot soldiers! The elites poured money into these various groups—and captured all the media to help promote them.

Oh, you want some proof, Ms. Factchecker? You want to see some *documentation*? Just look around. How else could a massive army of angry, pussy hat–wearing, #MeToo wine aunts all find cat sitters and descend on D.C. in the buttcold at 2017's Women's March? How else did they shoehorn shrieking women in Handmaids costumes into every senator's office to protest the Kavanaugh hearings? How else could you orchestrate simultaneous looting and burning campaigns nationwide in the summer of 2020? The dogma lives loudly in them, and the checks mailed from the Cayman Islands P.O. Boxes always clear the bank. (I don't actually know where the checks come from, but let's go with it.)

Author James Poulos calls this groupthink "mental terraforming,"[3] and it's hard to escape it, no matter where you and your kids hide. Philosopher Curtis Yarvin famously refers to this elite narrative control as "the Cathedral": "At one and the same time, the Cathedral is simply a name for the uncanny degree of agreement between the media, universities, and other organs of elite culture, and a theory explaining how the aggregate effect of that agreement is a system of Orwellian mind-control that projects an illusion of freedom so powerful it blinds people to reality."[4]

This force is corporatized, industrial-strength mental grooming on a mass scale. Not just grooming in the old sense of preparing innocent children for sexual abuse. I mean grooming for compliance. For obedience. For unquestioning acceptance of the Current Thing—whatever it is.

"Shut up and eat your bugs!" as Tucker Carlson put it.[5]

This includes mainstream consensus on abortion, pointless foreign wars, putting little kids on puberty blockers, putting men on women's sports teams, the idea that teachers are more qualified than parents to decide how to raise your child, that climate change is going to kill us all in five years, and so on. Once they can get you to go along with these ideas, they can get you to do . . . well, anything.

Now, forgive me for stepping into what you might consider no-go conspiracy theory territory, but it sure seems like the bloodless, sterile behemoths running the country want to seize control of our families, our minds, and our bodies so completely that we have no choice but to surrender to their openly stated goal: a zero-emission, zero-child, zero-family, infinitely gendered Uniglobe.

You, of course, get to be one of the pod people powering the paradise they enjoy far from where you toil.

Submit to being groomed—or get the broom.

Your survival depends on accepting these stakes and taking action to change your lifestyle so that you are impervious to their predations. You must adopt a lifestyle that makes you and your children ungroomable. You must reject their plans for you absolutely, non-violently, and peacefully, with love for God and our fellow man. (We must always love our enemies and pray for their conversion, no matter how they torment us. Most will face eternal torment eventually.)

But reject it you must. Your grandchildren—if you get any—are counting on you.

The next time one of their humanoid bots accuses you or a politician you support of being a "racist" or a "sexist" or a "bigot," understand that they have been programmed to parrot these words, without knowing why or what they mean. They are simply obeying their master's programming. In response, you should laugh and ask, "I know you are, but what am I?" over and over until they short circuit and smoke pours out of their ears.

None of these attacks are real, and none of them have anything to do with what you think or who you are, so you are free to ignore them totally.

The punches don't hurt if you know when to duck!

This Sounds Like an Unwinnable Battle. How Can We Possibly Win?

It's true. Sadly, there is *almost* no way to defeat the immense forces deployed against us, against tradition, against parents and children, and against the nearly dead American Dream. And it is almost too late. The army of craven villains is virtually omnipotent, omnipresent, and omniscient. They track your every move via your phone, monitor your Facebook posts, and put you on Government Enemy Lists if you do dangerous things like offer a contrary opinion at the local school board meeting.

But note: I said "almost." Because I have wonderful news for you: there IS a way to fight back, wage total war against them, and win. Yes, *win*. The path to victory is clear, and all of us can take it, starting this minute. Best of all, my strategy is 100 percent nonviolent and requires just a few basic tools *you already possess*.

It is also completely free (minus the price you paid for this book, of course).

Here is my plan: if I can convince just a few more of you to become ever so slightly more domestic, we will win. Living a more domestically extreme lifestyle will carry you and your family safely over the gaping abyss!

It's that simple. I promise.

In Part One, we will review the shrapnel damage to our hull. Warning: the damage is extensive. Brace yourself. We will examine all that has been taken—and the world we thought we were inheriting. The liquidation of the Kulaks never ended, it just changed forms. We will speed run through the main spoils of feminism and review all they stole from us.

In Part Two, we will learn anew how to reclaim what is ours. There is no time to lose, so let's begin!

Chapter I

Your Fleeting Fertility

Extinction Event Incoming

Sic transit gloria. Glory fades.

— Max Fischer, Rushmore

If people don't have more children, civilization is going to crumble. Mark my words.

— Elon Musk, car salesman and father of nine

What They Took:

☑ **Your Fleeting Fertility**

Committing Estro-Genocide

The first item on the list of priceless human artifacts that have disappeared is natural female fertility. American fertility rates used to be the pride of the nation. We kept outbreeding other so-called first world countries, like France and Germany, which cratered to below-replacement levels long ago.

No more. We've finally sunk as low as the Europeans. Maybe you've noticed the average age of the graying mothers at the local playground. Or the rampant childlessness among the smart set. There are so many missing never-born children that their faces may soon start appearing on the backs of milk cartons.

Jill Filipovic is an attractive, glossy-haired American journalist with an illustrious résumé. A contributor to fake news giants the *New York Times* and CNN, she appears in unreadable feminist anthologies like *Nasty Women: Feminism, Resistance, and Revolution in Trump's America*. She's the type who cleans up at journalist award shows for "reproductive health reporting."

She is the Extinction Event Planner of feminists. Jill smiles as she tells the caterers where to put banquet tables for guests who will never be born.

You will be shocked to learn she lives in Brooklyn. It's not her fault—if you are a famous feminist with at least two bylines in *Cosmopolitan* or Bustle, it's the law. I'm frankly grateful to Mx. Filipovic for providing me with so much fodder. My mother clips her articles for me, and we have a good laugh, so I thank her for bringing us closer together. One of Jill's opinion pieces that caught my mother's eye was titled "The Birthrate Is Falling? That's Not Bad." Did an AI write that unintentionally hilarious headline?

In her essay, Filipovic works hard to celebrate this hypothetical as a success story: "The 24-year-old who says she wants children someday but is focusing on her career can easily turn into the 30-year-old who says she wants children but with the right partner. Later, she can easily become the 45-year-old who has a meaningful career . . . and a life rich in pleasure and novelty that she doesn't want to surrender."

A life rich in pleasure and novelty? Okay, I guess that's one way to describe a life spent robotically swiping right on younger and younger men. Hard to be a MILF without the M, though. Or is "pleasure and novelty" a setting on the high-tech male sex robots Amazon is surely launching soon? Filipovic doesn't know this, but her feminist hypothetical is not a fairy tale—it's a cautionary tale.

"Growing numbers of young women have opportunities to travel, live independently, pursue a career, and simply spend many more years of their adult lives asking themselves who they are and what they want, instead of being slotted, early, into a narrow set of gendered expectations."[1] *Live, Laugh, Loveless: A Memoir.*

Encouraging young women to spend their fertile years trying to figure out "who they are" is terrible advice. No one will know or care who you were when you die alone, girls. Jill the Pied Piper needs to put the pipe down.

The total fertility rate in the U.S. went down from a fairly robust 2.12 in 2007 to an anemic 1.64 in 2020.[2] Remember, the minimum viable replacement rate is 2.1 kids per woman, which gets you just enough people to outweigh the number we lose naturally. "Over 38% of households have at least one dog. [Only] 30% of households have at least one child."[3] The replacement rate is now too low to sustain the population in every Western country, and it's dropping fast everywhere. By 2100, the fertility rate of nearly every nation on Earth is projected to fall below the replacement rate, even below 1.5 children per woman.[4]

Why is it happening? Microplastics? Pollution? Lower sperm counts? Wearing tight pants? "It has nothing to do with sperm counts or the usual things that come to mind when discussing fertility. Instead, it is being driven by more women in education and work, as well as greater access to contraception, leading to women choosing to have fewer children."[5] If the history books told the truth, feminism would beat out Mao, Stalin, and Hitler as the most successful genocider.

Fanatics like Jill Filipovic are girlbossing themselves straight into swift genetic suicide, and they're taking all of us down with them. Her powers have grown so great that she has transcended labels like "wine aunt" and "girl boss." She now bestrides the Earth as the Final Wine Boss.

A terrifying 2020 study in *The Lancet* projects that the global number of children under five will fall from 681 million in 2017 to just 401 million by 2100. Meanwhile, the number of people over eighty will increase from 141 million in 2017 to *866 million* by 2100. Social Security and Medicare solvency? That's so 1990. Brace yourself, Grandpa!

The study concludes with this:

> Our findings suggest that continued trends in female educational attainment and access to contraception will hasten declines in fertility and slow population growth. A sustained TFR [total fertility rate, or the average number of children a woman will have] lower than the replacement level in many countries, including China and India, would have economic, social, environmental, and geopolitical consequences. Policy options to adapt to continued low fertility, while sustaining and enhancing female reproductive health, will be crucial in the years to come.[6]

The study was funded by the Bill & Melinda Gates Foundation, where it was probably received with cheers. No wonder Bill is buying up American farmland: one might suspect he knows we're going to need thousands of acres of packed graveyards that no one will ever visit.

In the United States, things are just as dire. "Birth certificate data for 2020 show wide-ranging declines in childbearing in the United States. . . . [B]irth rates fell among women of all age groups from age 15 to 44; the decline in the birth rate for women aged 40 to 44 was the first since 1981." The Census Bureau estimated that "the U.S. population grew by just 0.1% in the year ended July 1, 2021, the lowest rate since the founding of the nation."[7] In other words, the last time the population growth rate was this low was . . . never. It's never been this low.

Turns out that telling girls to delay motherhood in favor of work may have some extremely unpleasant side effects.

But don't worry, it's probably nothing.

Involuntarily Child-Free

I concede that not *everyone* needs to have kids. Most of the people on the kid-free diet are dug in too deep to be helped. They are well beyond even my power to rebuild them into plausible maternal figures. Enjoy the cats, have fun Instagramming your vacations, Godspeed. You, your genes, everything you ever did, and everything you ever were will vanish like a fart in the wind, and there's nothing I can do to help you avoid that tragic fate.

The corollary is this: everyone who *does* feel that tug on their heart must listen to it. Do not ignore the voice calling you to become a parent! I am saving you a load of deathbed regret here. Just look at the heartbreaking results of this Pew Research survey from 2021 indicating that many people want children but can't make it happen:

"A growing share of childless Americans say it is unlikely they will ever have children. Some 44% of non-parents ages 18 to 49 say it is not too or not at all likely that they will have children someday, an increase from the 37% who said the same in 2018." Of the 44 percent who say they probably won't have children, 56 percent of them say it's because they don't want to. But almost 30 percent said it was because of financial reasons or not having a partner. In other words, they *wanted* kids but couldn't make it happen.[8]

Someone should start a dating service so this 30 percent of adults who want children can pool their resources and start getting busy!

This is a real crisis eating away at the fleeting fertility of young women—and men. The inability of young-ish Americans to build financial security is a key reason they aren't reproducing. Dating apps and porn are cheap and immediate, and kids cost money, so the urgency of waning fertility dissipates. The death of despair is real, only it's not just the adults' death; it is the death of future generations who die with them.

What would it take to trigger a massive baby boom? Certainly not what the U.S. government has been doing. In fact, every law they pass and every policy they promote only makes it harder to raise children. It's family unfriendliness all the way down. Why, it's almost as if the nattering nabobs of anti-natalism at the top *want* to keep you from having the children you desperately crave.

I'm not saying they're doing it on purpose . . . it just seems *exactly* like they're doing it on purpose. "Just drive an electric car to save money!" (They know perfectly well there are no electric minivans.) "Just take the bus!" (Sure, with a toddler, a double stroller, a newborn, and all your Costco shopping.) "Just ride a bike!" Just bite me, how about that? Walkable neighborhoods, pedestrian-only streets, bike lanes, and more unusable public transportation are obstacles to creating big families. You can't fit five kids on a bike or in a tiny electric car. You can't walk home with more than a single bag of groceries. You can't commute to and from school and your errands via the Homeless Lunatic Local subway. They know this, which is why we're going to be getting a lot more of these family-unfriendly options.

Our childless overlords who hope to usher in a magical fossil-fuel-free future are convinced that every child born is a massive, unsustainable waste of nonrenewable energy. Don't even get them started on diapers.

It turns out that the climate they wish to change most of all is the *economic* climate that allows large families to feed themselves.

The big question remains: can we *actually* breed our way out of American population collapse? Why not? If every young family had just one extra kid, that would add up to—sorry, I'm bad at math—a lot more kids! Each new child we produce represents one more cork in the leaky lifeboat ferrying us into the future. Every baby is a promise that maybe we can make it to shore after all! The longer you wait to get started, the lower your boat sinks in the water.

Why would you let people who hate you tell you how many kids you get to have? Think about it: the same people who hate children, loathe cisgendered heterosexuals, and despise the traditional American family are the very same people telling you not to have kids. Why would you *ever* listen to them?

I wonder, what could be their motive? The climate? Or is that the smokescreen they're using to shrink the size of the next generation?

Meanwhile, your life and your waning fertility slip away! The most unsustainable, nonrenewable energy is your own body's fertility. Squander it, and it's gone forever. Like sand through the hourglass, so are the days of your ovaries. But don't worry, Bill Gates owns almost three hundred thousand acres of arable land in the United States.[9] Plenty of room for the mass graveyards of the future beyond the Gates of Hell. (We all know he isn't going to bother growing food to feed us.)

Female Youth Matters

The inconvenient truth of human fertility is that it fades, just like youth and beauty and my husband's fancy dress socks I accidentally bleached. *Sic transit gloria*, ladies. Fertility evaporates even faster than the rest of you, in fact. A woman's twenties are prime baby time, and it's all downhill from there. One of the first things they stripped from us was this primitive, ancient truth. For decades, academics and the media have been chipping away at this hard biological rule. You probably have read article after article about the "myth" of the bio-logical clock, and have seen glowing stories in the news of women "having it all" by having their first baby in their fifties. Go ahead—ask any Beverly Hills fertility doctor driving a $400,000 car if women tend to struggle to get pregnant after a certain age.

This is the big secret you are not allowed to discuss in polite society. You are forbidden from telling young women this inconvenient truth. The last thing you want to do is encourage them to start early! Feminists dismiss the fertility decline as "outdated science" and boast about the "reproductive technologies" that will make you pregnant into your eighties, even your nineties one day! There's nothing science can't do!

If you argue, they get very upset and accuse of you wanting to turn young women into sex slaves from *The Handmaid's Tale*. (After a close reading of *The Handmaid's Tale*, I have concluded it is a thirst trap for sexually frustrated women who fantasize about virile authoritarian men having their way with them. They should have called it *Fifty Shades of Scarlet*.)

What these ladies don't know is that they *already* live like the sex slaves in *The Handmaid's Tale*. They may not wear the red robes, but their sexual slavery has simply been rebranded "sex positivity" and "planned parenthood."

The myth that you can easily get pregnant any time you want, whenever you're ready, is reinforced by aging celebrities having babies in their late thirties and forties. What the Instagram stories don't reveal is that many of these celebrities have undergone intensive IVF (in vitro fertilization) and even used surrogate mothers to carry and deliver their children—which can cost hundreds of thousands of dollars.

Women are instructed over and over that they can simply *delay* parenthood until they reach "financial security" (LOL, what's that?) and feel "ready for children."

Life tip: You will never have enough money. You will never feel ready. Which is why you might as well go for it while you still can.

Meanwhile, the push to delay motherhood has been a gold mine for the fertility industry. This multibillion-dollar "health care" cartel is actively marketing the benefits of delaying babies—to turn you into a future client. Why in the world would you teach young women to get married and start families early when that would deprive you of massive profits? They need to mint more customers. The easiest way to do that is to produce millions of infertile women who are desperate enough to pay any price to achieve a family.

This perverse incentive has lulled millions of women to sleep and made them deaf to their inner clock. When they wake up and discover that their wombs are barren deserts, their eggs desiccated husks, these baby serum merchants will be ready. They will take women by the hand, lead them into the little room, and tell them to undress from the waist down so they can work their magic.

Of course, it's not just advanced maternal age that can affect fertility. There are lots of people who are relatively young and still can't get pregnant. This is a heartbreaking situation; infertility causes unimaginable pain. The only demons here are the cynical fertility clinic CEOs and doctors taking advantage of the older women who missed their motherhood window on their way up the corporate ladder.

Birth Control as Mind Control

As a Catholic, I am officially not allowed to use chemical birth control. Catholics are called to remain "open to life." But that doesn't mean you have to spit out a new kid each year. Catholics I know who need to space out their children or avoid pregnancy for various reasons use a method called Natural Family Planning, or NFP.

Warning: do not confuse NFP with NFTs! NFP lets you plan a pregnancy without drugs. NFTs let you plan a bankruptcy without money.

Natural Family Planning is a wonderful tool to have in your arsenal. It's a chemical-free alternative to America's favorite recreational drug: the birth control pill.

To paraphrase Orwell, when it comes to "reproductive rights," freedom really is slavery. Even the name—birth control—is straight out of a dystopian horror movie. Who is controlling whom? It sounds like a eugenics program for a herd of sheep. The birth control pill, in theory, puts you in control of your own body. From now on, *you alone* get to decide when and if you ever have a baby. No one else will get a say! No one else will *ever* influence your decision in any way. Especially not big pharmaceutical corporations that carefully market and package their products to appeal to young women.

Instead, you, a sixteen-year-old high school sophomore clutching your packet of pills wondering what they will do to you: *you* are firmly in control!

Or are you?

"Birth control," framed as health, justice, and liberation, has turned a nation of innocents into ignorants when it comes to sexual dynamics and successful approaches to family formation.

At the heart of the birth control—and abortion—marketing industry is an elite cultural distaste for children and motherhood, at a deep ideological level. It enrages them aesthetically—women with crying babies are messy, offensive, earthy, and worst of all, *middle class*. Our supervillains' exciting plans for resetting our society involve *liberating* mothers from their resource-sucking children as much and as early as possible, by any means necessary, at every stage of their lives. The New Childless World Order has got you covered, girls!

This probably sounds overdramatic to people with mainstream pro-choice views. (If any of you are reading this book, welcome! If you are hate-reading it, good for you for trying something new.)

Having a contrary opinion about something as ubiquitous as birth control outrages even milquetoast feminists. They throw out arguments about preventing teenage pregnancy and abused women mired in poverty. As of 2017, 40 percent of U.S. high school students reported ever having sex, the lowest rate since the numbers first got tracked in 1991. Most of these kids used a form of birth control, usually condoms. So by condemning birth control, I must want all these teenagers to get pregnant, right? "Who's gonna take care of all those babies, Peachy? *You?*"

To these people I say, do you think it's *healthy* for minor children to be exploiting and using *other, even younger minors* for sex? If not, then why are you making it easier for them to do it? Call me crazy, but giving children free and easy access to every type of birth control under the sun is *not* a great way to prevent them from using each other for sex. If trusted authorities are teaching children how to use condoms, and handing out condoms in health class, and encouraging them to have "safe sex," chances are many of them will get busy getting busy.

Frozen Eggs, Frozen Future

Once you are fully vaccinated against pregnancy with the contraceptive of your choice, you are free to enjoy the infinite array of loveless encounters beckoning you at the heaping buffet of sexual consumerism. It's all-you-can-eat, but you will never be satisfied. Plus, it's hard to truly enjoy it if you can hear a biological clock ticking away while you stuff yourself (so to speak). Fear not: the egg-freezing industry is here to help! Yes folks, step right up to enjoy as many random hookups and dead-end relationships as you like.

One day, when you are old and gray, you can call up the cryogenic clinic, get some of those eggs you froze thirty years ago fertilized and implanted via IVF, and maybe—after a few years of failure—you can end up hiring a surrogate to make one last attempt at a viable pregnancy!

Of course, you will have spent your entire retirement savings on the process, and if a child is born you won't live to see it graduate high school, but who cares? You were practicing *birth control*, which is a sacrosanct woman's right!

What they don't tell you at the egg-freezing office is that women over forty have just a 7.5 percent chance of giving birth to a live infant with each IVF cycle. 7.5 percent! You're going to need a Costco-sized walk-in freezer to store all the eggs you'll need to chip a frozen kid out of that tundra.[10]

The odds are already against anyone who delays motherhood too long. But I guess the egg-freezing ladies be like, "Never tell me the odds!"

Freezing your eggs doesn't just delay your fertility—it puts it into deep freeze for good.

"Between 2009 and 2016, the number of women in the U.S. who froze their eggs rose by more than 1,000%. As more women become more ambivalent about having kids, egg freezing is becoming borderline mainstream. Celebrities like Chrissy Teigen, Khloé Kardashian, and Rebel Wilson have all spoken publicly about freezing their eggs."[11] Oh, well if it's good enough for Rebel Wilson, how could you say no?

Egg freezing has also become a popular corporate HR perk. Big companies have started offering to pay female employees the cost of harvesting and freezing their eggs. Of course, they are only doing it to prevent you from going on maternity leave, but don't worry your pretty little head about that! "Employees are increasingly enjoying a full suite of fertility benefits as companies look for new ways to attract top talent and boost their DEI credentials. As of 2020, more than two-fifths (42%)

of large U.S. employers offered coverage for IVF treatment, while almost one-fifth (19%) offered egg freezing."[12]

Egg freezing has another benefit for corporate HR departments: it also lets them hire more lesbians. "[Egg freezing] could be a win for employers as they seek to improve their female and LGBTQ+ representation, particularly within their more senior ranks."[13]

A fly-by-night egg-freezing operation called, no joke, Progyny, is ready to help you harvest and freeze your eggs as a hedge against your own bad decisions. "These benefits are increasingly seen as central to DEI objectives," said Progyny's CEO Pete Anevski. "Fertility benefits can help companies improve *gender diversity* while also showing they value their female workforce."[14] [Italics are mine.]

Got that? Fertility treatments increase a company's *gender diversity.* The last time I checked my government-issued list of the ninety-eight official human genders, there was still just one gender that can, you know, gestate other humans. I'm no expert, but "lesbian" is not a gender, okay? 100 percent of lesbians who have eggs available for freezing are female! It's really not a very diverse group. But what do I know? I'm not the fertility expert CEO of a scientific science company like Mr. Anevski.

I'm sure the HR departments at Google and Apple and Disney and Amazon are not asking these questions in their quest to recruit single women—especially *lesbians of all genders*—to work for them.

Progyny will even save the frozen vials of any unused, ancient oocytes and toss them into your coffin with you, at no charge. Your kids won't visit your grave; they'll be buried with you.

Escape from Hookup Hell

My personal views on all this have shifted dramatically over my lifetime. In my teens and at college, I eagerly accepted the idea that birth control was necessary for you to "be anything you want to be." The idea of an accidental pregnancy derailing your weekend plans, disrupting your career ambitions, or getting in the way of looking hot up in the club—these terrors stalked me and my friends for years.

On more than one occasion, sloppy birth control use among my friends led directly to a traumatic abortion, which haunted them (pro-choice, liberal feminists all) for years.

In high school, I was given explicit instructions on using birth control pills, diaphragms, condoms, dental dams, foams, jellies, IUDs, and long-term birth control implants. I was warned about the dangers of forgetting to use your preferred method: a disgusting STD or two, certain death from AIDS, or the worst nightmare of all, a baby.

I arrived at my freshman dorm room with a computer, extra-long twin bed sheets, and a prescription for birth control pills, which they were handing out like candy at orientation. "Can't be too careful!" we'd tell each other.

Birth control was like wearing makeup and a push-up bra: you looked much more attractive to guys when you weren't carrying hopelessly lame baggage like "fertility" around with you. Or so we thought.

You could tell yourself that it was *safe* to do literally *whatever you wanted* with anyone, without any unpleasant side effects. No cute frat boy would be able to resist the allure of your sterilized loins! Our parents weren't paying $50k a year for us to stay home and study—that's what nerds were for!

After a while, I realized that all I had gained from the pill was an extra ten pounds. I never actually put my prescription to the test, if you know what I mean. Despite my best efforts to throw myself into college social life, I was held back by two awkward traits I didn't know I had: a deep resistance to loveless intimacy (i.e., wasted hookups) and extreme pickiness about who I wanted to "date." Despite enormous peer pressure, I did not fully participate in the elite drunken culture sloshing around me, despite the vodka sodas sloshing in my gut. (This was at a college consistently ranked in the top ten in the country. Parents: the *U.S. News and World Report* college rankings don't tell you the important stuff!)

Don't get me wrong—I *did* participate. I was an enthusiastic participant in many aspects of the decadence, and a regular partygoer. But I realized fairly early on that what I *really* wanted was not on offer at the bacchanal. I wasn't interested in playing Musical Crotches, or in the late-night-only, love-free relationships my female classmates settled for.

I made it out alive by the skin of my teeth!

The problem with *any* form of birth control is that it acts like Chekhov's Gun. Regarding playwriting, Anton Chekhov is quoted as having said, "If in Act I you have a pistol hanging on the wall, then it must fire in the last act."[15] If you put a young girl on birth control, she will eventually be tempted to test its efficacy.

It's the parental equivalent of your daughter telling you she plans to scale the outside of a hundred-story skyscraper with her bare hands, and instead of talking her out of it, you just hang safety nets around the building and tell her to go live her best life.

Eventually, I groped my way out of this dark house of cards. It collapsed around me, cards falling from the sky, wafting away in the breeze, when I finally figured out that without birth control, more girls might try harder to do the unthinkable: *avoid intimate acts with people who didn't love them.* Who didn't care if they lived or died. Who would not remember them in a month, let alone a year. Imagine!

Of course, "chastity" is not a message that college girls want to hear, now or in my day. *But it is still a message worth teaching.* There's no way to stop them all from diving into a drained pool headfirst, but we can stop *more* of them. All that "liberation" does is liberate you from your fertility, your agency, and your joy. It's a giant lie, a brainwashing cult, and a mass mind-control exercise. Once you break free of it, toss out the birth control, rip up the egg-freezing flyer they hand out on campus, and take control of your life, you may be called a "misogynist" and an "extremist" and a "religious fundamentalist." But *true* ownership of your fertility is the real superpower.

Pharmaceuticals and feminism have now turned at least two generations of young women into—I need to choose my words carefully here—extremely affordable concubines. Ninety-nine-cent escorts. Human Fleshlights for the price of a few drinks. Is this what liberation looks like? Unsatisfactory naked encounters, the extreme risk of communicable disease, and the inevitable crushing heartbreak that follows?

You may be the one who gets ghosted by guys, but in a cruel plot twist, *you* end up becoming the phantom who never really lived.

CHAPTER 2

Your Role

The Feminist Mistake

*Feminism is the revolt of women against the outrage
of democracy. They have been in a revolt against the
inability of the bugman to command authority or respect.*

— BAP, Bronze Age Mindset

*Whenever you remove any fence, always pause long
enough to ask why it was put there in the first place.*

— G. K. Chesterton

What They Took:

☑ ~~Your Fleeting Fertility~~
☑ **Your Role**

Triumph of the Shrill

At my local bookstore, the Women's History Month table was piled high with books that were supposedly about women. I perused titles like: *Rude: Stop Being Nice and Start Being Bold*, 100 *Nasty Women of History*, *The Nasty Women Resistance*, *Bad Girls*, *Shrill: Notes from a Loud Woman* (by the author of *The Witches Are Coming*), *Bitch: On the Female of the Species*, *In Defense of Witches*, and a very slim book called #*VERYFAT* #*VERYBRAVE*.

The display prominently featured several books about mothers who were finally able to achieve full self-actualization by cheating on their husbands. For example, *Blow Your House Down: A Story of Family, Feminism, and Treason* is an unreadable memoir about the rage that drove a middle-aged writer to have a secret affair and destroy her daughters' lives. I also passed on several other titles, including *Unladylike: A Field Guide to Smashing the Patriarchy and Claiming Your Space*; *Witches, Sluts, Feminists*; and *Against White Feminism*, which frankly sounds a lot better than it is.

I walked out of the bookstore feeling #VERYALONE. I don't recognize any of these hellacious female archetypes. Women like me are not represented on any Women's History Month book table. Who are all these loud, shrill, fat, nasty bitches (their words, not mine)? I don't want to share a *month* with them, let alone an entire gender. I'm not a biologist, but based on these titles, a woman is something I hope I never encounter in a dark alley.

Do not taunt Slutty Nasty Witch! She'll cut you.

From Suffrage to Suffering

The second item on my litany of lost treasures is your role in society—the traditional position women played until a few decades ago. It has since been obliterated in the name of "liberation." Historically, women could be queens, explorers, and inventors *without* relinquishing their power over domestic affairs. Thanks to the political movement we call "feminism," they are now mostly powerless over both their families and society, having handed their innate power over to the State and the guy who pays the rent on their office cubicles.

Feminism is perhaps the most successful war ever waged on our well-worn human pathways to lasting happiness. The feminist cry to "smash the patriarchy" accidentally smashed the matriarchy instead. Oops!

By matriarchy, I don't mean the barren pantsuit-wearing harpies who rule the globe. I mean actual female matriarchs: mothers. The feminists in charge of you, your body, and your choices took over the matriarchy and deformed it into their ideal woman (who may not even be a woman these days). We are ruled by a different sort of matriarchy now: women and their male feminist allies imposing rigid and suffocating rules on the rest of us. American society has been feminized to the point of castration. If you resist, *you* will be smashed next.

So how did we get here? There is nothing more boring than reading about the history of feminism, so I will spare you the details. After all, the history of feminism is a tale as old as time. It's what happened when undateable bores, bitter about not being asked to the prom, decided that if *they* can't have a man, you don't get one, either.

But these unmarriageable women, bitter and alone, are *themselves* victims. This is not "women's" fault, entirely. It's also the fault of men, who somewhere along the way abandoned their natural roles as leaders of societies and families. When everyone is put in charge, no one is in charge. Ancient human social structures collapse. In the modern age, women were suddenly empowered to lead, thrust into roles that did not quite fit, and then found they were not able to mate. Their anger and dissatisfaction with this state of affairs simmered and festered. Could this be why so many young women self-harm through high "body counts" (their gruesome term for a list of lifetime sexual partners), chemical birth control, and abortion? Are those cries for help in a world where men have forsaken them?

It's a mystery worth contemplating: How did a ragtag group of shrill, grating hags get their way? Why is there only one acceptable mainstream cultural blueprint for female life? Why?

On her podcast, *GirlBoss, Interrupted*, writer Helen Roy asked, "Whose idea *was* feminism?"

Good question. How *did* we get to this blighted place?

Like other virulent viruses that plague humanity, feminism came in waves. We have suffered through at least four waves so far. In first-wave feminism, ladies who still wore corsets and carried parasols fought for women to have the right to vote and work so poor women could quit resorting to prostitution when they got hungry. These early pioneers were militantly against "sex work," and saw it for what it was: desperate women forced to sell their bodies to avoid starving. Their battle for voting and labor rights was wildly successful: women started voting for liberals and prioritizing careers over families. They were somewhat less successful at abolishing prostitution. (When you can't beat 'em, join 'em: in a neat trick, subsequent waves of feminism successfully turned young feminists *into* prostitutes by turning it into a socially acceptable career choice. Problem solved!)

Second-wave feminism, the hippies and boomers, decided liberation for women actually *had* to include sexual liberation. No more oppressive patriarchal rules telling girls to stay virgins until marriage. That's no fun, Grandpa! And what did their male peers think when they found out their nubile college classmates wanted to embrace "free love"? The stoned, long-haired dudes in bell bottoms were only too happy to accept this gift. They could enjoy the best of both worlds: declare themselves firmly on the side of women's liberation, while also partaking freely of liberally available women. Summer of love, baby!

Our boomer ancestors—your parents and grandparents—accidentally created an industry of unpaid prostitution, or what is now called "dating." Instead of desperate, hungry women forced into prostitution to make money, liberated career girls could enjoy a full Rolodex of Johns. Hey, if men could do it, so can we, right? Your right to sleep with anyone, any time, was freedom. A predictable tidal wave of STDs, unmarried parenting, single motherhood, and divorce soon followed.

Are ya feeling free yet, girls?

The pill and legal abortion were new absolute rights that enabled the liberated female lifestyle. You're lonely, have an oozing crotch rash, and no husband, but hey, those are the blessings of liberty.

Third-wave feminism decided these wondrous innovations weren't enough, so they invented "sex positivity," which glorifies "sex work" as liberation. Paid prostitution was back in style! Instead of burning your bras, you will remove yours, slowly please, live on camera from the comfort of your living room. They brought us full circle. You've come a long way, baby!

Third-wave feminism also brought us the rise of gender studies programs at college and mass rape paranoia. Women reclaimed the words "bitch" and "slut" and turned the old-fashioned walk of shame into the Slutwalk, where college girls celebrated their sex-positive liberation from the patriarchy by stripping down to their plus-sized undies and proudly parading around campus topless. If you were (un)fortunate enough to attend college during this era, you may have seen a Slutwalker or two. They were hard to miss!

In other words, a movement originally founded to free women from prostitution to survive has become a movement that actively seeks to recruit young women to become prostitutes. Paid in the streets, unpaid in the sheets. Young men, for the most part, are only too happy to go along with the ruse. It takes two to tango, as they say. They've all been forced through the same feminist indoctrination and rendered powerless to rein in their female peers.

How'd we get to this awful place?

Female Liberation Theology

These days, we are in the muscular grip of fourth-wave feminism, also known as "wokeness." The fourth wave kicked off with the #MeToo movement, which was about protesting biological men who assault women. It then devolved into a movement celebrating psychological and physical assault on women by biological men who think they're women.

Confused yet?

Fourth-wave feminism also rejects liberal "white feminists" who demand equality. LOL, equality. Remember that? Instead, fourth-wavers are mostly focused on *replacing* women with men. On the plus side, women's college sports teams have never been better!

Fourth-wave feminists gave us the full flowering of rancid gender theory, which posits that there is no gender binary—no more male and female. A remarkable scientific discovery! Have these people ever been to a zoo? According to the theory, everyone exists on some sort of gender spectrum. You can see fourth-wave feminism at work when a large man is dominating a swimming pool full of petite girls; at the spa where fully nude people with male genitalia walk around ladies' lockers rooms; and at lesbian nightclubs, where biologically male lesbians (formerly known as straight dudes) demand biologically female lesbians sleep with them, or else get called bigots.

Fourth-wave feminists are hard at work doing important things for women: for example, trying to destroy liberal second-wavers like J. K. Rowling and smearing her as a "TERF" (a "trans exclusionary radical feminist"). Fourth-wave feminism is also busy co-opting other far-left movements, including the billion-dollar Black Lives Matter, Inc. This is why you quickly saw the 2020 BLM protests mutate into "Black *Trans* Lives Matter" protests.

Fourth-wave feminism is also actively transforming formerly Catholic countries with abortion-on-demand legal wins. Argentina, Ireland, Colombia, and Mexico each loosened their formerly strict abortion laws in the last few years.

Fourth-wave feminism: the undefeated Final Boss (same as the old boss).

Third-wave feminists: "Women need to act more like men!"

Fourth-wave feminists: "Hold my beer."

Fourth-wave feminists have helped women achieve their final liberated forms as women who were born male. The ideal woman is now a transgender woman, just as the ideal man is now a feminized soyboy who has been stripped of his "toxic" masculinity.

Nowhere has this change been more visible than in the United States military. Fourth-wave feminism has transformed the World's Finest Fighting Force into a feminized freakshow.

To honor Women's History Month, the United States Air Force posted an interview on its official social media accounts with the sole woman in all of the Air Force they chose to honor: Lt. Col. Bree Fram, the highest ranking openly transgender woman in the military. She currently serves in the Space Force (insert punch line here). Despite her girlish ponytail and flirty high heels, Fram cuts an imposing figure. She stands well over six-foot-two and boasts a powerful frame, jutting jaw, and deep voice.

In an interview, Fram revealed that her wife of sixteen years, Peg, the mother to their two children, has suffered from deep depression due to her inexplicable inability to accept her husband's new identity as . . . her wife.[1]

Another win for fourth-wave feminism! Is there no end to the victories feminism delivers to women? Well, to some women. After all, some women are more equal than others.

I look around and see a ludicrous world where female athletes are relegated to second and third place as biological males power their way to dominance. But you can't blame the biological men for this. Their glide path to gold medals was carved for them by women. Male sports coaches, to their great shame, are only too happy to reap the trophies and accolades. Yet again, feminism delivers the goods for men!

Feminists fought for decades to help girls succeed, but they overshot the goal. They crossed the finish line and then hit the gas and drove the car right off the cliff. The early feminists who wanted women to be treated as equals under the law would spin in their graves if they saw where their descendants have gone.

Sure, I'm glad I can vote (though I suspect in California my ballot is tossed straight into the trash). It's wonderful that girls can demand to be treated with respect by male college classmates—and also get in free to the freshmen orgies on campus. I'm sure they are treated with the utmost respect at those orgies.

We can all agree that voting and equal rights for all people, including women, are good. However, "equality" and "feminism" are now just weasel words obfuscating nasty outcomes for your innocent daughters. The kindly, maternal figure of the traditional grandmother has been swallowed whole by the wolf—and she/they plans to eat you next. Too many of America's boomer grandmothers are more likely to teach their granddaughters to make "My Body My Choice" signs than how to bake a pie. Grandmother, what sharp curettes[2] you have!

In every way, the term "women's rights" has been warped and hollowed out, a total misnomer, like one of those hilariously euphemistic government names for bad laws.

Your "right" to be treated equally quickly turned into your "right" to demand an abortion at nine months, your "right" to brag on social media about your lucrative career in socially acceptable sex work, and your "right" to be one of hundreds of jilted girls ghosted by a single male user on Tinder.

Somehow, along the way to making our lives easier, feminists made them harder. They set out to allow women to have more fulfilling lives, but our lives became less fulfilling. We were supposed to be happier with all these "freedoms," and yet, rates of depression and suicide among young women have never been higher. Liberation from the pressure to get married and have children was supposed to free us to grow old unencumbered and living in a paradise of independence.

Instead, older women have skyrocketing rates of depression. White women over the age of forty-five have the highest rate of antidepressant use. "Older white women account for 58% of adults who have used antidepressants for at least five years."[3]

Where is the happiness feminism promised them? Where is the thrill that childlessness and no-fault divorce guaranteed? Can't all those cats cheer them up?

Feminists promised us that we could "have it all" and achieve all our professional and personal goals—with no more mean old patriarchs and their big, swinging glass ceilings to stop us.

It's true that it's easier for a woman to become a CEO in the twenty-first century than it was in the nineteenth century. For those twelve female CEOs in the Fortune 500: hope the sacrifice was worth it!

For the rest of us, things are not going that well. It's never been harder to have the kind of life most women still say they want: to fall in love, be happily married, to raise children, and to enjoy grandchildren one day. These simple, timeless things have never been more out of reach for more women.

Not only are these dreams more difficult to achieve—loyal husband, fulfilling marriage, babies—they are treated as backwards, out-of-fashion trends that you, as an enlightened, modern woman, must reject. Your heart may tell you to seek domestic fulfillment, but the culture at large has erased this desire from public view. Nowhere in popular media do you see examples of young married couples devoted to each other—beholden to their own family culture, not to mainstream American culture.

If you follow Christian mommy bloggers on TikTok or Instagram, you will see no shortage of homesteading homeschoolers with lots of children. But this lifestyle is a curio—a tiny fringe that cultural arbiters regard with total disdain and study like anthropologists examine the indigenous Sentinel Islanders who throw spears at them from the ground when they fly overhead in helicopters. There are some homesteads in this country that I would advise feminist gender studies professors not to try to invade.

Anyways, we can't all buy farms. Few of us are equipped or prepared for the off-the-grid dissident life, including me. Despite my inner domestic extremist, I'm still outwardly the same city slicker I've always been, more comfortable at a lively cocktail party than a barn raising. However, foundational female roles don't require you to transform into a tradwife stereotype, or Ma Ingalls.

Despite that, getting married and having a child is now Mission: Impossible for many young women, so they're simply opting out. For the first time, the majority of British women under age thirty are childless.[4] Feminists, take a bow.

If politics is downstream of culture, then culture is downstream of the family unit (as Ed, Holly Hunter's character, calls it in *Raising Arizona*), and the family unit is downstream of the mother—which makes her enemy number one.

Women: the cause of—and solution to—all the world's problems!

Cue the Tsunami

I propose a new wave of feminism: a mega-tsunami that will crash ashore and wash away all the other waves with its magnitude. Imagine a "wave" of women who, after being lured by the false promises of liberal feminism, eventually arrive at the bitter dead end. They were sold on a vision of earthly delights, only to find out they bought a one-way ticket to the Feminism Fyre Festival—complete with moldy bread and overflowing sewage. These disenchanted travelers will be ripe for a new way of being. Ladies, gaze upon the wreckage wrought by a century of female "progress," your broken dreams and dashed hopes, and choose another path!

This nascent movement has already begun. British writer and vanguard Mary Harrington calls herself a "reactionary feminist." She likes to lob hand grenades like this into mainstream feminist front lines:

> We need a movement grounded in pragmatic realities. Male and female bodies are different; humans can't change sex; most women want to have children; heterosexuality is the default human condition; outsourcing domestic chores is a movement to reintroduce a servant class; children do better in stable two-parent families; and our hyperfocus on individual freedom is a central factor in the plummeting of birthrates worldwide. Against technological developments that promise to free us from love, longing, and human nature itself, restating these truths is an act of feminist resistance.[5]

Here's an inconvenient truth: the authentically female-centered movement Mary and others like her are proposing is your best chance at achieving lasting happiness.

Reject mainstream feminism. Come with us if you want to live, laugh, love!

CHAPTER 3

Your Gender

Gone: Girls

Vagina. The word itself makes some men uncomfortable.

— *Maude Lebowski*

A woman is someone who claims that as their identity. It could be many things to many people.

— *Dr. Michelle Forcier, pediatrician*

What They Took:

- ☑ ~~Your Fleeting Fertility~~
- ☑ ~~Your Role~~
- ☑ Your Gender

Replaced and Erased

The singer Adele got in trouble at the Brit Awards for using the word "woman" in her acceptance speech. Her crime? She'd just won the first-ever gender-neutral Artist of the Year award after the separate male and female categories were replaced with one all-gender category. She said onstage, "I understand why the name of this award has changed, but I really love being a woman and being a female artist. I do!"[1]

Yikes. It's a miracle she wasn't stoned to death on stage for this transgression. Her choice of words sparked a raging "transphobia debate." How dare a woman express joy for . . . being a woman!

The only conclusion one can draw is that women—Women Classic, not the trendy new brand—are no longer permitted to have a separate category in any human endeavor. The word "woman" is taboo. The N-word has been replaced with the W-word.

Your gender is the next item on the list of stolen goods, after your fertility and your role in society. It's also the funniest thing on the list. Even the definition in Merriam-Webster's dictionary was given gender-confirmation surgery. "Female: having a gender identity that is the opposite of male." Well, at least they reinforce the gender binary by calling female the opposite of male, but that doesn't really help much.

There was a brief, shining moment when we were told to call ourselves "uterus-havers" instead of "women," but that's problematic, too, since some "men" have uteruses. Then they tried out "menstruators," but here again we run into trouble, since "men" can menstruate these days. Bloody hell! Okay, how about "front-hole-havers"? Does that fit (no pun intended)? Well, no, because there are women who have not had their neo-vaginas surgically constructed yet.

Sweat pouring down their foreheads, they search for a new term for this amorphous group of humans with no defining physical characteristics of any kind. "We are adult human females," you inform them.

They shriek and break their nail extensions as they try to scratch your face. "We know what to call you. How about *bitch*?" Well, a bitch *is* an adult female, so I guess I'll take it!

The Goodbye Girls

After a hundred years fighting for the rights of biological females, mainstream feminism quit. We got ghosted. In a few short years, feminists went from worshipping the girlboss to worshipping girls with balls. Feminists stopped helping girls compete on a level playing field; instead, they literally leveled the playing field, destroying sports for a generation of young women.

The reason is simple. Feminists discovered a new kind of woman they like better: men. That is, people "assigned" male at birth who later identify as women. These newly minted women shot right to the top of the food chain, fast-tracked to the front of the line and the highest echelons of political power. The glass ceiling has been replaced with the trans ceiling.

And lo, the perfect feminist Platonic ideal of a woman has been birthed. She arrives like Venus on the half shell, a resplendent, glimmering queen. Behold her muscular arms. Her ripped abs. Bit of stubble on the chin, but how dare you for noticing. She is six feet and three inches of shining womanhood.

It starts at birth, the erasure of your biological nature as a female. "What gender would you like the doctor to assign your baby?" is a question mothers are starting to get asked in the delivery room. Only the most careless, nearsighted doctor would randomly "assign" a baby's gender at birth after the most cursory glance at their bodies. How could they make baseless assumptions about your newborn's gender like that?

Good news: gender activists have strong-armed hospitals into including multiple check boxes on birth certificates, so you can choose your child's gender, or choose none of the above. Because . . . science!

I used to eagerly await the moment I would find out what I was having—we never waited until the delivery. I needed to know as soon as possible! "It's a boy!" they would announce, pointing to the proof right there on the ultrasound screen.

What do ultrasound technicians tell expecting parents now when they can see the fetus is a boy? "The fetus presents with stereotypical male genitals, which has absolutely no connection to its actual gender, which you will discover many years from now."

Women who object to the "male-bodied" showing up in their most intimate areas, like locker rooms and saunas, in bathrooms and dressing rooms, are the villains. Complain about naked penises in the women's spa, and establishment feminists accuse you of committing violence against transgendered people. Some women's rights groups, who have fought for years to support women in prisons and allow them to have greater access to their children, now stay silent as rapists with male bodies are locked in jail cells with female rape survivors. Sorry, ladies, this is what equality looks like: prison rape is now equally distributed at the men's and the women's penitentiaries.

The irony is that, yet again, story of our lives, women are getting pushed aside by natal males and their feminist handlers. The loudest (and deepest) voices won. Let's face it—if you were on the school committee making the rules for who gets to be nude in the teenage girls' locker room, but the head of the athletic department is a lady with five o'clock shadow and thighs like Honey Baked hams, what would you do?

You'd let him win, that's what you'd do.

Athlete Delete

In the world of sports, once the larger, stronger competitors are allowed to play against natal females, it's game over. Real women's dreams of collegiate glory get snipped and tucked right before their eyes. If an athlete has the advantage of getting to adulthood in a male body before switching to the other side, the competition does not stand a chance.

Lia Thomas, the former superstar swimmer on the University of Pennsylvania women's swim team, has shown the way. With her size (six-foot-one) and spectacular wingspan, she easily won both Ivy League and NCAA Championship races against her puny competitors. NBC cheered her victory as historic, saying, "Lia Thomas' NCAA Championship performance gives women sports a crucial opportunity. Anyone who cares about the advancement of sports, and women's sports in particular, should celebrate her win."[2]

In ten years, the United States Women's Olympic Team will be dominant in every sport worldwide—except perhaps in gymnastics and figure skating. We will dominate the competition in track using our huge, muscular backsides. We will destroy the best female tennis players in the world with our massively powerful forearms.

Women will finally rule the world.

Only, not *all* women. If your daughter is hoping for an athletic scholarship, she'll find this out the hard way.

Unfortunately, the lunatics are running the sporting asylums.

The chief medical advisor to the NCAA and the International Olympic Committee is a French doctor named Dr. Eric Vilain (a little on the nose, isn't it?). Here's his bio: "Eric Vilain, M.D., Ph.D. is an Adjunct Professor of Human Genetics, Pediatrics and Urology at UCLA, and the Institute for Society and Genetics. He is also Chief of Medical Genetics, and an attending physician in the Department of Pediatrics."

Dr. Vilain runs a laboratory where he "explores the genetics of sexual development and sex differences, focusing on the molecular mechanisms of gonad development, as well as on the genetic determinants of brain sexual differentiation. An internationally renowned expert in the field of gender-based biology, he has identified a large number of mutations in sex-determining genes, developed animal models with atypical sexual development, and identified novel mechanisms of sex differences in the brain."[3]

Get that? He's an expert on genetic differences between men and women and was instrumental in crafting the NCAA's gender-blind participation rules—where genetics don't matter.

As far back as 2009, Dr. Vilain said:

> There is no strict or obvious definition of what sex is in humans. It's quite a complex definition. There are many different parameters that are not always concordant. There is chromosomal sex, genetic sex, hormonal sex, gonadal sex, the way your external genitalia look like or the way your internal genitalia look like. And there is even now an anatomic brain-sex definition. So, it's really a constellation of parameters that define sex. And in the end, what really counts, in my opinion, is what we feel like we are, either male or female.[4]

For some odd reason, Dr. Vilain has yet to weigh in on the shameful lack of gender diversity in men's sports. When will the good doctor break down the barriers preventing transmen from playing college basketball? Let's get transmen into the NBA and see how they handle *those* balls.

According to Science, we must coddle the group most able to curb-stomp a girl in a street fight. Serena and Venus Williams should be grateful they cashed in while they still could; in our lifetime, women's tennis will be "trans" formed.

Abigail Shrier, author of the bestselling book *Irreversible Damage: The Transgender Craze Seducing Our Daughters*, wrote an essay in *Newsweek* about the erasure of women in sports. In it, she lays out the stakes in stark terms. "To force young women to compete with male-bodied athletes will bring about the collapse of women's sports."[5] Why do women need their own spaces and sports competition? Just look at the science. When you compare the records of male high school athletes against female Olympians, "in the 100-meter, the 200-meter, the 400-meter and 800-meter races, the male high school players handily dominate the female Olympians, claiming all the top spots."[6]

Lia Thomas is already planning to try out for the 2024 U.S. Women's Olympic swim team.

Not only does the emperor have no clothes, he's wearing the empress's bikini.

Miss Gendered

You may think you can avoid this abject humiliation, since you'll never be in the Olympics or play competitive sports. You assume you'll be able to live your life in peace, birth gender intact, identity secure.

Except . . . your boss just told you to put your pronouns in your work bio and in your email signature. Your sons were required to write their preferred pronouns on the name tag they had to wear at college freshman orientation. If they fail to repeat their pronouns on demand, they will be corrected and eventually punished.

This is the work of a tiny but mighty group of political activists who do it in the guise of protecting women's rights. Because close to zero transgender men can plausibly pass as biologically female in person, they are forced to angrily correct anyone who refers to them as "he." Their greatest fear is to be misgendered. Each time someone uses the correct (to them, incorrect) pronoun, it's like pointing and shouting that they have no clothes. It only reminds them of the great lie they are living and the comical futility of their attempts to pass. What they call gender dysphoria is actually bitter self-doubt awakening deep in their lizard brains, and no amount of lipstick can silence it.

But because *they* are forced to speak their neo-pronouns, to tattoo them on their foreheads, then we *all* have to do it. We are a country held hostage by an angry, vicious mob that likes to refer to itself as "tolerant." Look, I feel their pain. Getting misgendered is hurtful. I was once misgendered! When I was seven, I got sick and had to stay in bed for days. When I finally emerged, I had the worst case of bed head in history; my long hair was tangled in one giant knot. Instead of waiting for my mom to brush it out, I took matters into my own hands and found a pair of scissors. I inadvertently gave myself a gender-affirmation haircut. My mother saw my butchered 'do and rushed me to the salon, where I emerged with a cute pixie cut. I didn't care, I was seven. But when I walked into the girls' bathroom at the park, some older girls screamed and told me to "get out" because I was a boy.

When you put your pronouns in your bio to signal that you are an "ally," you have surrendered to the mob. You might as well shove your head into the nearest guillotine and call for the executioner to let the blade drop. That's how over it is for us as a society if we are forced to do this pronoun dance. I know someone who is the last person in her department at work who has not yet added her pronouns to the company intranet. She might as well replace her headshot with a picture of Hitler, or one of her in blackface. That's how obvious it is that she is not one of them.

I told her she should tell her boss she is "challenging norms" at work, since she is instructed to "challenge norms" in all fifty (!) of the corporate struggle sessions she is required to attend each year. "This year, I am challenging norms by not putting my pronouns in my bio."

I was on the phone trying to schedule someone to repair the HVAC, and the lady asked me what gender I was. I laughed and asked, "Do you *really* not know what gender I am?" The lady sheepishly replied, "Well, we are required to ask every customer." My local *HVAC repair shop* wanted to make sure they knew my gender and pronouns.

I told her, "Just take a guess, you'll be right." She chuckled! All is not lost!

If you are *not* transgender and someone asks you what your pronouns are, you should be insulted! Horrified even. Do they not know? Can they not tell? Consider a haircut and a makeover, maybe. As offended as a transgender woman may be by getting called "he" or "sir," I am *equally* offended when asked my gender. Where is my *equality*?

No one ever asked Marilyn Monroe for her pronouns. No one ever wondered what gender Cindy Crawford was. It's all just a humiliating exercise in compliance you are forced to play at work or school, like rats in a maze at a laboratory. "Which one will get to the pellet first?"

Here is my suggestion: instead of forcing us all to play this little game, how about no one is required to ever put their pronouns anywhere, and we all just use our best guess. If someone calls you "he" and you wanted to be called "she," just politely ask them. It may shock you, but if a transgender person was polite and friendly, I would have *no problem* calling them whatever they wanted me to call them (other than "mommy"—I have to draw the line somewhere). I am not into public confrontation or being an A-hole. I like to get along with people! I like to model civility and friendliness for my children! You want me to call you *she*? Fine. Just don't force me to tell you *my* pronouns. Fair?

If you are ever unsure what gender someone is, here's an easy way to find out: carry a jar of pickles in your purse and ask them to open it for you. That should clear up any confusion right away. Unless they are hostile and vicious, in which case—run!

Although that may not work—they can run a lot faster than you.

Girl Powerless

This is all funny, except it's not. Scores of male domestic abusers and rapists are suddenly "becoming transgender" and requesting transfers to women's prisons. I'm pretty sure that, like the contestants on *The Bachelor*, they're not all there for the right reasons.

On July 23, 2007, two depraved felons broke into a family's house in Cheshire, Connecticut, beat the husband unconscious, and spent the next twelve hours terrorizing, raping, and finally killing his wife and two daughters; the daughters were eleven and seventeen. Stephen Hayes, the mastermind, had a long rap sheet with over thirty arrests. He was sentenced to death in 2010. In 2019, Hayes declared that he was a woman and demanded to be transferred to a women's prison. To date, it is unclear if he—excuse me, she—has been transferred, but he/she is on female hormones. I heard a prison interview with him a few years ago. He whined that not everyone in prison had accepted his new identity. "A lot of people accept it, but in this facility here you have a lot of racist and bigot [*sic*] staff, and they're not happy with it."[7]

According to some studies, half of transgender prisoners are violent sex offenders.[8] It's one thing to have strapping swim queen Lia Thomas walking around with a semi in front of her female teammates in the UPenn girls' locker room. It's quite another to have male predators locked up with young women, most of whom have been subjected to abuse in their lives.

The State is allowing female prisoners to be brutalized in jail. Fight back and you get canceled, smeared as a bigot, or worse. Boomer feminists used to chant, "I am woman, hear me roar!"

Now their poor daughters have had their vocal cords snipped.

CHAPTER 4

Your Virtues

Femininity: The New F-Word

*Your clothes should be tight enough to show you're a
woman but loose enough to show you're a lady.*

— Marilyn Monroe

What They Took:

☑ ~~Your Fleeting Fertility~~
☑ ~~Your Role~~
☑ ~~Your Gender~~
☑ **Your Virtues**

Girls Gone Wild

Feminine virtues: the next item on our litany of loss. When they quietly seized your virtues, I bet you never even noticed. I certainly didn't, until it was almost too late. The definition of "virtue" is "conformity to a standard of right; a beneficial quality or power." That power is a woman's natural femininity, which conforms to a standard that, until recent memory, was considered uncontroversial, undisputed, and hotly desired. Today, classic feminine virtues like chastity, modesty, and beauty are punchlines to be mocked and ignored. They have been replaced by liberating new virtues that create long lines outside the orgy tent at Burning Man—or as I like to call it, Burning Crotch.

Enormous energy has been poured into a multipronged effort to defeminize girls. It starts at birth, with gender-neutral baby clothes. God forbid you get a pink frilly dress from Grandma—burn that before anyone sees! It continues with the push to show girls they can "do anything boys can do," including wear the same clothes and act "masculine." (Masculinity is no longer allowed for boys, of course.) Your teenage daughter will be encouraged to be "loud," to "demand" her "rights," and to reject archaic and unfashionable "feminine beauty standards." She will be encouraged to be confident and fearless, which means getting up in someone's face for any perceived slight or "microaggression."

Unfortunately, acting more like a stereotypical male can quickly lead to having promiscuous sex like a stereotypical male, as soon as she is of age.

Writer Bridget Phetasy published a brave, heart-wrenching essay called "I Regret Being a Slut" about the feminist lie behind promiscuity. "I doubled down on being a proud slut and internalized the biggest and most damaging lie: that loveless sex is empowering. I basked in the girl-power glow of that delusion for decades, weaponizing my sexuality while convincing myself I was full of the divine feminine. I was full of shit."[1]

Her experience is all too common—being "a slut" is now the default setting of most young American women. Shame, regret, and introspection have been forcibly bred out of them. They are heaved right into the fetid swamp as soon as they are legal, with no life vest—but a lifetime supply of birth control. They are promised power via promiscuity, but find themselves nearly powerless to escape their fate.

Teenage girls are left with two lifestyle options: style themselves as hypersexualized pleasurebots with OnlyFans pages, or transform themselves into sexless, genderless, confused he/theys with strange hair and clothing.

For the first type, her role models are social media stars who practice extreme hyper-femininity and have a revolving door of boytoys and baby daddies. This lifestyle can require pricey body modifications: three-inch fingernails shaved to talon-like points, unnatural plastic surgery, butt implants, fake tans, and fillers. The Kardashians have perfected this faux-female look. The results turn a normal-looking girl into something resembling a robotic sex doll with inflatable, interchangeable parts. When I used to listen to Courtney Love (lead singer of the proto-feminist band Hole) sing "Doll Parts," I never dreamed she was predicting our future!

Why spend all that money to look like a blow-up doll if you're not going to amortize those costly implants and your BBL (Brazilian butt lift) over lots of sex partners or your live sex cam business? You're going to spend fifty grand on a state-of-the-art body, and *not* sell tickets to every Tom, Dick, and Pete (Davidson)?

For the other type, the situation is even worse. These gender-neutral, nonbinary, or asexual young women reject all traces of girlhood in favor of social-media–driven propaganda that leads them into their own baroque sexual explorations, including a total rejection of all sex.

If femininity eventually goes extinct, it's taking the species with it.

Pimped from Puberty

This misguided effort to seduce, distract, and delude young women with powerful lies about their own femininity has deformed our culture in ways that are only now becoming clear. It's nothing but another form of grooming. Defeminization teaches young girls that traditional femininity equals weakness, frailty, and obedience to an imagined patriarchal tyrant. They are coached to rid themselves of their God-given femininity so they can claim the modern mantle of Female Empowerment.

It starts with getting them to despise and sabotage the natural attributes that make them female: natural modesty, natural beauty, and natural body parts. Is it any wonder that so many teenage girls who don't look like camera-ready porn stars want to have their breasts surgically removed and grow mustaches?

Although society has taken it upon itself to teach girls to defeminize themselves, young men cannot be so easily retrained! It's an immutable fact of the universe: heterosexual men are *designed by their Creator* to prefer feminine women. All the forces at work desperately trying to reprogram young men to be attracted to shrill women, masculine women, genderless women, or artificial simulacra of women will fail. No matter how many times they put a man in drag on the cover of the *Sports Illustrated* swimsuit issue, most men will stubbornly refuse to fall into the uncanny valley of fake femininity, for they know it is a barren caldera where your libido goes to die.

The male operating system—God bless it—keeps stubbornly reverting to its 1.0 code. The richest men in the world aren't hanging around with nonbinary blobs who want to shout their abortions loudly. They aren't hanging around with bizarro fembots. They've reverted to the same female archetype that the poorest medieval European serf was also into: the cute milkmaid in the haystack.

Turns out that it's hard to get honeybees to land on dead flowers.

Sorry about this biological fact. It's a shame, I know. You'd think all the Gaia worshippers and climate change militants would respect Mother Nature when it comes to What Men Really Want, but I guess not.

This is why embracing, instead of rejecting, femininity matters. Girls need to know how—to put it crudely—to present themselves in ways that will attract heterosexual, marriage-minded men. The fate of the species literally hangs in the balance! Undateable girls become unmarriageable women, who become genetic dead ends for humanity. Natural selection, working exactly as it's supposed to.

The Female Binary

The world is now clearly divided into two types of women, and not between the biological ones and the transgender ones.

Type A: This girl is groomed to believe she should be in charge of everything. She is taught to be a "rule breaker," to "smash the patriarchy," and to spend her twenties finding out who she "really is." She is placed on birth control at puberty, encouraged to explore every nook and cranny of her sexuality as early as possible, and given directions and a punch card to the nearest Planned Parenthood. Your fifth STD or abortion is free, just like at Jamba Juice!

She will spend her life demanding more government support for her "reproductive health." She will be a shrill "voice for change" wherever she goes, loudly denouncing those she disagrees with, including friends and loved ones. She will proudly take charge of her multidimensional sexuality and collection of kinks and fetishes by practicing it with as many partners as she can, the more the better. Only a patriarchal oppressor would tell her to slow down and keep her dating body count low. Don't you care about her reproductive health?!

She will happily sacrifice her youthful fertility for a career of any sort—or just because she's too busy. When she looks out at the future stretching before her, she sees herself confidently striding through life without tiresome encumbrances like children or spouses holding her back. If they get a little too clingy, she can always ditch them and start over.

Type A is the dominant femo-type in America. You see Type As on TV, in movies, awards shows, filling the dorms at every college's freshman class, and at all your local public schools.

However, there is a smaller group that is nothing like their more visible peers. Type B women teach their children exotic notions like it's okay to be female, men are actually good, intimacy should be saved for your spouse, marriage should be monogamous, and parents are the primary educators and role models for children.

Type Bs understand and appreciate their natural feminine power and don't suppress it in favor of either artificial hypersexualization or masculine attributes. Type B women recognize that men and women are different, and that's a good thing. They believe women should be treated equal to—but not the same as—men.

Nobody puts Type B in a corner!

The Three Filthiest Words in the English Language: Beauty, Chastity, Modesty

When I say they have taken your "femininity," does anyone know what that word even means?

"Do you mean archaic, ridiculous, cringe things like . . . modesty and chastity? LOL, gross. We threw those out a while ago, Grandpa! You want us to be pure and virginal, until a man comes along and unlocks our chastity belts? Too late, we're liberated now. We are empowered by our Tinder dates. We operate by one rule: Always Be Swiping. Yes, we picked up incurable chlamydia and had our heart ripped out and stomped on fifteen times by people we had crushes on, but hey—that is what equality looks like."

The rebranding of classical feminine virtues as dorky, lame, and out of date has successfully stripped young women of the very things that made them *different* from men. The same thing is happening to classical masculine virtues as strength is tossed out and replaced with weakness. The fabric of both genders has been torn, shredded, rejiggered, and stitched back together into an ugly patchwork costume that fits no one, itches, and makes everyone look fat.

What are these magical disappearing female virtues? Things like beauty, grace, compassion, and yes, modesty. In ancient Greece, the seven classical virtues were prudence, fortitude, temperance, justice, faith, hope, and love, or charity. These virtues were adopted later to form the basis for Christian theological virtues and, yes, they underpin the entirety of Western civilization.

Trigger warning: the word itself is from the Latin *virtus*, meaning force, power, strength, high character, and valor. I'm sure legions of graduate students have written dissertations on how virtues like these "uphold white supremacy." No wonder so few people exemplify these anymore.

The misinterpretation of beauty as a core feminine attribute has caused all sorts of problems. Those who run away from beauty also tend to shuck off their other feminine virtues. Some women may decide that since they aren't physically beautiful, they don't have to bother with *any* feminine virtues. They rebel against their own perceived "ugliness" and double down with purple hair, shaved heads, and extreme body modifications. If you won't gaze upon them in admiration, then they will force you to gaze upon them in horror.

The eternal impulse to *épater la bourgeoisie* strikes again—only instead of Bernice the flapper bobbing her hair, she decided to become another lumpy, topless, screaming college chick with sleeve tattoos and a giant hoop through her nose, like the obedient bovine she has become.

These girls have it all wrong. Almost none of us look like old-school supermodels (you know, the hot ones) on the covers of the magazines. Good luck finding a pretty face on a magazine these days. Thanks to Photoshop magic, even cover girls don't look like cover girls. Cover girls are just as likely to be cover boys.

No wonder everyone is so confused.

Whither true feminine beauty, then? As Saint Peter reminds us, beauty has to shine from within. A cliché, but one born of old truths.

"Your beauty should not come from outward adornment, such as elaborate hairstyles and the wearing of gold jewelry or fine clothes. Rather, it should be that of your inner self, the unfading beauty of a gentle and quiet spirit, which is of great worth in God's sight" (1 Peter 3:3–4 NIV).

Inner beauty—perhaps that, then, is *the* crucial feminine virtue. True inner beauty can transform even the very plain into paragons of loveliness. You don't need lip injections and hair extensions. Saint Peter doesn't explicitly condemn the practice of injecting five pounds of liposuctioned belly fat into each of your butt cheeks, but I'm pretty sure he wouldn't approve of that sort of "outward adornment," either.

Kill the Virtue, Kill the Soul

After feminism has its way with a young woman's soul, twisting and warping her inner beauty into grotesque abominations, her outer beauty usually follows suit.

In 2018, I stumbled onto a disturbing photo blog that documented young Brazilian women before and after they got to college and discovered feminism. It was called "Before and After Feminism" (in Portuguese, "Antes e Depois do Feminismo").[2]

In the "Before" photos, you see a lovely young teenage girl. She is slim, smiling, long-haired, and feminine. In the "After" photos, the difference is shocking. Feminist, Marxist indoctrination had turned her into an unrecognizable Orc. At least fifty pounds heavier, shaved head, hairy armpits, face tattoos, wearing a man's tank top with no bra—and dead, lifeless eyes. "Like a doll's eyes," as Quint says about the shark in *Jaws*. Something terrifying has devoured this girl's soul and carried it off to the depths.

College is the culprit that has transformed her and many others into a clone army of terrifying militant radicals—and debrided their flesh of any last bit of femininity. The Twitter account Libs of TikTok exposes an incredible collection of young American feminists who look like their Brazilian counterparts. They seem almost purposely freakish in appearance; the more offensive to your wretched, patriarchal sensibilities, the better. The point is to disgust you, the despised normie, aka, their parents. Imagine mutilating your appearance solely for the purpose of upsetting people you hate!

Despite their state of perpetual rebellion, these young women are nothing but slaves, held captive by the very thing they fight against: an invisible patriarchy they blame for their plight. Their minds are in chains, and every inch of their bodies shouts their enslavement. Their identity as "nonconforming to beauty norms" seems instead wholly dependent on their perceived enemy's reaction.

My *actual* reaction? Extreme pity.

You can spot militant young feminists like this in every town in America, red or blue—publicly displaying their inner turmoil in the form off excessive tattoos, exotic piercings, strange haircuts and hair colors, and showcasing as much skin as possible.

It strikes me as a form of self-harm, even masochistic humiliation. Aren't they just telegraphing their self-hatred to the world? "I was taught to hate myself, so I did everything I could to transform myself into something you hate, too."

People who love and respect themselves and others do not mar their natural selves in such ways. If this is just a "fashion trend," then I pray it goes the way of low-rise jeans as soon as possible.

A Modesty Proposal

There is no bottom when it comes to the rejection of another crucial feminine virtue: modesty.

I mean that literally: there are literally no bottoms on women's swimsuits anymore. Every time I visit the local beach or hit a hotel pool, I'm shocked all over again by G-string bathing suit bottoms. I grew up with "high cut" bathing suits, okay? The kind Christie Brinkley and Pamela Anderson wore.

To paraphrase Tony Soprano, I like "some" butt cheek showing, not "lots of" butt cheek showing.

Perhaps a worldwide Spandex shortage spawned the Brazilian-cut bathing suit, which is a suit that no longer bothers with any fabric. How else are you gonna show off your butt lift? Instead, you get a fashion-forward, one-inch-wide strip that disappears deep within the nether regions. I guess it functions like a stirrup holding the rest of the suit down.

I don't know why I'm always surprised by these bottomless bikinis. Modesty, like other virtues, has been tossed out in favor of increasingly disturbing public displays that would make a 1970s street pimp blush. The obscene is now the norm in women's fashion—and behavior. From time immemorial, women have known that leaving something to the imagination is the most effective way to present yourself for maximum attention. There is a way to dress that is alluring and sexy—without veering into crass or trashy or, frankly, butt naked.

Sadly, crass and trashy are all we have these days.

If you watched the video for Cardi B's and Megan Thee Stallion's 2020 hit rap song "WAP," first, are you okay? And second, you might have been left wondering where women can go from there. Feminists, of course, hailed the video as a powerful reclaiming of women's sexual dominance. Alyssa Rosenberg at the *Washington Post* wrote, "'WAP' is completely filthy. We could use a lot more pop culture like it."[3]

No, Alyssa, we really can't.

To top their triumph, Ms. B and Ms. Stallion will have to recreate the final scene from the movie *Requiem for a Dream*. They've left themselves nowhere else to go. The only thing missing from their music video is a money shot. We are very close to a moment where live, penetrative intercourse with a herd of *real* stallions onstage at the Grammys will be required of all female nominees. You've come a long way, baby. Neeeiighhh!!!

When I see young women on the street wearing just enough fabric to keep their iPhones tucked into something, I have to suppress the urge to reconsider the burka. To rethink the niqab. It's a clothing-optional world; you may wear either a bra or a T-shirt, but never both at the same time. Why bother? It just creates more laundry.

Imagine choosing *not* to display acres of pasty, tattooed upper thigh. I get it, you want to be noticed. People also crane their necks to look at car crashes. Noticing you is one thing, noticing you for the wrong reasons is something else entirely.

Put your pants on. Please.

Modesty also means moderation in *behavior*. Drunken debauchery has its place, trust me, but that place is usually at your college roommate's Las Vegas bachelorette party, and lucky for you, no one will remember what happened. I'm not telling you *not* to have fun—I'm telling you not to have *too* much fun. I spent my twenties at parties and bars, as did 100 percent of my college peers, but I am here to tell you that the hardcore "party" lifestyle will chew you up and vomit you out into the gutter.

You can always pick out the ones at the bar who have taken the fun too far—their hardened faces and glassy eyes tell you the whole sordid backstory. Just say no to that sixth margarita, girls—and the offer to do lines in the bathroom. Learn to moderate, or learn the twelve steps.

Camille Paglia famously enraged '90s-era feminists when she declared that girls who get wasted at college frat parties are partly to blame if they are assaulted. "A girl who lets herself get dead drunk at a fraternity party is a fool. A girl who goes upstairs alone with a brother at a fraternity party is an idiot. Feminists call this 'blaming the victim.' I call it common sense."[4]

If a sophomore gets drunk and ends up in a "consensual" situation she later regrets, is it rape? What if the frat bro was equally blotto? Equal rights, equal responsibility? As Dean Wormser said, fat, drunk, and stupid is no way to go through life. A little self-control is not only more attractive, but also contributes to your physical and psychological health.

I don't judge anyone who's acted in unspeakably immodest ways; after all, I am a survivor of an elite party school where free-flowing alcohol and drugs of every kind were plentiful. (*I Am Charlotte Simmons* by Tom Wolfe was like reading a nonfiction account of my college years.) A friend was once given a drink on her way home for Christmas break. She didn't know it was spiked with medical-grade ether a premed student had pilfered from the esteemed medical school. Everyone had gone home for vacation, so she was unconscious in her apartment for three days before anyone knew.

She lived, thank goodness, but "partying" has a price, and we have all paid it, in various amounts. It's all fun and games until someone develops a serious substance abuse problem, and I'm sure you, like me, have witnessed friends or family caught in this web. "Partying" can lead to a lifelong hangover, friends.

I am here to report that I escaped elite college culture *by the skin of my teeth.*

Chastity: The Gravest Sin of All

Chastity is the final and perhaps most hated of the three key feminine virtues. Teenagers may be having less sex than ever, but the *culture of chastity* as a virtue among millennial women is nonexistent, practically unimaginable. Wanting to have sex, having the opportunity to do it, and saying no? Inconceivable. You are not allowed to waste a perfectly good opportunity to increase your body count. You want your body count number to be *high*. The higher it is, the more desirable you must be. Trust the Science™.

Still, even the most liberated sex-positive sisters can sometimes sense that a gruesome body count may *not* be what men want in a future wife. A helpful article called "How to Hide a Promiscuous Past from Your New Man" includes this body-count affirming advice. "First of all, let's make one thing perfectly clear: There is absolutely nothing wrong with being a slut. The fact is that you have to kiss a lot of frogs before you find your prince."[5]

The writer neglects to mention that her readers aren't just kissing these frogs, they're sliding into home plate on every lily pad in the pond.

The article recommends the following as strategies to hide excess notches in your belt: lie to a new boyfriend, tell him previous lovers abused you, etc. But why would a feminist who *rejects* the patriarchal concept of chastity want to date a man who preferred a chaste girlfriend? Because even these liberated women know that the good boyfriends don't want a girl who was the last hat on the rack, the one that's been tried on and put back by every greasy head of hair that walked into the store.

A marriageable man is probably not super comfortable with the idea of his future wife wasting her best years as a fluffer for every rando who swiped right. Ladies, here's a tip: the trick is to *try to keep your body count low*. Much lower than Hillary Clinton's (according to her conspiracy theorists, who are definitely wrong). Lower than Charles Manson's. Aim for the sweet spot, which is somewhere between the number O. J. Simpson and Alec Baldwin are each accused of having.

Abnormalizing Normal Things

Some young people, in their own sad way, have invented a refuge from having sex with random strangers. Some hide behind asexuality, a newly invented sexual orientation. "Asexuals do not experience sexual attraction and or sexual desire."[6] Okay, if you say so. Hard to know, of course, if their libido vanished because of a soy-heavy diet, antidepressants, or other mood-stabilizing drugs—or if they are simply not comfortable with promiscuity but are too ashamed to say so to their friends.

Of course, nearly all healthy young people are supposed to experience some form of sexual attraction in their lives. Haven't these people ever seen an '80s teen movie? Blockbuster Video had to devote enormous sections of their stores to house movies made about a single topic: the horny American teenager. I guess Netflix must have ditched all the movies we watched, like *Risky Business* and *Weird Science* and even *Zapped*, starring Scott Baio. How come none of the teenagers in those movies ever, *ever* report feeling "asexual"? Let's be real: how could you stay asexual after seeing Rebecca DeMornay, or Kelly Lebrock, or Jake Ryan from *Sixteen Candles*?

Those old movies, full of good-looking young people, affirmed healthy teenage sexuality. They also had romantic happy endings—they all end in some form of true love (the less said about *Porky's*, the better.)

Things have, uh, changed a bit. Traditional attraction to other people your age is out. Breeding kinks are in. These are impregnation-based fantasies where girls indulge in the thrill of risky, procreative sex. Participants are "excited and possibly aroused by being intimate without protection, without condoms because the idea behind this kink is to inseminate someone."[7] That's right: young women have rediscovered their maternal instinct—and turned it into an edgy sexual fetish.[8]

Old-school feminists hate the breeding kink because it is "internalized misogyny." According to a militant publication you haven't ever heard of called *Fem Magazine*, "internalized misogyny is the involuntary and often unknowing acceptance of sexist ideas by women, the very people the patriarchy was built to oppress. In breeding kink, the contention is that you desire pregnancy or to be utilized as a tool for reproduction because society has taught you to want that."[9]

Yeah, okay, if you say so.

To me, it's pretty obvious that the "breeding kink" is just plain old-fashioned clock-ticking with a trendier filter. "Wanting to be pregnant is for boomers, so I'll make my desire for children into something weird."

Hey, I'll take it!

CHAPTER 5

Men

Masculinity Goes Extinct

We make men without chests and expect of them virtue and enterprise. We laugh at honor and are shocked to find traitors in our midst. We castrate and bid the geldings be fruitful.

— C. S. Lewis, The Abolition of Man

A woman simply is, but a man must become. Masculinity is risky and elusive. It is achieved by a revolt from woman, and is confirmed only by other men. Manhood coerced into sensitivity is no manhood at all.

— *Camille Paglia*

What They Took:

☑ ~~Your Fleeting Fertility~~
☑ ~~Your Role~~
☑ ~~Your Gender~~
☑ ~~Your Virtues~~
☑ **Men**

Where Have All the Young Men Gone?

A good man is hard to find these days, and you didn't need Flannery O'Connor to tell you that. This is the next item on our list of vital national resources that have been depleted nearly into extinction. The Great American Male used to roam our towns, prairies, beaches, and forests in large herds. They built big cities and small ones. They constructed railroads, freeways, highways, and byways, tamed the wilderness, mined the copper, founded empires and industries, and invented, well, almost everything. They walked on the friggin' moon!

Do they ever get so much as a thank you?

If this kind of talk triggers you, you might want to stop reading, because it's about to get worse.

Roughly three hundred sixty-five thousand men died freeing slaves in the Civil War. Around four hundred thousand more died freeing Europe and the Pacific from Nazi Germany and Imperial Japan. Countless thousands more fought, bled, and died in our other wars, many (all?) of them ill-begotten and futile efforts that should never have been fought.

The thousands who survived these horrors and managed to get home were never the same.

American men conjured the car, the airplane, the spaceship, the skyscraper, the steam engine, internal combustion, satellites, the television, the radio, the computer, the internet, modern medicine, the microchip, the flush toilet, the dishwasher, the washing machine, the assembly line, moving pictures, musicals, baseball, football, barbecues, the iPhone, and nuclear power.

They wrote excellent novels and poems and plays, invented jazz, composed the Great American Songbook, made art, founded the entertainment industry, directed all the classic films, and founded museums and theaters from coast to coast to showcase these wonders.

They even came up with the concept of "childhood," and produced the toys and theme parks to go with it.

They also, crucially, swept millions of women off their dainty feet and helped produce enough sons and daughters to carry on their legacy of American greatness—far into a future they could only imagine.

Here we are now, living in the bright, safe future they built for us. Or are we?

We get to live on the land they paid for with their blood, in the cozy bosom of the freedom they secured for us, surrounded by the marvels they left for our convenience and amusement.

Does anyone appreciate these gifts ancestral American men left for us?

No, they do not.

Instead, these great men are being methodically erased from history and our collective memory. The famous statue of Teddy Roosevelt was recently torn down from in front of the American Museum of Natural History in New York City. A 9/11 memorial to *firefighters* was defaced and its American flag destroyed.[1] A Thomas Jefferson statue at Hofstra University was hidden from sight because it offended students.[2] In San Francisco, the idiotic city council—in the middle of a pandemic and a crime wave—drew up plans to rename schools named for problematic men like Francis Scott Key, Thomas Edison, Paul Revere, Robert Louis Stevenson, William McKinley, James Garfield, James Monroe, and Herbert Hoover.

Books written by disfavored male authors are banned, deleted from university English class curricula, and forgotten.

Even Dr. Seuss has been tossed onto the ash heap of literature.

The short-sighted historical illiterates pushing to erase great men and their achievements from memory never offer to give up their comfortable homes in the land those men built. Instead, they are content to continue to live and work in cities and towns founded by these legions of awful "toxic" males. Curious, that.

If any of you decide to abandon this befouled land of toxic masculinity, call me—I'll help you pack. I hear North Korea is very nice this time of year.

Going on a Manhunt

Of course, men are also to blame for our present situation. Some men willingly relinquished their dominance and authority over society and their own families. They were complicit in putting women in charge of everything, maybe out of fear of being called misogynists or "male chauvinist pigs" by their own wives and daughters. Perhaps husbands got tired of the constant noodging and took their hands off the steering wheel, threw a brick onto the gas pedal, and bailed out of the family station wagon. Liberal politicians who were early adopters of the women's rights movement probably saw a vast new voting bloc they could instantly capture. The barons of industry who supported the early movement saw eager hordes of low-wage employees to fill their sweatshops and factories.

By the time second-wave feminism crashed onto the boomer shores in the '70s, it had become a full-blown destroy-the-patriarchy call to arms. Mallory Millett, the sister of Kate Millett, feminist icon and founder of NOW, wrote about a consciousness-raising meeting Kate hosted in 1969:

> We gathered at a large table as the chairperson opened the meeting with a back-and-forth recitation, like a Litany, a type of prayer done in Catholic Church. But now it was Marxism, the Church of the Left, mimicking religious practice:

"Why are we here today?" she asked.

"To make revolution," they answered.

"What kind of revolution?" she replied.

"The Cultural Revolution," they chanted.

"And how do we make Cultural Revolution?" she demanded.

"By destroying the American family!" they answered.

"How do we destroy the family?" she came back.

"By destroying the American Patriarch," they cried exuberantly.

"And how do we destroy the American Patriarch?" she replied.

"By taking away his power!"

"How do we do that?"

"By destroying monogamy!" they shouted.

"How can we destroy monogamy?"

"By promoting promiscuity, eroticism, prostitution and homosexuality!" they resounded.[3]

These women raised their sons to be the first generation of "male feminists," and now we're living in the charred rubble.

With no more obstacles, women eagerly filled the vacuum at the top of the food chain. Somehow, despite their claims to lifelong oppression by men and the Patriarchy, women now enjoy complete dominance in American society; indeed, across the developed world.

Celebrated feminists now dominate our institutions, academia, politics, government, media, culture, medicine, and tech. Their every utterance and proclamation is grist for a glowing profile in *The Atlantic* or *Newsweek*. "The Year of the Woman!" the news proclaims, every year, year after year. Every time, the cover photo is Georgia gubernatorial loser Stacey Abrams, the gap between her teeth wide enough to park her inflated sense of herself.

Men had their chance, now it's the gals' time to shine! "Behold our competence," the ladies chant, pulling on knit caps shaped like their own genitalia.

Meanwhile, young men, especially straight young men, and particularly those from disfavored racial groups, are finding their applications tossed in the trash at college and grad school admissions offices. They are deemed unhireable by corporate HR departments—treated like an untouchable caste by the lavishly paid Diversity, Equity, and Inclusion gatekeepers who now run the world.

The deletion of men from the ranks of elite society is only speeding up. Women have dominated men in college admissions since 1979, and the gap is growing. "Women in the U.S. are now more likely than men to have a four-year college degree. Among those ages 25 to 34 specifically, women are now 10 percentage points more likely than men to have a bachelor's degree (46% vs. 36%)."[4]

Lower education levels usually mean a lower lifetime income, which brings with it the negative baggage poverty always does. How are men with less education, who make less money, going to woo and marry babes in higher tax brackets? "The college gender gap...reflects women pursuing higher education at greater rates than ever before, while college-going rates among men have stalled for reasons that mystify experts." LOL, we know the reason. "The gap in graduation rates is even larger, because male undergraduates are less likely to complete their degree.... [W]omen have also edged ahead in prestigious programs like medicine, law, and masters and doctoral degrees."[5]

The reasons men are lagging behind should not mystify the "experts." The reasons are clear: everywhere, from birth on up, girls are celebrated and cheered, encouraged to do anything, to be anything, to code, to enter traditionally male-dominated STEM fields, and to replace men in every profession.

Boys, meanwhile, are ignored, shamed, dosed with ADHD meds, and treated like second-class citizens in the classroom. For years, I have been reading about the "war on boys" at schools, where boisterous boys are medicated and punished for acting like . . . boys. In history class, they are taught that the great men of history only accomplished what they did because they trampled on some woman's rights. Alexander the Great, Caesar, Napoleon, William the Conqueror, Shakespeare, Charlemagne, George Washington, Thomas Jefferson—actually, kids, they were a bunch of sexist pigs who only got where they were thanks to the *unsung females* in their lives. Don't try to emulate these bad men, boys. Try to be more like, like *Hillary Clinton* instead!

When you see a man driving around with an "I'm With Her" bumper sticker on his Nissan Leaf, say a prayer for his mother, because she ain't getting any grandchildren. The "with" part is purely platonic.

Unfortunately, the war on men and boys has been won. It's over. Men have been replaced, from the cockpit to the gravel pit. Women can do *anything*, we were told.

What they didn't mention was that women were going to do *everything*.

After all, they can't just double the number of available spots in the MIT or Harvard freshman class, or double the number of new hires at JPL or Morgan Stanley or Amazon. Sorry, boys!

There is just one American institution where men still dominate: the prison system. "Out of 185,000 federal inmates, 93.2 percent were made up of men, and only 6.8 percent were females."[6] Ladies, you're just going to let men overrepresent like that? We need more women represented in the C-suites—and the cell blocks.

Of course, women cornering higher education and high-paying careers has had some ugly unintended consequences. "The simple mathematics of more women than men earning college degrees means that many highly educated women will either have to partner with less educated men or forgo partnership. We currently live in an era of work and family, but this might presage a harder choice between work or family, and consequently a lower birthrate."[7]

You'll have lots of framed degrees hanging on your wall, but no framed wedding photos. No family photos, no husband, no children. But as head of HR, you'll get to start a Bring Your Fur Baby to Work Day!

Fatherless Boys, Dangerous Mothers

Not that long ago, little boys were encouraged to do traditionally boyish activities. Sports, Boy Scouts, hunting, carpentry, Navy SEALS, strapping dynamite to your little sister's Barbie doll and trying to launch it into space. The character Sid from the first *Toy Story* movie is an evil villain who torments toys, but he's macho and tough compared to that wuss, Andy. And look what happens to poor Sid: he grows up to be Andy's family's garbage man.

Of course, neither Sid nor Andy has a father in the home, as far as I can tell from the movies. The trend of fatherless boys raised by single mothers is not a new one, but it is no longer just a trend—it's a massive cohort. According to the 2020 U.S. Census, 30 percent of all American children grow up without a father at home.[8] When broken down by race, things look stark. "While 74.3 percent of all white children below the age of 18 live with both parents, only 38.7 percent of African-American minors can say the same."[9]

That's over twenty million children. Millions of little boys are living in mini-matriarchal societies with no male energy to temper all that estrogen—no one to play catch with them, teach them how to deal with bullies, treat girls, and warn them away from pornography, drugs, and other dangers.

Is it any wonder so many boys fail to launch?

The other side effect of boys growing up without dads is the forced feminization that occurs. Without a pesky dad around, a single mom can paint her son's nails and put him in fun hairdos for her Instagram reels. Whenever you see the latest transgender "girl" feted on toxic morning talk shows, he is almost always being raised by a single mother. I can't find any studies on this, but anecdotally, it seems that the most egregious cases of boy feminization—like the abusive "drag kids" trend—seem to be mostly propagated by oddball, bipolar single mothers.

It makes perfect sense. A single mother is *by definition* someone who probably had a profoundly negative experience with *at least* one man. Is it any wonder these moms love getting their cute little boys to wear pink, to try on princess dresses, and to experiment with lip gloss? The social media clout, the likes, the dopamine hits, are almost too much for lonely, befuddled older women to resist.

Anyone who pressures a young boy to try on a dress and pose for a photo or take part in a "drag queen" event starts to approach symptoms of the mental illness-induced child-abuse disorder known as Munchausen by Proxy syndrome. These are disturbing cases where a mother (it's almost always the mother) invents a fake sickness or injury in her child in order to enjoy the emotional rewards that come with victimhood. It's powerful—and frightening. A perfectly healthy woman named Gypsy Rose Blanchard is serving ten years in prison for murdering her mother after enduring decades of Munchausen-induced abuse, including being forced to use a wheelchair, have twenty unnecessary surgeries, and get fed via feeding tube because her mother craved the attention.[10]

Now imagine the temptation for an insecure, unstable woman to conjure for herself a transgender child. With a transgender "daughter" by her side, she will be catapulted into a new life via social media. After life as a wallflower, she will finally be popular and adored, showered with affirmation, likes, and compliments like "You're so brave" and "Wow, what a super mom." There is no other way for her to generate this level of deep societal acceptance—and love for herself. So Timmy puts the dress on, the likes roll in, and his mom is hooked on dopamine hits. Is Timmy truly transgender? Or is his mother making up a fake condition for status?

We will never know, and once Timmy is Tammy, it's too late.

I once witnessed a conversation at an extremely progressive, monied preschool between the Mommy-and-Me teacher (a middle-aged white boomer who wore nothing but Indian saris and fancied herself some sort of enlightened child guru) and a young mother. The mother told the teacher that a preschool boy she knew had asked to try on an item of girls' clothing. The young woman's face glowed as she spoke, like she was announcing the Second Coming of Christ (that news would *not* have been welcome, I'm sure). The teacher's face lit up with a beatific glow. True enlightenment had been reached by both women; their hard work had paid off. They had tears of joy on their faces as they held each other. Powerful waves of estrogen-induced spiritual ecstasy emanated from their bodies; I was nearly blown over by its force.

When these boy-destroying women are married, it is usually to feckless "male feminists." These are husbands in name only. They behave like submissives caught in the grip of suburban dominatrixes who crack the whip, wear the pants, and rule the roost. She is the queen in her castle, and he is but her lowly jester.

You probably know a few couples like this. I knew a little boy with parents like this. At some point, the parents divorced (shocker), and almost immediately after the dad moved out, the mother proudly started posting photos on Instagram of her little boy (age four) wearing clip-on earrings. I watched as thousands of people liked her post, posting hearts and flowers and rainbows in honor of her poor little boy's "bravery."

Folks, it's not bravery when your mother makes you do it.

Forcing little boys to temper their own masculine impulses and sometimes *literally* neuter themselves to please overbearing, insecure mothers is just old-fashioned child abuse in drag. Isn't this what the movie *Psycho* tried to warn us about? It's about a boy raised by a domineering woman ("Mother"), and the boy grows up to dress like a woman.

I wouldn't be surprised if *Psycho* is soon shown to children as a feel-good, trans-affirming, mother-son love story.

Feminizing Men

Men are getting curb-stomped from birth by their mothers, their teachers, their professors, their bosses, their wives, and the culture at large. But there is another factor causing the "shrinkage" of male power and dominance in American society: falling testosterone levels and cratering male fertility.

Why are more men low T, as they say? Why are sperm counts crashing? Were these guys forced to watch too much *Dora the Explorer* and *Blue's Clues* as children? What is causing the collapse not just of masculinity, but biological *maleness* itself?

Scientists cite a range of diet and health issues to explain this problem. Poor diets with too much soy and seed oils (proven to lower testosterone and even shrink testicles), being overweight (fat cells lower testosterone), and guzzling all those "xenoestrogens" in our food and water supply. These are artificial female hormones that have built up in the environment thanks to sixty-plus years of chemical birth control in urine being flushed into the water supply. This estrogen-infused water is used to grow crops, feed farm animals, and fill your baby's bathtub.

It's the circle of life: birth control pills your mother took to try to prevent your birth will, in a wild plot twist, render you incapable of having her grandchildren.

Our boy babies are literally swimming in a toxic environmental stew of feminizing chemicals from birth. It's no wonder so many boys grow up to be man-boobed Marvel superfans.

There is another obvious reason behind the testosterone shortage in American society: feminism itself! Scientists—trust science, remember!—recently *proved* what I always suspected: male feminists have much higher rates of erectile dysfunction. "Feminist-identified men were substantially more likely to report EDM [erectile dysfunction medicine] use than non-feminist men, even after controlling for alcohol use before sex, erection difficulties, sexual arousal, sexual health, mental health, and physical health."[11]

As a Christian, I must remember not to laugh at people suffering from tragic medical conditions caused by feminism.

The experts behind the study noted that they were mystified as to the reason *why* male feminists can't achieve erections. "One explanation is that feminist men may use EDM to bolster their masculinity when it is otherwise threatened by their identification as feminist."

Okay, I mean it, stop laughing.

Allow me to offer my own rigorous scientific explanation for why male feminists cannot become aroused by their feminist girlfriends: it's because *they have feminist girlfriends.*

Have you ever *seen* a feminist? Are you telling me those shrill, pasty women with shaved heads and hairy pits and unshaven legs, who proclaim on your first date at the Ruth Bader Ginsberg biopic that they'd abort your baby and never tell you about it—are you telling me those alluring sex goddesses are *unattractive* to straight men? Incapable of arousing even the most liberal-minded male ally?

The rigid, rock-hard truth is that no matter what the hapless, hollow-chested male feminist does or says, no matter how many "I'm With Her" bumper stickers he slaps on his Prius, no matter how many plant-based soy drinks he sips, no matter how many Lizzo songs he forces himself to listen to, no matter how many sympathetic menstrual cramps he pretends to have when his *grrrrlfriend* is on her period—he will never be able to eradicate his God-given, hardwired, natural attraction to . . . *feminine-looking women.*

The male feminist's plight is tragic. It's Shakespearean. It's like the Gift of the Magi: his love of feminist women has rendered him incapable of *expressing* his love for them. Pray for this poor "man" who has been psychologically tormented to the point of impotence and permanently gelded by Girl Power.

Maybe this is why feminist women feel so safe with male allies—they know these guys will never bust a move.

Enslaved by Smut

There's one more force that is perhaps the most potent man-killer of all. It destroys teenage boys' minds, damages grown men's ability to form healthy relationships with women, and yes, lowers testosterone. Writer Pascal-Emmanuel Gobry published a mind-blowing report on how pornography permanently alters the developing male brain, and it is terrifying.[12]

Most boys first encounter porn at age eleven on their "smart" phones, and thus begins a lifelong love affair with trafficked sex slaves on their screens.

Pornography is not only highly deformative to the male psyche—it's also one of the most addictive substances on earth. It does all sorts of awful things to your brain and makes permanent changes to your cortex. It has basically the same effect as a meth addiction and is just as hard to quit. It's well documented that a pornographic stimulus quickly loses its ability to excite the viewer, so he or she is forced to seek ever more extreme or taboo content. Like drugs, the porn user needs a bigger hit to get the same high.

At the end of this descent into the abyss await truly demonic horrors like sissy porn (where straight men are subjected to "forced feminization" sadism), torture porn, and then, the final circle of Hell: kiddie porn. Pornography is not a harmless way to satisfy urges when you're alone. It is truly a portal to selling your soul to the devil—for both the performers and the consumers.

OnlyFans is a wildly popular website where young women post lewd videos of themselves for paying fans, and then brag on social media about all the money they've made. It's billed as female empowerment and financial independence to young, poverty-stricken, college-age girls. I even saw a video of a young man recruiting OnlyFans girls at a *college job fair.* The important thing is to get young women *working* early—who cares if it involves stripping on the internet? Men get to take advantage of these poor, deluded girls and enjoy the whole Girlfriend Experience—except you are alone in the dark in your filthy apartment. Sexy!

Could anything be more demeaning to men *and* women? OnlyFans turns users into pathetic homunculi, caged eunuchs, and neutered voyeurs. This is not a habit or a hobby or a fun way to relax after work—it is a sickness that will slowly devour your masculinity and your humanity.

I briefly considered lowering myself into the septic tank and making an OnlyFans account to conduct some research. For *research* purposes, okay? After all, maybe OnlyFans has a bad rap. Maybe it really *is* empowering for young, double-D-cup women! But then I remembered the time I watched *The Exorcist* and couldn't be alone in a dark room for a year without feeling an overwhelming sense of dread. If I innocently browsed OnlyFans, would I be forever haunted by images of busty ex-baristas wearing fluffy pink kitten ears and asking me to send them five dollars a month? I cast you out, unclean spirits!

If you have been caught in the web cast by these cheap online strippers, it's never too late to quit. The male sex drive is not necessarily the problem here. God knew what he was doing when he invented it. It had to be utterly invincible, or it could never have kept the genetic line going through natural disasters, plagues, famines, fights with the neighboring cave, extinction bottlenecks, and smelly cave chicks who didn't own perfume, razors, or toothbrushes.

The tireless male libido, along with the equally mighty maternal instinct, has saved humanity's skin many times over the eons. Now men's libido and latent masculine energy are weaponized against them. The pornography industry is monetizing their "horniness" and turning them into return customers and helpless addicts. The male sex drive is being diverted away from real relationships with live women towards a spiritual, romantic, and genetic dead end. Men's healthy instincts are driving them right over the edge and into a blighted abyss.

It's sadly out of fashion now, but there is a very good and smart reason for the ancient chivalric virtue of chastity. When you're a young, chaste male, you are *much* more likely to lock down a nubile and willing bride—and then get her alone, fast. It's an excellent system for the modern young man to adopt. It can save you from the ugliness that your natural urges may lead you toward.

You must resist, or else you risk transforming into a pale wraith alone in the flickering screen light, covered in lotion, your shorts around your ankles, awash in shame. If you drop dead mid-session, that is how they will find you. Is this how you wish to spend your precious time on this planet? Rejecting porn is real masculine power—and the timeless way of great men. But beware: living a porn-free life makes progressives and feminists angry! How dare you stop looking at porn! Are you some sort of . . . domestic extremist?

Just look at the reaction to the popular "No Fap" movement.[13] It started on the right but has taken off in online circles everywhere. ("Fap" is slang for "masturbate.") "No Fap" is a movement and a support group for young men trying to abstain from pornography. Feminists, predictably, accuse these men of believing in the "pseudo-science" behind abstention. NoFappers are accused of being Christian fundamentalists, misogynists, and even racists (!). You know femi-nism is completely fake when men who choose *not* to interact with pornography are vilified. Real male feminists spend at least eight hours a day supporting sex workers—by watching them get abused on camera.

In college, I was forced to write English papers about the oppressive "male gaze." Now, if you *aren't* addicted to gazing at exploited females all day, you are literally a white supremacist. In a neat trick, the oppressed and the oppressor have changed places. "The Male Gaze: Why It's a Good Thing, Actually."

Make Men Great Again

Our civilization hangs in the balance. We desperately need men to be great again. To woo women again. To form families again. To assert themselves as patriarchs. No, not the tyrannical patriarchs that femi-nists have wet dreams about "smashing." I mean wise paterfamilias who act as the loving and devoted heads of their own little kingdoms. The other day, I found an old Mickey Mouse–ear hat from Disneyland buried in a box of kid dress-ups. My husband had had it personalized with his first name at the park: "Dad." Is there any better crown for a family's king?

Humanity requires strong men who are attracted to fertile women, successfully entice them into marriage, and vow to spend their lives protecting them and their offspring. Some of you are out there, doing the work, being good men, and raising good boys. I applaud you. I'm doing my part, too. My husband and I are doing our best to raise boys who will become men like this.

There is a scarcity of role models for them in the wider world. Teenage boys can't exactly model themselves after the Gigachad meme guy. The ephebic pop stars Harry Styles and Lil Nas X comically appear on the covers of magazines modeling ball gowns, feather boas, and nail polish. Elon Musk is a hero for speaking about the fertility crisis, but he is not exactly a poster boy for monogamous pair breeding. He's doing his part to save the world—one baby mama at a time.

How can a young boy learn to be a man when his father is either M.I.A. or changes his name to "Mia"? Yes, there are wonderful, quiet heroes all over America raising their sons to be normal men with their body parts and hormone levels intact, their minds uncontaminated by progressive viruses, but they toil in obscurity. There are countless other examples of brave "toxic males" coming to the rescue during natural disasters, carrying women and toddlers to safety through waist-deep floodwaters, rescuing babies from burning buildings, and, perhaps most courageously, remaining loyal to their wives and families.

There are a few simple things men can do to reclaim their latent powers. For example, stop dressing like six-year-olds. Stop projecting mental infantilization when you go out in public. Take off the cargo jorts and put on a well-fitting pair of pants. Project masculine power and watch the world react accordingly.

I asked a few like-minded fellas to tell me what they think has gone wrong with modern men. Their responses are enlightening:

"I've been watching old *Miami Vice* episodes, and it is making me think about men. Part of what men have lost is swagger. The ability to walk around like kings. The vibe a real man projects is 'Stay the f*ck out of my way, I am a man and there might be something dangerous about me. Perhaps not physically dangerous. Perhaps I will buy and sell you, perhaps I will mog you with my comfortable life, but I am going somewhere that doesn't concern you, and I advise you to stay out of my way right now.'"

"A man must live above the world. 'I need a table inside for four. You will give it to me, now.' A man is constantly sending out Jedi mind tricks."

"A culture is largely defined by what in that culture only men do."

Well, I guess masculinity is not dead yet! There used to be a deodorant commercial in the '80s, and the tagline was "Never let them see you sweat." That would be a good masculine ethos to bring back. In times of grave peril, everyone will look for the one guy who is not panicking, who is calmly directing people to the exits. Be that guy.

Perhaps more than anything else, our masculinity crisis is a crisis of *confidence*. We need to stop telling our boys, "It's okay to cry and wear a dress," and instead start telling them, "It's okay to be strong and act brave, even when you're scared." One reason the story of United Flight 93 has become legend is because of the incredibly brave actions of four normal American guys: Jeremy Glick, Todd Beamer, Mark Bingham, and Tom Burnett. They gathered a team, said a prayer, and stormed a cockpit filled with armed terrorists during a hijacking, in midair, with no weapons other than their fists.

If that flight had been full of squishy male feminist allies headed to an abortion rally, they would have remained seated until the plane crashed into its intended target.

I am not exaggerating when I say that the survival of the species depends on getting masculinity back on track. Are you man enough to save humanity from itself? If you are reading this book, chances are you and your sons are gonna make it.

CHAPTER 6

A Soul Mate

The Wedded Abyss

More good women have been lost to marriage than to
war, famine, disease, and disaster. You have talent,
darling, don't squander it.

— *Cruella de Vil, textile aficionado*

No man or woman really knows what perfect love is
until they have been married a quarter of a century.

— *Mark Twain*

What They Took:

☑ ~~Your Fleeting Fertility~~
☑ ~~Your Role~~
☑ ~~Your Gender~~
☑ ~~Your Virtues~~
☑ ~~Men~~
☑ **A Soul Mate**

Marriage Disparaged

L ittle-known fact: the Disney animators based the Cruella de Vil character on actual middle-aged feminists. She did have a point, though: marriage is a partnership in which both people gain, but each must also give up some part of their old life. When you're single, there's no one else to worry about, to ask permission of, or to deal with when you're in a bad mood. You can do exactly what you like, when you like!

Which will mostly involve eating meals alone with your cats, who will return the favor by devouring your body when you die alone in your apartment.

Finding a soul mate is hard enough—but what are you supposed to do when the entire notion of marriage has gone out of date? The gays fought for the right to get married; now they're the *only ones* getting married. The delicate two-step process of falling in love with your soul mate and then committing to each other for life *legally*—it would be easier to get two average singles to build their own rocket and fly it to the moon. Marriage has simply been removed from the ideal fantasy life plans of everyone under forty.

By marriage, I mean two things: first, your own personal marriage-ability, and second, the concept of making a lifetime commitment to another person. These are dire conditions in which to find a suitable spouse. There is a severe soul mate crisis among both men and women. Most single people under thirty are not exactly what I would call mar-riage material. Single men are probably watching porn, playing video games, or prowling dating apps—sometimes all at the same time. Men are simply reaping the benefits feminism sowed for them: plentiful, abundant, even overflowing opportunities for sexual encounters, on demand. Hookup apps serve as your own personal streaming platform—only instead of TV shows, you get a steady stream of liber-ated, empowered girls. Netf*cks, if you will.

Meanwhile, young women—trained from birth to avoid monogamous romantic entanglements—are simply behaving according to their programming. Bad news: spending your prime years collecting STDs and broken hearts is not the most productive path to true love, a long-term relationship, or deep and lasting intimacy with another person. But young women and the men they "date" are both victims of the same vicious feminist propaganda. Never settle down, never accept compromise, never sacrifice, do what feels good in the moment without fear of consequences, and stop looking for a man to make you happy.

It's no wonder everyone treats marriage like it's lava.

Til Death or Whenever Do Us Part

It's all fun and video games until civilization starts to crumble under our feet. Folks, the U.S. marriage rate is at rock bottom. In 2020, it hit a 50-year low.[1] What a wonderful achievement, thank you! "A growing share of U.S. adults are neither married nor living with a partner. In 2019, roughly four-in-ten adults ages 25 to 54 (38%) were unpartnered. This share was up sharply from 29% in 1990."[2]

This is a feature and not a bug of modern American society. Did you think the girlboss army was just going to sit back and take it while they watched their prettier, more feminine friends get engaged to the few men alive not yet addicted to porn? They may be miserable, but they're smart. These people are supervillains. Their plan was brilliant:

> Step 1: Rebrand marriage as something bad men do to oppress women.
> Step 2: Remove the stigma of unwed motherhood.
> Step 3: Always be swiping!

Step 4: Invent expensive and invasive reproductive technology that renders marriage—and men—unnecessary.

Mission accomplished. What we are experiencing is a contemporary reboot of *Cinderella*, as told from the stepsisters' point of view. "No one wants to marry us, so now no one will marry *you*, either." It's the female remake of *Revenge of the Nerds*, and it's a blockbuster hit. If only sex appeal were more evenly distributed!

Young women are not the only ones opting out of wedded bliss; young men are fleeing the altar, too. Is it harder than ever to find a suitable mate, or do people in their twenties just not want to get married? Is it the proliferation of dating apps, easy access to pornography, and the fear of getting called a sexual harasser if you try to flirt with a stranger?

Sixty years of unchecked feminism convinced young women marriage is a trap and a prison—and gave permission to several generations of young men to collect digital harems of cheap concubines.

Divorce Porn

We find ourselves in a situation where many young women of marriageable age are no longer interested in finding husbands. Worse, women with perfectly good husbands entertain vivid fantasies about leaving them. While some studies say that 30 percent of divorces are initiated by women, others put the figure even higher—a mind-blowing 80 percent![3] The main reason behind this startling statistic seems to boil down to . . . housework. "There's still a lack of equality regarding domestic labor within the average American household, and it's a gap that might make marriage seem less advantageous for a woman who is career oriented. If the wife makes more money but is still expected to do more of the housework and childcare, what's the point?"[4]

The point? The point is . . . oh, never mind, just dump the guy already and get it over with. Lately, I've come across essay after essay by miserable wives who divorce their husbands and blow up their kids' lives because . . . they make messes in the kitchen. "Divorce Porn," as I call it, is now an entire literary genre. Books, essays, plays, poems, and screeds of every type celebrate the lucky marriage escapees who found a magic key that unlocked them from the prison of their marriage to a loving, loyal husband.

Escapees describe the harrowing details of their wretched married lives, which tend to include atrocities like their husband's failures to put his dishes in the dishwasher, do an equal amount of the laundry, or to teleport home from work to sweep up spilled Cheerios in the afternoon. Divorce porn always ends with a happy ending: the newly divorced middle-aged woman kissing her children goodbye and leaping into an Uber with a younger man, one of many she will subject her kids to post-divorce.

Perhaps you know some women like this. We all do.

One heartwarming essay in *The Atlantic* called "How I Demolished My Life" documents Honor Jones's decision to essentially abandon her marriage and flee from her country house to—where else—Brooklyn. In part, it reads:

> I didn't have a secret life. But I had a secret dream life—which might have been worse. I loved my husband; it's not that I didn't. But I felt that he was standing between me and the world, between me and myself. Everything I experienced—relationships, reality, my understanding of my own identity and desires—were filtered through him before I could access them. The worst part was that it wasn't remotely his fault; this is probably exactly what I asked him to do when we were 21 and first in love, even if I never said

it out loud. To shelter me from the elements; to be caring and broad-shouldered. But now it was like I was always on my tiptoes, trying to see around him. I couldn't see, but I could imagine. I started imagining other lives. Other homes.[5]

I feel for this poor woman. It sounds like her life was causing her extreme distress. Yet I can't help but wonder: did no one ever explain to her that once you have children, their emotional well-being is, like, more important than yours? Staying home with messy kids all day can absolutely drive you crazy. This should not be a surprise. Sorry to break this to you, but parenting is hard, and no amount of money or liberation from your domestic shackles can change that.

Maybe I'm reading too much into these Divorce Porn writers. Maybe b*tches just be crazy.

A True-Life Divorce Story

My equation for happiness is pretty simple: maximize your number of children and minimize your number of spouses. I'm going for a lifetime total of one spouse. One seems like plenty, at least for me. My siblings and I survived a dramatic and shocking parental divorce. There was no abuse in our home, and our parents had an uncontentious split. We didn't have to pack pathetic little suitcases and shuttle between two homes. We were lucky—we got to stay put in our childhood house while our father got an apartment we rarely visited.

Then why was it dramatic and shocking? Because we discovered, in a single moment, despite having outwardly privileged childhoods in a nice neighborhood and going to good schools, we lived in a house of cards built on quicksand. It was sudden. No warning. The mental shock was brutal.

To my fellow Generation X veterans of boomer divorce: I salute you.

Somehow, we all did okay as adults. We managed to survive, and even recover. We maintain good relationships with both parents, who remain friends with each other to this day. We avoided falling into ruin. Nobody picked up a drug addiction or landed on a stripper pole (yet).

Some people fear marriage because they experienced divorce in their childhoods. What if shunning marriage to avoid divorce simply perpetuates dysfunction in your life? What if the cleanest way to erase generational chaos and broken home pathologies and not pass them on to your descendants is . . . to do life the right way?

In other words, surviving divorce as a child is all the more reason to strive for a happy marriage. Instead of letting my parents' mistakes scare me away from marriage and potentially ruin my life, I decided sometime in my twenties that their foolishness would end with me. Long before I met my husband, I promised myself that marriage-ending choices would never be a part of my life. I vowed to do what I could to prevent any future children from enduring what we had endured. My children would be free!

Note: I am aware that divorce, like pulling a rotten tooth, is sometimes necessary. Unavoidable, even. Yes, I am a Catholic and a traditionalist, but good people (these days it's usually the men) can find themselves facing divorce though they have committed no sin. If any mistake was made, it was perhaps during the original mate selection process, when numerous red flags were overlooked and an "I can fix him/her" mindset crept in. No sane person sets out to be divorced, and yet, sometimes, one party takes its vows less seriously than the other party. No one ever talks about the many Widowers of Feminism: decent men who end up divorced after their wives decide that marriage is "oppressive" and decide to "go find themselves."

How many intact families has feminism taken a wrecking ball to? It's almost as dangerous as infidelity. Women who get bored with their marriage and their husband and throw them overboard to chase a mirage of self-discovery rarely find a pot of gold at the end of the rainbow. Instead, they tend to end up alone with a weed dealer on speed dial.

I can think of a few reasons when you must risk jumping out of the burning building, lest you perish. (One might be tempted to apply my divorce gray-area dispensation to abortion. To that I say, in the case of abortion, a small child is dismembered, so it's quite a different matter.) Even your best-laid plans can go sideways.

Children are the main victims of divorce, however amicable it may have been for the adults. So do your best. They're counting on you. I can think of a couple reasons why I would consider divorcing my husband, but they mostly involve scenarios where he becomes Jack Nicholson in *The Shining* or asks me to start calling him Jackie. If he comes at me holding an ax or wearing heels, I'm outta here.

The Path to Matrimony

Don't misunderstand: I'm not arguing that everyone has to get married. Like ill-tempered dogs who do best as the only pet in the home, there are plenty of people who should remain single. I'm sure you've met some of them. My position remains this: while many people have painted themselves into unmarriageable corners, some who seem to be heading that way can still be guided away from that dead end. Not everyone needs to get married to save the world; we just need more people to try it.

Nobody had to tell my generation of women to get married. When pressed, we would admit to being feminists, but we weren't militant. We were hyper-focused on getting cool jobs after college and *definitely* delaying marriage and a family until we had either made it big or had met "the one." The consensus was that marriage was something you do only once you turn thirty, and sure enough, that was when the bachelorette party save-the-dates started rolling in.

Not a single one of my college girlfriends met their future husband in college, but every single one ended up getting married—after at least a decade sowing wild oats.

There must have been wild oats shortages up and down the East Coast in the '90s as swarms of *Sex and the City*–addled female college grads descended on Manhattan, ravaging its crops of fresh MBAs and tormenting its club bouncers. Lubricated by barrels of Ketel One vodka, the drug of choice, these well groomed American Psycho-ettes had zero concerns they would end up single and alone. They could sip the wine of youth, slurping it down to the lees, secure in the knowledge that a future husband was their birthright.

They made risky choices knowing they would stick the landing when it was time to come down to reality. The difference between my peers and contemporary women in their twenties is that despite our wannabe–*Sex and the City* lifestyle, we all *wanted* to settle down. Just like Carrie Bradshaw, we would find our own Mr. Big one day and live happily ever after. The fact that Carrie failed to live happily ever after, season after season, didn't deter us. Maybe we'd had too many Cosmos.

Settling down with one person is no longer an aspiration for many. How can monogamy compete with an infinite menu of sexual partners, positions, and polyamorous propositions? Why would anyone restrict themselves to one Mr. Big when they can date Mr. Large, Mr. Extra Large, and Mr. Huge, all at the same time? How can you think about marriage when you must first spend years, decades even, staring into your navel (and other places) to uncover the unique quirks, fetishes, and arcane sexual subcultures that excite you the most?

You may end up living with a man, a woman, both, or a multi-player polycule. You may have children, or you may not, and who cares? You are in a cult of one, and as cult leader, your every whim is law. There is no higher purpose than experiencing the most pleasure possible, every single moment of every day. You're married to your desires, and that's the only relationship you'll take to your grave.

CHAPTER 7

Your Unborn Children

Aborting the Future

*We must not be surprised when we hear of murders,
killings, of wars, or of hatred. If a mother can kill her
own child, what is left but for us to kill each other?*

— *Saint Teresa of Calcutta (Mother Teresa)*

What They Took:

☑ ~~Your Fleeting Fertility~~
☑ ~~Your Role~~
☑ ~~Your Gender~~
☑ ~~Your Virtues~~
☑ ~~Men~~
☑ ~~A Soul Mate~~
☑ Your Unborn Children

Planned Parentlesshood

Those eggs you were born with? You don't own those. That fetus growing in your womb? It's not yours until you decide to keep it. Just relax, lie back, and think of Margaret Sanger. We'll take it off your hands and strip it for parts. Maybe one day you'll be ready for children. But not now. Trust us, we're doctors.

Democrats spent the last few years of the Trump presidency screeching about Central American mothers getting separated from their children at our Southern border. (Of course, many of those mothers willingly separated from their own children, some as young as two, when they handed them to depraved human smugglers who dropped them forty feet over the border wall or left them to wander the desert alone.) We can all agree that separating yourself from your *own* children is even worse than some government agency or institution taking them away from you, right?

Right?

Among all that has been stripped away from us, perhaps nothing is as traumatic as this: innocent children some adults decided were not worthy of being born. There is one region in the world where government officials and other authorities are only too happy to convince mothers to separate themselves from their children. And that region is your body. Any genetic material in your loins that could be used to create a child one day is fair game. Young women are subjected to intense psychological indoctrination from early childhood to disconnect them from any genetic legacy they may produce.

I was carefully coached by the media and my teachers to believe lies like "It's just a clump of cells" and "It's just a few eggs, you don't need them, you have tons." It's truly a miracle that any young woman not raised in a religious community escapes the gauntlet we are forced to run.

The abortion industry, and all its works, and all its empty promises, exists to trick young women into thinking an invasive, gruesome medical procedure is about female freedom and equality. The only people liberated by abortion? Men. They became instantly free to abandon anyone they impregnate and enjoy the company of women—without worrying about getting chased down for marriage proposals or child support.

As you probably know, Margaret Sanger, founder of Planned Parenthood, was a fanatical eugenicist. She was open about wanting to reduce the number of people in the world, especially people of color. Planned Parenthood of New York went as far as removing her name from one of their buildings, because, as they themselves admitted, "Margaret Sanger's concerns and advocacy for reproductive health have been clearly documented, but so too has her racist legacy. There is overwhelming evidence for Sanger's deep belief in eugenic ideology, which runs completely counter to our values."[1]

Everyone knows that historically black neighborhoods don't have a lot of Whole Foods markets, but they are positively littered with abortion clinics. Meanwhile, there is not a single abortion clinic on the entire West Side of Los Angeles, which is where all the liberal white feminists live. These are the Hillary Clinton–donor zip codes, where CAA agents and movie stars rub shoulders at the acai bowl shop after Pilates. But as soon as you cross the 110 freeway that bisects the city in half from north to south, you will find at least a dozen abortion clinics in the poorer neighborhoods.[2]

Beyond racial genocide, young women seduced into giving up control over their bodies and their fertility in the name of "health" are pawns in a great game. Women of all races are being encouraged to forgo, delay, deny, and minimize their own magical reproductive powers all over the world. Charitable organizations are causing mayhem wherever they go, convincing the women of the world to go along with it.

Country after country in South America is busy overturning longstanding abortion restrictions. On December 30, 2020, giant crowds of college-aged women in Argentina filled the public squares, cheering and screaming as the new law was announced. "With the legalization of abortion, Argentina, the birthplace of Pope Francis, deeply impregnated by Catholicism, marks with its seal the history of Latin America and joins Cuba, Guyana, and Uruguay, where abortion is already legal."[3] On the news, I watched as topless, stoned young feminists with shaved heads and pierced faces jerked around like zombies in the street dance party that followed. They were celebrating "freedom," but it all looked so bleak and ugly. The mark of feminism!

The abortion industry is racking up win after win. We know what the real long-term project is, and it's not to abort babies and sell their organs on the biomedical black market; that's just their extremely lucrative side hustle. ("Recently unsealed documents reveal Planned Parenthood charged a biospecimen company nearly $25,000 for fetal tissue."[4]) No—the real goal is to abort the nuclear family.

To do that, they must attack the traditional center of the family, its beating heart: Mom.

Once you can convince a young woman to dispose of her own child, literally into a medical waste bin, you have helped render her less equipped to raise a family. What happens to the river of maternal love when the spring has been poisoned?

Even if a woman never actually gets an abortion, just being an abortion supporter can warp you in ways that are hard to quantify. It can affect how you feel about children and make you question your own desire to start a family. Pro-choice mothers who get pregnant and decide to keep it walk around knowing that the poor kid is strapped into an ejection seat. One wrong move, one small defect, and she can just press EJECT. A baby in the womb of a pro-choice woman is standing in front of the villain's desk as he strokes his cat, unaware he is standing on a trap door above the piranha tank.

Most babies with even minor defects are instantly aborted. Over 90 percent of Down syndrome children are ejected.[5] But the babies aborted most often are perfectly healthy.

Their only defect is congenital inconvenience.

Reduction Ad Absurdam

Pro-choice propaganda has not only made parenthood less desirable, but it has also convinced women to reenact *Sophie's Choice* using their wombs as the setting. In that 1979 novel by William Styron (and the 1982 movie starring Meryl Streep), a woman who survived the Holocaust is haunted by the choice she made when she arrived at a concentration camp: she was forced at gunpoint to hand the guards one of her two small children, so she handed over her baby and kept her older child.

The novel is heartbreaking. It is unthinkable that a woman could be forced to choose which of her children lives and which one dies.

But today you can enjoy the *Sophie's Choice* experience right in the comfort of your obstetrician's office! *Sophie's Choice* is now *Sophie's Reduction*.

"Selective reduction" is yet another horror-movie phrase posing as a clinical medical term. It sounds like a fun diet you go on to reduce the size of your post-pandemic rear end. (We could probably all use a little reduction, am I right?) A selective reduction is a procedure in which a multiples pregnancy, like twins or triplets, is "reduced" to a single baby by killing and removing the unwanted fetuses. Calling the practice of selectively exterminating one baby in a set of twins a "reduction" is a euphemism only a supervillain could come up with. Ladies and gentlemen, I give you the American College of Obstetricians and

Gynecologists: board-certified MDs who are sworn to do no harm to their patients—unless the largest of the patients commands them to murder the smallest one.

Warning: if you attended a selective college, you may be more likely to experience a selective reduction.

Learning about "selective reductions" was one of my first wake-up calls to the reality of abortion. A female medical resident who was staunchly pro-choice told me about the time she witnessed a reduction during her OB rotation. She was so upset by it that she decided on the spot to choose a different specialty—one that did not involve pregnancy.

Years ago, a family friend found out she was having triplets. Unfortunately for her babies, she was an obedient pro-choice feminist, so she chose to have one of the three "reduced." She gave birth to healthy twins.

I have often wondered if those two fortunate abortion survivors, whose limbs narrowly avoided the doctor's vacuum suction tool, are aware that their own mother killed their missing sibling.

I once read about a similar vomit-inducing scenario in a *New York Times* opinion essay called "One Is Enough."[6] The author's list of reasons for deciding to reduce her natural set of triplets down to *just one baby* included her strong desire not to move to Staten Island, drive a minivan, or shop for bulk foods at Costco. Talk about a horror movie—how are you supposed to store all those giant Costco packages in your tiny Brooklyn walk up? (All abortion writers live in Brooklyn; it's an iron-clad law of journalism.)

The true collateral damage of abortion can't be measured by the number of tiny bodies incinerated as medical waste by the millions each year. That biosludge is just a messy byproduct of feminism. The lifestyle entire generations of young women are signing up for is underwritten and insured by the fetal biosludge safety net. Good vibes only—no babies allowed. When a lifestyle underwritten by abortion stretches out to fill a young woman's twenties and thirties, she can become nearly incapable of handling the sudden shift into committed, married motherhood later on. It's like a longtime street junkie thrown into involuntary rehab who is forced to quit drugs cold turkey: things can get ugly. Some pro-choice women will relapse into old habits, and the relationship—and family—will fail. "I can fix her" quickly becomes "No, I guess I can't."

I was once a liberal pro-choicer who finally woke up to the lie—right before trying to have my first baby. It takes a radical mindset shift to survive this transition. The cognitive dissonance is massive. Witness how women who have had abortions are forced to convince themselves, over and over again, how beneficial those abortions were. Actress Busy Philipps shouted her abortion at a rally and credited her past abortion(s) for helping her reach the bottom tier of Hollywood. "At rally [*sic*] outside the Supreme Court Wednesday, . . . Philipps delivered a pro-abortion rant in which she thanked her abortion for her professional success."[7] I'd never heard of her before that abortion rally, so I guess it worked!

Leggo My Eggo

Let's talk about your eggs. It's like the old riddle: What came first, the baby or the egg? This is not an "every sperm is sacred" screed. I am fully aware only a tiny fraction of female oocytes will ever become living babies, even under the best conditions. However, many young women who are tricked into donating their own eggs do so without complete understanding of what it can do to their future fertility. Egg donation, ladies, may scramble all your future plans.

The separation between a woman and any future offspring starts early. News stories about how kids cause climate change have never triggered anyone to dump their carbon-emitting kids by the side of the road. You have to target girls before they have families—long before they understand exactly how their bodies work and what oocytes are.

You get them at the source: their eggs.

Oviraptors know how to attract prey. Egg "donation" clinics, like escort services, target their marketing to very young women, ages twenty-one to twenty-nine, who need the extra money and don't have a complete grasp of how delicate reproductive biology is. It's an ugly combination of capitalism and compassion. Young altruistic women are lured to clinics with heartbreaking testimonials of infertile couples desperate for children. They are preyed on with promises that the process is risk-free. It's also pitched as the most wonderful gift you can give another suffering person. It's just like donating cans of beans to the hungry. You weren't going to eat those beans anyway.

You are an impoverished college junior with crushing debt. It's the eggs or the sugar-baby life. Since clinics can't legally buy your eggs, the money is called "compensation for your time and suffering." Plus, you can let a worthy couple experience the joys of parenthood—raising your child! You don't need all those eggs; they're going to waste, stuck inside your body. Give them to us!

Note that they call it egg donation when it is a sale, pure and simple. But the word "donor" reminds you of the time you donated blood, and you have an organ donor sticker on your driver's license, so it's a nice word. It makes you feel good.

Except the young egg-seller doesn't realize she is walking into a catastrophic, irreversible trap. Once you donate your eggs, their fate is entirely up to the recipient. You have no say about what happens to your biological offspring. Your maternal bond to any future children is severed for good.

Just thinking about a stranger giving birth to my biological infants—siblings to my children—and not being able to, you know, raise them myself—it's like having a night terror. Once you donate, that's it—no backsies. The eggs are gone forever, and no matter what happens to them, your rights as their biological mother are zeroed out.

Here is the nightmare scenario laid out for all to see on, of all places, the New York State Health Department website:

> You cannot be certain when a genetic child of yours may be born—it could be nine months or even years after your donation. More embryos may develop in the laboratory than can safely be transferred to the woman's uterus. The remaining embryos may be frozen and kept in storage for later use. The eggs may go to more than one recipient. One or more women may conceive, using your eggs, now or years from now. Or, no pregnancies may occur. The original recipient may never use the frozen embryos. The program may ask the recipient to: donate the embryos to another couple; donate the embryos to research; leave the embryos frozen indefinitely; or allow the embryos to be destroyed. Once you donate your eggs, their fate is entirely up to the recipient. You have no say about what happens.[8]

Eh, who cares? Look, over there: a chai latte! Coachella tickets! A big dent in your student debt!

Student debt has played a key role here. Your gender studies degree cost you $200,000, but your starting salary at the nonprofit is $36,000 a year. How else are you supposed to pay off that degree? Plus, thanks to your dedication to your career, you are not going to need your eggs any time soon. The only eggs you'll worry about are the poached ones on your avocado toast at boozy brunches with your roommates.

Clinics pay donors up to $10,000 per cycle, and even more for your second and third times. You're allowed to donate up to six times.

Payments can go up to $50,000 if you're special, like a supermodel who went to Harvard and got 1600 on her SATs.

A clinic called Beverly Hills Egg Donation has a list of rules and guidelines called "Responsibilities of an Egg Donor." Things like eating right, not smoking, and not getting AIDS. Almost like you're the mother or something! Egg-donation clinics target naive, cash-strapped young women who think of themselves as empathetic and caring—and who have already been carefully groomed by the pro-choice industry. These girls go into the donor process already convinced that their eggs have no relation to their own future human children ("It's not even a clump of cells, each egg is just one cell, you won't miss it"). They have zero emotional connection to the potential child each egg represents. Otherwise, how could they do such a thing?

You may enjoy the affirmation of getting picked, since it means you are nice, smart, and pretty. Almost like getting asked out by your crush. Imagine: someone picked you to be the mother of their baby! What an incredible ego boost!

Unfortunately for these ladies, the maternal bond is not so easily torn asunder. Nature, as they say, finds a way. One day, maybe years later, donors may wake up and realize they have real live children somewhere out there—but will never see them or even know if any exist. Just Google "egg donation regret" and you will see some of these stories. Over and over, older and wiser women rue the day their younger selves allowed doctors to rob them of their eggs. They believed the "experts" who told them there were no risks, no risks at all, step right up, and here is your check!

Leah Campbell developed severe endometriosis as a result of the grueling process, which included giving herself dozens of powerful hormone injections daily before she was plucked. She became perma-nently infertile, unable to have children, and eventually resorted to trying IVF—with donor eggs from a stranger. Her IVF attempts failed, and she eventually adopted and became a single mother:

> I have become increasingly bothered by an industry that seemed to profit off of my donations and then shut me out when I was no longer a commodity they could sell. I also struggled a bit more with the anonymity of my donations. I guess I'm more curious now because there are two children out there who look like the children I could have had if not for donating my eggs.[9]

It's the circle of life—in the seventh circle of Hell.

The only two biological children Leah will ever produce are being raised by a stranger. She will never meet them, touch them, or know them, and they will never know her.

Regret can also plague the recipients of donated eggs. *The Atlantic* published a story a few years ago called "Uneasy about the Ethics of Egg Donation," in which a woman who married in her late thirties resorted to donor eggs to have a baby:

> I can't get around the fact that we effectively "bought" a baby. . . . I also worry about the financial pressure on the donors, who are generally young women trying to pay off student loans. Being walked through the donor database was surreal and icky. Much like a dating site, we could review donors' photos, medical histories, eye color, height, etc. As we searched the list—trying to find a donor who bore at least a vague resemblance to me—I felt like I was in a sci-fi movie picking out a designer child. . . . It just felt too much like eugenics for comfort.[10]

I checked out some of these donor websites. They look exactly like dating sites, with airbrushed photos of young women posing provocatively in bathing suits and sexy outfits, like they're recycling their Tinder photos for their donor profile pages. You can search by race, hair color, and ethnic origin. Curiously, they break out "white" into over a dozen European subgroups: Danish, Swedish, Russian, Ukrainian, German, French, Irish, and so on. Options you will not see on your child's college applications.

On one major site, I tried searching for "African American" and was surprised to see zero potential donors found. Is the egg-donation industry perpetuating white supremacy?

Some argue that almost all the eggs that get donated would have otherwise gone to waste and never resulted in a child. Well, okay. But they are your eggs. Maybe the only thing worse than being haunted by the child you aborted is being haunted by the child you gave away and lost track of. Those donated children will spend the rest of their lives wondering about you, maybe seeking you out. Imagine not knowing who your biological mother is—but someone out there knows and is keeping it secret.

In some adoptions, it's impossible to trace a baby's parentage. I get it. But imagine erasing your own baby's lineage on purpose. You're not going to let your own child ever know where they came from?

What kind of parent are you?

Youth Supremacy

If you bother to investigate why all these clinics limit donors to young women in their twenties, you will accidentally uncover the painful truth propping up the fertility industry. Popular San Diego–based egg clinic A Perfect Match inadvertently reveals the secret to the spike in female infertility in the fine print on their FAQ page:

Q: If I donate my eggs, will I still be able to have my own children?

A: A little motherly [!] advice: women should not wait too long to have their own babies[!!]. The uterus may remain healthy for many years, but medical data shows that the quality of the eggs starts to diminish after age 29 [!!!] and steadily decreases with every year after that. If a woman waits much past that age her eggs could be of such poor quality that she may have trouble becoming pregnant, or may suffer miscarriages, or may have a child with Down Syndrome or other developmental issues. Unfortunately, most physicians do not inform women about the risk of waiting until they are older to have children [!!!!]. APM's average intended mother is a woman who started fertility treatments when she was about age 36 or so, and who had treatment and attempted use her own eggs for years before she had no other choice than to get an egg donor.[11]

Translation: the egg-harvesting factory *knows* that donating eggs puts you at risk of aging out of your own fertility. Spend too long giving your eggs away to strangers, and before you know it the only children you'll ever have will be raised by strangers. Silver lining: you can become an egg donor customer yourself one day.

Tiny Orphans

The worst waste products of the fertility industry? Excess embryos. Thousands and thousands of them; millions even. Since IVF can create dozens of embryos for a single couple, most will never be implanted. Couples who create extra unwanted embryos have few choices: they can pay to keep them on ice indefinitely, they can tell the lab to destroy them, or they can abandon them. Abandoned embryos are then available to childless couples at no or low cost.

A friend recently told me about a nice older couple at their child's school; the older woman confided that she'd adopted and given birth to someone else's discarded embryos. The unknown parents of the abandoned embryos had done IVF, had one child, and told the lab they had no use for their other embryos. No use for their own biological children. The older couple adopted three embryos, lost one to miscarriage, and is now happily parenting two living, healthy children orphaned by their biological parents. These children have several full siblings in another state who are being raised by their biological parents, but they will likely never have the chance to meet them—or even know their names.

It's hard for me to imagine my biological offspring, or frozen siblings, lingering in cryogenic sleep for decades, tossed into an incinerator, or sold to literally any rando off the street. Do they vet potential embryo adopters? Do they do background checks? Who is claiming these forgotten frozen babies? Into whose hands will they be entrusted, your discarded, supposedly worthless children? How are so many women able to make this ugly choice, over and over and over again?

Pro-choice psychological persuasion is so powerful and pervasive that women who take part in this think nothing of it. After all, they have been carefully groomed to shout, "It's my choice!" when anyone questions their ethics.

Let's think about *Sophie's Choice* again for a moment. This time, imagine an empowered, modern-day Sophie standing outside the boxcar at Auschwitz, shivering a little in the cold, merrily handing her crying baby to the Nazi guards for extermination.

"It's my choice!" she shouts, secure in her rights as a woman.

"One is enough!" she gloats as she marches to the barracks with her only surviving child.

Her little boy looks back and catches a brief glimpse of his baby brother disappearing forever into the death chamber.

CHAPTER 8

Your Maternal Instinct

Maternity Turns Terminal

A mother's love for her child is like nothing else in the world. It knows no law, no pity. It dares all things and crushes down remorselessly all that stands in its path.

— Agatha Christie

What They Took:

- ☑ ~~Your Fleeting Fertility~~
- ☑ ~~Your Role~~
- ☑ ~~Your Gender~~
- ☑ ~~Your Virtues~~
- ☑ ~~Men~~
- ☑ ~~A Soul Mate~~
- ☑ ~~Your Unborn Children~~
- ☑ Your Maternal Instinct

Whither Maternal Love?

The power of a mother's devotion to her offspring was no mystery to Agatha Christie. The impenetrable, God-given bond that ties a woman to her children cannot be severed by any craft we here possess. It is truly one of the strongest forces on Earth. Heroic mothers have been known to lift cars off toddlers who get pinned underneath them.

Which is why you must give our current supervillains credit. They've done a masterful job chipping away at the maternal bond women have with their unborn and born children. Most of the children who make it out of the womb alive are instantly funneled into the Childcare Industrial Complex. Millions of mothers voluntarily shed their innate maternal instincts in ways large and small; some in ways they aren't aware of—or don't figure out until it's too late.

This is why "maternal instinct" is next on my list of purloined treasures they've taken from us. How did they do it? Easy: they simply convinced *women themselves* to sever their own maternal bonds. Instead of getting kids to turn on their parents, they get women to turn on their own kids. You are allowed—encouraged, even—to reject your own helpless dependents as impediments to fulfilling your true destiny. Children are *in your way*, okay?

They even convinced some smooth-brained liberals that your natural maternal instinct is fake, a right-wing conspiracy theory being perpetrated on us by, yes, the Invisible Patriarchy. The trusty *New York Times* supplies these women with all the moral support and scientific evidence they need to ease the psychological distance they must create between themselves and their offspring. "Maternal Instinct Is a Myth That Men Created" is one unintentionally hilarious headline that appeared in the *Times*.[1] The author, Chelsea Conaboy, is naturally a "journalist specializing in health." At exactly the moment when a woman is forced to make the heartbreaking decision whether or not to sentence her tiny infant to full-time daycare so she can resume her career, she is told that any hesitation on her part is just the Patriarchy talking. "The notion that the selflessness and tenderness babies require is uniquely ingrained in the biology of women, ready to go at the flip of a switch, is a relatively modern—and pernicious—one."[2]

Pernicious! Hand over the kid, lady, nice and slow, no funny stuff, and get back into your work pod.

Here's another eye-watering example from the Shitty Mother genre in (what else) *New York Times* magazine: "The Abortion I Didn't Have: I never thought about ending my pregnancy. Instead, at 19, I erased the future I had imagined for myself."[3] The author, a novelist named Merritt Tierce, writes about her deep, lifelong regret . . . over *not* aborting her son, who is now grown. "I love my son, and I am not at peace with the sacrifice I was required to make."[4]

It will not surprise you to learn that the author was a graduate student at Yale at the time.

I know I'm the crazy extremist here, but anyone who regrets not aborting the child *they are currently parenting* should maybe not brag about it for clout in the paper of record, where said child can read it. It's much easier to just hand your child the phone number to a psychiatrist and a suicide hotline.

Tierce's essay provides us with a nightmarish glimpse into the mind of a woman who has had her natural maternal instinct surgically removed by our malign culture. If you were compiling artifacts to leave in a time capsule for future visitors to Earth to explain how we caused our own extinction, you would include her essay. This passage should be engraved on humanity's gravestone:

> It's not about the yes/no of a child's existence; it's about what kind of life the child will have, and what kind of life the family will have together. When I help someone get an

abortion, or even help someone think about abortion in a new way, I'm going back, choosing an alternate future, and affirming the worth of that concept itself: it does make a difference to wait, to grow, to mature, to decide. I had two abortions after my children were born, and I don't regret those abortions or think about who those people would have been. I also realize that if I had continued those pregnancies, I would have loved those people. But my life would have been harder and I would have lost more of myself, because people don't have unlimited resilience. If I imagine the counterfactual, I can say I have strong and loving relationships with both of my children now, in large part because I didn't have those other children.[5]

I wonder: How *does* it feel to find out your mother aborted your siblings? I doubt mothers bother to ask their living children if they would mind if she got rid of a baby brother or sister. She's simply exercising her *reproductive rights*, after all. But what about sibling rights? This blinkered mindset makes it possible for mothers to not only send their own children to the glue factory, but also to deprive living children from meeting family members. It's almost too sad to contemplate—but not if you have cauterized the place where you contemplate those sorts of inconvenient feelings.

It's all part of the plan, of course. Progressive Utopians, Green New Dealers, Great Resetters, and New World Orderers can't make any real progress transforming human civilization into the Me-Topia of their dreams—and our nightmares—if women stubbornly cling to their maternal instincts.

They are right to fear you. Our supervillains know that mothers control a rare and precious power they only wish they had: true influence over children. I'm not talking about the power to make them clean their rooms or stop bothering their sisters—I *wish* I had that kind of power. No, I mean the ability to guide kids away from the worst excesses of the culture, teach them a better way to live, and inspire them to have their own families one day.

Mothers also have the power to *not* sentence their kids to local progressive reeducation centers. They must be stopped!

If only our cultural overlords could find a way to somehow weaken, even permanently sever, the bond a woman has with her children. That would make it a lot easier for the State to swoop in and get its hooks into kids. All kids love their mothers, so the State has to target broken adults instead.

And if they're not broken yet, they will be.

Motherhood in the Crosshairs

The dark, unmentionable secret about babies is this: they want to be with their mother, like, all the time. Dad will do in a pinch, but Mom is where the action is. To deny this is to deny nature itself. And yet, at every step in the contemporary motherhood journey, the desires and needs of the baby come last. Society's needs come first, then the mother's boss's needs, then the mother's needs, then her husband's needs. Of course, you are legally obligated to feed a child, but what does the child desire most? Don't tell them I told you this, but your kid just wants . . . you.

I remember feeling most at ease as a child when I was in my mother's presence. I could finally stop being "on" with a babysitter, or at school. I was fortunate to have a physically affectionate mother, and I know some people tragically don't feel this way about their mothers. My own mother had a difficult childhood, which is probably why she compensated by trying to make ours so comfortable. But if you do it basically right, your baby will just want to be with you, period, end of discussion.

Everyone else is just keeping it alive until the next second it is mercifully put back in your arms.

Studies back this up. Babies and young children have the lowest levels of cortisol and highest degree of relaxation and happiness when in the presence of their mothers. Erica Komisar's "controversial" 2017 book *Being There: Why Prioritizing Motherhood in the First Three Years Matters* makes the case that babies who are with their mothers the most do the best in life.

"Spending more time with your child during this critical period of development means she will have a greater chance of being emotionally secure and resilient to stress. . . . But a mother's physical presence is not enough. What is vital for both the short-term and long-term well-being of your child is your emotional presence. And . . . if you are not with your child, you cannot be emotionally present."[6] Believe the Science, unless you're a feminist.

This obvious, commonsensical fact, so uncontroversial for all of human existence, is now a forbidden truth. Komisar was excoriated by feminists, as you can imagine. Her book is an exhortation to women to do their best to prioritize their young child over their careers. "Your baby does not care if she has a bigger room or a Florida vacation; what she wants is you and the safety and security of being in your presence."[7] The issue we face today is that, although the baby doesn't care how big her room is, the mother does, and is only too happy to hand her newborn to a hired surrogate parent to pay for it.

We can see everywhere the long-term consequences when children are raised by daycares, babysitters, or each other. Well-to-do children "raised by maids" will comfort themselves with narcissistic addictions to early promiscuity and designer drugs. Children of single parents raised by low-quality daycares, or each other, have exponentially higher rates of mental illness, drug use, dropping out, incarceration, and violence.

I practiced attachment parenting, which is a fancy term for what mothers have been doing forever, i.e., trying to be with your baby as much as possible. This means nursing on demand, probably co-sleeping or sleeping in the same room as the infant, and doing a lot of baby-wearing. Hospitals have gotten better about this, and by the time I had kid number three, instead of taking the baby straight to the nursery for whatever they do to babies there, they put the newborn right on my chest for skin-to-skin contact, which helps with some sort of alchemical bonding magic.

Not everyone can nurse or run around with a baby in a pouch, and that's fine. But my friends (at the time) thought I was crazy for not having something called a "night nurse." All the new moms I knew who had the extra cash hired professional nurses to come to their house in the evening and take over with the kid. What an unimaginable luxury! The nurse stays up with the baby, feeds it, changes it, and rocks it so the mother can get some sleep. Just imagine! The rich are . . . different.

I love sleep. Ask anyone who has tried to wake me up early in the morning how I feel about it. But a night nurse felt like a strange out-sourcing of something that I was willing to do—that I *wanted* to do. It wasn't like I was going to start mowing my own lawn, okay? (No one in California does that, guys.) But still, I resisted indulging in what my friends considered an essential luxury item—the in-house, all-night nanny. When the baby wakes up and cries, are you supposed to lay in bed listening, hoping the strange woman in the nursery knows what to do? That sounded stressful to me.

If you want to breastfeed, your nocturnal servant will have to bring you the baby when it wakes up to eat, so you're going to get woken up every few hours anyway.

I didn't get it. I still don't. Two able-bodied adults would be in the home, just a few feet away, but they were not to be disturbed by the precious child they had spent months eagerly awaiting.

After surviving a combined several years of newborn all-nighters, I am confident that those long nights with a tiny child are prime bonding hours, especially for the baby's dad. Why do you want to give that gift to a stranger?

Maybe the reason my friends needed night nurses was because they were well into their thirties with the first kid and, you know, tired. Another reason to start young, friends.

Pulling an all-nighter with a baby when you are in your forties hits different—trust me.

Outsourced Motherhood

Once you and your expensive night nurse are through the newborn period and she moves on to her next pampered postpartum employer, don't panic! You can seamlessly transition to handing your older baby off to underpaid timecard-punchers who can't wait for their next break. Daycares beckon new mothers from every strip mall and office complex. All ages! Newborns welcome! Late hours! Affordable!

If you have the money, you may prefer to hire a nanny to raise your baby for you. Nannies are trustworthy and loving strangers who you allow into your home to spend all day alone with your baby. Parents trust their nannies, which is why there is a multibillion-dollar industry of spy cams and snooping technology you must install in every room of your home so you can watch the trusted nanny the whole time she is with your child. Leaving your baby home alone with the nanny is so liberating and safe that Amazon sells over two thousand different types of hidden nanny cams!

In your empowered, baby-free state, you will spend hours at work watching live hidden camera feeds, scrutinizing each frame for signs of neglect or abuse being inflicted on your small child, who will not be able to report these things to you when you get home.

When the pandemic began, I was amazed at how many women bitterly complained about having to work at home. You'd rather be in an *office* all day? Wearing shoes? Having school-age children doing Zoom school was not ideal, of course, but any little kid who no longer had to go off to daycare or spend all day with a nanny was probably relieved.

None of the people involved in getting new mothers back to work as soon as the bleeding stops ever seem to wonder what might be best for the child. You went to all this trouble to conceive, you put together a crib, you waddled around for nine months, and you actually delivered the thing, but you won't consider for a moment what this little creature would prefer? Raising your own baby is sustainable, cruelty free, organic, non-GMO, and gluten-free. It is better for the environment (no commuting to a daycare required!), and it introduces fewer germs and viruses into your home.

Raising your own children is also FREE. Crazy, right?

I am not talking about using babysitters. We had help from babysitters and from grandparents, and it was wonderful, but they were not the *primary caregivers.*

I worked at home with babies and toddlers underfoot for years. I still do. I wrote this book at home, with a kindergartener on my lap. It's hard, distracting, and, some days, feels nearly impossible. But to me, it is much easier than leaving them alone all day with strangers. The only thing worse than hearing a shriek in the family room when you're on a conference call in the bedroom is hearing the shriek on your phone after getting a Nanny-Cam alert at the office.

This profoundly destructive symptom of modernity has been totally normalized, but it never ceases to shock me. You spend more time planning the gender reveal than you do planning how to raise your own baby.

The Free-Time Cope

Parents of both sexes may hear the siren song of the culture calling them back, and sometimes they make the choice to return to their previous child-free lives. Abandonment, divorce, and abortion get a whole lot easier once you have experienced early separation from your baby. There is a lot of coping that goes into talking yourself into this, however. I've heard it.

"They didn't mind the nanny or the daycare. They won't mind if I leave them in after-school care until 7:00 every night and all day during Christmas break. Kids are resilient. I can't be home, okay? And if I leave their father to have an affair with my Kundalini instructor, maybe move to Bali for a few months and leave them at home, they'll understand. Do they really want a mother who isn't happy? Who feels repressed? Who isn't living her dream? One day, my toddler will understand. Hey, if I have to put them all in therapy, that's probably a good thing."

I've heard nearly all of this from intelligent women I know, including glowing and graphic descriptions of infidelities with younger boyfriends. (Of course, they might have been swingers, and I was too naive to understand at the time.) I would nod and smile and suppress the chill shivering up my spine.

Maybe because I experienced firsthand how parents' selfish pursuits of their own interests affects a child, I can't imagine *choosing* to do something that would hurt my kids. Some things are outside my control, obviously, but I can at least control my own decisions. For now. Until our societal overlords update my operating system and fix that stubborn maternal bug in my code. But my rule is pretty much, if it's not good for kids, I try to avoid it.

Another way to think about this is: What would the child want? No, I don't mean giving in to demands for a second bowl of ice cream or to watch the latest Pixar atrocity. I mean asking yourself, "Would my toddler like it if I left him for twelve hours a day in this daycare?" or "If my teens find out about my affair with their friend's dad, would they mind?" Doing what's best for the kid is conveniently what's best for you, too. It's what your inborn, God-given maternal instinct is telling you to do.

You are born with all these answers; all you have to do is listen to your gut and follow it. I am woman, hear me growl!

Daycare Nightmares

Imagine explaining the concept of "daycare" to an alien. "See, you finally have your baby, the one you spent $75,000 on fertility treatments to create, and then as soon as it's born, you're supposed to count down the seconds until you can drop him off at a store, usually in a strip mall, where minimum-wage unregistered felons you wouldn't trust to walk your dog are in charge of infants from age six weeks and up, along with up to a dozen other crying babies at a time. Feel free to leave your baby for eight hours, nine hours, whatever. Then you pick up your baby and spend an hour or so with him before you repeat the process the next day (and every day for five years!) until he starts kindergarten.

"Daycare frees you to spend more time answering emails and reviewing documents, which you could do on your phone from literally anywhere, but then you would be forced to admit to your zealot girlfriends that you would rather spend the day nursing your baby in the nursery you lovingly designed and painted yourself—instead of pumping and crying in the lactation room at work. Daycare is freedom!"

But not for you.

It's a trap for parents and a prison for tiny inmates. Daycare is just an essential release valve for the liberal world order, exactly like abortion is. Without "quality affordable childcare," as the Democrats in D.C. call it, women can't achieve any real worth or value. *Work* is where women belong—not tending their own children. Let the government-subsidized childcare union take that noisy six-week-old off your hands! You have more important things to do that bring glory and honor to the sisterhood, like prepare Google Slides presentations.

Lots of babies that manage to make it through the Great Filters of birth control and abortion will get caught by the Daycare Filter. It catches all the kids Planned Parenthood missed. Women can start preparing for their return to work as soon as they tell their bosses they're pregnant. You are required to submit your "return date," which will be whenever any meager state maternity benefits run out, or when your boss says it is.

You will get your unborn baby on the waiting list at every decent daycare you can find. You will do some quick math and be shocked to discover that even at the bargain-basement daycare in the bad neighborhood, your daycare bill will wipe out at least 40 percent of your after-tax income. You realize you will be working for two bosses: yours, and your baby's unsmiling caregiver.

Meanwhile, these strangers are going to do the actual parenting, only without any parental affection. Daycare workers are sort of like prostitutes, but not the kind who offer the Girlfriend Experience. Most daycare workers are banned from even providing the Mom Experience. Your child won't get hugs, kisses, affectionate words, or love. A daycare worker's only job is to keep your child alive without running afoul of state regulations. They will feed it, diaper it, put it down for naps, and discipline it, and that's it. You're *lucky* if that's what you get.

"I check the daycare website camera all day to see what my eight-month-old is doing. And I dread drop-off every morning," one woman told me. I remember talking to a young mom at work right after she dropped off her four-month-old at daycare for the first time. She called the daycare "school," which tells you how hard she was compensating to cope with the situation. "Elijah started school today! He loves it; he only cried a little when I said goodbye."

Elijah will be away from his mother approximately eleven hours each day. She will spend that time doing graphic design for a corporate website. Elijah understands this; he is a Feminist Baby and wants his mother to work. He knows work makes her a *better mom*. It is a sacrifice he is happy to make. Who is he to force her to care for him by herself?

Again, I don't judge her for surrendering her child to the daycare gulag. She is a victim of the same system her baby is. How else can she and her husband support themselves without the half of her paycheck left after paying for daycare? They would be forced to make uncomfortable sacrifices, even move, rethink their lives, and maybe wonder if anything had gone wrong in the wonderful modern society where women can be anything they want and have fulfilling careers like their husbands. Hey, don't start going down that rabbit hole! Look, over there: a raise!

It's not their fault. I have coached several friends out of the daycare mindset, and it's like deprogramming a cult victim. A nurse cried and told me she was dreading going back to work when her newborn turned twelve weeks old. She didn't know how she was going to do it. A colleague made the mistake of asking me why I had never put a baby in daycare. After calmly explaining that the idea of leaving my baby for ten hours a day felt like sawing my arm off, that I simply could not physically do it and would have happily lived in a trailer park to afford not to for a few years, she nodded.

After having her first child, this coworker resigned. A year later, she had a second baby. I hope those kids know Auntie Peachy is the one who saved them from doing hard time.

A final data point if you are rolling your eyes at this. To underscore how unnatural it is to take young children to a baby warehouse and leave them there all day, it's instructive to look at hot-car deaths. How do these relate to daycare, you ask? If you read the tragic news stories about young children who die after being accidentally left in their parents' cars for hours and hours, in nearly every single story, the death occurs *when the parent forgets to drop the child at daycare.*

Truly, only Satan could have invented the concept of daycare. "How dare Trump separate children from their mothers!" but also "Please hand us your six-week-old so you can contribute to our economy."

Reality Check

I'm aware that single mothers and struggling families have no choice but to bundle their tiny children off to daycare as soon as mom's episiotomy stitches are healed so she can get back to bringing in paychecks. I get it. The huge structural economic issues at play that force young mothers into that lifestyle are real. I hate them as much as you do. If I could return us to a country where one parent can earn enough to support a large family, I would. What I can do is try to expose the real cost of this unsustainable corner we've painted ourselves into.

And there is a cost. "Affordable" childcare is a myth. Even the cheapest childcare has a profound hidden expense—one you may only start paying when your children are older. I understand that daycare is a "necessary evil" of the modern era. Fine. I'm not going to outlaw it or stop you from outsourcing your maternal devotion to strangers. All I can do is suggest that more of you *choose not to.*

Breaking the maternal bond releases more negative energy than splitting an atom and is even more destructive to the fate of humanity. This precious bond must be preserved and protected, and that starts with keeping mothers in close physical proximity to their offspring for as long as possible. You may not like it, but deep down you know this to be true: the nest is best.

Maternal Dysphoria

I must remind myself to pray for non-abortion-having regretters like Merritt Tierce and all the other women who have rejected their maternal instinct and spend their lives grappling with feelings of cognitive dissonance around motherhood.[8] I call this "maternal dysphoria," and like body dysphoria and gender dysphoria, it seems to come from a deep discomfort with the raw, biological, physical fact of their own humanity. They run from it in fear.

It's true: the female body is imbued with something as close to supernatural magic as it gets. With great power, however, comes great responsibility. Rise to the occasion, or you will eventually sink into the abyss.

CHAPTER 9

Your Real Job

Lean Out

*It [feminism] is mixed up with a muddled idea that
women are free when they serve their employers but
slaves when they help their husbands.*

— G. K. Chesterton

*The equal contribution of women and men in this
process of deep economic and societal transformation
is critical.*

— Klaus Schwab, executive chairman, World Economic Forum

What They Took:

☑ ~~Your Fleeting Fertility~~
☑ ~~Your Role~~
☑ ~~Your Gender~~
☑ ~~Your Virtues~~
☑ ~~Men~~
☑ ~~A Soul Mate~~
☑ ~~Your Unborn Children~~

☑ ~~Your Maternal Instinct~~
☑ **Your Real Job**

Girlbossaggeddon

We are "careering" right over a cliff. Rampant, mindless careerism has led to the disastrous feminization of American institutions and corporations, causing our present troubles. The Karen is out of the bottle; the Karen has been unleashed.

To mainstream feminists, a woman's true value can only be expressed *outside* the home, when she's earning a paycheck. In order to stuff as many women as possible into the corporate clown car, the government pushes subsidized childcare for newborns, free birth control, and, of course, abortion. Maternity leave is a dead end for companies, and a corporate value killer—you can't just *disappear* when there are all these emails to send! TPS reports to fill out! Come back! Before other women get the same idea!

Here we come to the next item on the list of things taken from us: our *choice* to stay home with our babies and not return to work right away. The *option* for your husband to support a family on just one income. The guilt-free embrace of the task of raising your own newborn, without shame, peer pressure, or extreme financial hardship. Take the "Stay Home with Your Newborn and Not Piss Off Your Woke Girlfriends or Starve" challenge: impossible!

When politicians talk about "quality affordable daycare," they are telling you about the choice they took from you. Well, I have news for you: outsourced childcare is rarely "quality" or "affordable." Quality affordable daycare for babies used to come *with* the baby—in the form of a lactating mother.

Do we really have a baby formula shortage—or is it masking a shortage of mothers able to nurse infants on demand from the comfort of their homes?

We have drifted far from the original feminist notion that women have the equal *right* to work to a nightmare world where women *must* work in order to have equal value. It is *abortion* that makes it possible for a woman to participate fully in society—because it enables her to work without interruption by pregnancy and demanding children. In other words, pregnancy and babies prevent you from being a full and equal member of American society!

When the Supreme Court reversed *Roe v. Wade*, Attorney General Merrick Garland issued this dystopian statement: "The Supreme Court has eliminated . . . a right that has safeguarded women's ability to participate fully and equally in society."[1] We know what Merrick *really* wants you to eliminate, ladies.

My smart friend Jeremy Carl said this about Garland's statement: "For the Democrats, women 'participating fully and equally in society' means destroying the most precious and unique thing that only women can do."

The rejection of motherhood as a worthy and acceptable vocation in favor of other, "more equal" career choices like marketing associate or attorney or sales representative is a colossal error. It has led countless families into the hell of "juggling" multiple jobs and children and has created millions of lightly (or barely) parented children.

Cue feminist screeching, but here is a truth: certain careers are indeed damaging to a woman's long-term happiness and her family's future—if she manages to eke out a family.

If you ask the bitter and lonely women who choose the corporate career path, they will confirm this for you, usually after their sixth skinny margarita.

Work Sucks, and Then You Die

Please note: I am not anti-work. Work is fine, good even! Work can keep you alive, fed, and even fulfilled. I always hated real work, so I did my best to turn my only hobby into a skill that paid, albeit somewhat meagerly. (I jettisoned career plans to be a doctor after hitting the skids in high school chemistry. Freelance writer it would be!)

Besides, "career" was always a vaguely terrifying word to me. It sounds too much like "careen," as in, to careen off a cliff at high speeds. A career meant years of extra school, a lifetime of hellish commuting, and finally careening straight into the pantsuit panopticon. No exit, no way out, no changing your mind once you signed on the line that is dotted. To my innocent ears, "career" sounded like a life sentence along a path that would cost me everything: youth, freedom, beauty, and babies.

For some women, their chosen career perfectly fulfills their heart's desire, and God bless them for that. Go ahead and be the corporate tax lawyer of your dreams and bill a hundred thousand hours a year. I won't stop you. Go ahead and choose neurosurgery, do some good. I am not against women seeking "careers" as their primary life path; I am merely saying that *fewer* women should, especially the ones who want to see their kids during daylight hours.

Fact: your children need you more than your customers, your clients, your patients, your investors, or your bosses do.

I dare you to go to any gathering of hard-working, mid-level career women, maybe at the wine bar during the sales conference, and casually opine, "You know, studies show young kids do best when their mothers stay home as much as possible during the early years." Remember to duck when they start throwing their wine glasses at your head.

Young women should, of course, be encouraged to do what they like for a living. Some women have particular skills and talents so vital to humanity that I would encourage them not to bother having a family and to keep at their careers until they drop dead. (I can't think of any of these types of jobs at the moment, but I'm sure they exist.) Not everyone is called to be a Joan of Arc. Working seventy-hour weeks as a BigLaw partner or hedge fund manager does not make you a hero. It will make you rich, stressed out, and a stranger to any children you outsource to surrogates and nannies.

I have yet to meet a female law school graduate who didn't quit after having kids. They learn the hard way that real life starts and ends *outside* the office, and deep and lasting fulfillment can only come from domestic—not professional—joy.

It's true that career women usually have more money, higher incomes, and much more impressive LinkedIn pages. Stay-at-home mothers make less money, if they make any. They are forced to wear comfy pants, watch cartoons, go to the park, maybe hang with other moms they like, and drink coffee. What hell! How could women be subjected to this nightmare?

"But Peachy, I need to make a living. What, you want me to be homeless? Starve?" It's true, one does need to eat. Not everyone has what it takes to make a living on OnlyFans.

Although if you do choose to become a sex worker, you will surely lose your appetite for food.

Leaning All the Way Out

Full disclosure: I am a housewife in the sheets but a working girl in the streets. It never occurred to me to get married in my twenties and get a golden ticket out of the salt mines. Instead, I worked full-time from the moment I graduated from college until shortly after I got married, and then again when my older kids were in school. But I was never a "girlboss." I hated having "direct reports." I had many female bosses, and I found every single one of them a role model of what not be. "Imagine wanting to still work here and do this at that age," I'd think with a shudder as they pitched yet another client in yet another board room. Anytime I was asked to "manage" a few underlings, I took that as my cue to leave the underlings alone as much as possible, since that was how I wanted my bosses to treat me.

The instant I held my firstborn, I fully realized the horror of having to hand a baby over to strangers and return to the office. It was unimaginable—I would have gnawed my arm off to stay home. I barely trusted my own mother to watch my baby on the few occasions I darted out to run errands.

The new baby became my boss baby.

There's a simple reason why there are fewer female CEOs than male: the sanest, smartest women have figured out what I figured out early on, and they don't want the job. Only 8 percent of the CEOs of the Fortune 500 companies are women.[2] Despite desperate corporate boards scouring business schools for eligible female candidates, the pickings are slim. There is just one area where female CEOs outperform their male counterparts—they are 45 percent more likely to be fired.[3]

To make sure no fertile young women are left behind to their own devices, single college girls are funneled along a path towards a sole destination. This is the "girlboss-to-wine-aunt pipeline," as Spencer Klavan calls it.

It is the virulent "Lean In" virus, and it is now endemic in our society. Former Facebook CEO Sheryl Sandberg famously wrote a bestselling self-help book called *Lean In: Women, Work, and the Will to Lead*. In it, she urged young, ambitious women to "lean in" to their jobs, to sacrifice everything to get ahead in their chosen career. Millions read her book; it became a thing, a movement.

This book, the one you are reading, could have been titled *Lean Out*.

As Sandberg puts it, "A truly equal world would be one where women ran half our countries and companies and men ran half our homes."[4] Which half of your own homes do you run, Sheryl? Do you even run a single home? In her mind, and in the atrophied minds of corporate feminists like her, "equality" for women means helping themselves to half of men's stuff and shunting onto men the tasks they don't want to do. "Look, honey! I took half your jobs and salaries, and you get to do more mopping. Now we're *equal*."

As others have pointed out, true female equality will not be achieved until women are half of all military casualties, half of all suicides, and half of all police officers killed in the line of duty. We must also close the gender gap in early deaths of despair!

Leaning in is easy when you are a gigajillionaire. With enough housekeepers, nannies, personal shoppers, personal macrobiotic chefs, Pilates instructors, executive assistants, drivers, groundskeepers, and bookkeepers, you, too, can "lean in" to your job without pesky distractions. Sheryl Sandberg got very rich leaning in, but on a mass scale her strategy would lead to mounting misery, and in the final act nothing less than the extinction of the human race.

Why was Sheryl so excited about getting young women to lean in, to choose career over their personal lives? Did she want to make sure her hardworking minions devoted their lives to the company that pays her millions, instead of bailing for a baby? *Lean In* reminds me of the old *Twilight Zone* episode where the Earthlings finally translate the name of the space alien's book and realize that the title "To Serve Man" is not a benevolent manifesto of space-age brotherhood, but a cookbook featuring recipes for cooking humans. When you lean in too hard at Facebook, you will fall right into the witch's bubbling cauldron.

Ms. Sandberg would like *you* to lean in a little more, so *she* can spend more time leaning back on the beaches of a private island in the South Pacific.

That One Time I Leaned In

Feminism had not yet tightened its bony grip on young women when I was in college. The concept of a "career" was still sort of alien to my Gen X friends. One applied to Wharton simply because she loved the Armani suits Sigourney Weaver wears in *Working Girl*. The Daryl Hannah character in *Wall Street* inspired another friend to become an investment banker. I have no idea what she did at that job, only that it involved arriving at six in the morning, sometimes on no sleep from being out the night before, and doing a lot of cocaine.

My friends and I had been raised by boomer housewives; we had no idea what we were supposed to do after graduation. Neither did our mothers. Mine told me to "do whatever you want and then get married." Marriage? That was absolutely out of the question, at least while I was in my twenties. Marriage was something gross old people did! With my plan firmly in place, I set off into the world armed with my college diploma:

Step 1: Graduate

Steps 2–4: ???

Step 5: Wedding

After I had my first baby, I worked from home, freelancing here and there and nursing newborns. I was living the pandemic lifestyle before COVID made it trendy.

Then, one day, I got a call from an old colleague about a job with incredible perks. My youngest (at the time) had just started real school. I had no more toddlers to wrangle or babies to nurse, so I headed back to the salt mines. Back to Big Corporate Life. At the time, my husband worked out of his home office, which was the clincher. It would be easy, and we'd pull in some extra dough to help support all these mouths. What could go wrong?

Navigating the rocky seas of remote parenting from an office is like trying to steer a ship through icebergs blindfolded. I remember the day I realized I'd made a terrible mistake. I was at my desk watching the clock. At 6:00, I could go home. Every second felt like torture. And it wasn't even a mindless dead-end job. It was a "dream job" for someone with my background. But it was never my *career*. I called all my jobs "day jobs," because my heart was always elsewhere. My titles and my paychecks got better over the years, but still—there I was, watching the sun go down behind the mountains on the other side of the freeway where my home and children waited.

Mind-numbing boredom, annoying coworkers, ridiculous dead-lines, and soul-crushing product reviews where incompetent managers would humiliate younger employees defined my experience. "Be a creative," they said. "Work in entertainment," they said. "Live your dreams," they said. "You can do anything," they lied.

A pregnant coworker, newly married, asked me how I managed work and kids. I told her I was not ever able to leave my kids with a nanny and I recoiled at the idea of daycare. She said she was feeling anxious about leaving her baby to come back to work. Guess what? You are *supposed* to feel like that. It doesn't make you weird. It makes you *a normal mother*. Extended separation from a child is *designed* to fill you with anxiety. That's nature's way of telling you to go find the baby you left back in the cave. Get it before the saber-toothed tigers do!

My coworker told me her girlfriends "got mad when I said I might not come back to the office." Tip: if your friends shame you into leaving your baby behind to go back to work, consider the possibility that *they* are saber-toothed tigers.

Our office had very nice lactation rooms on every floor. They were desolate and rarely used since so few of the millennials had any kids. They had mini-fridges for storing your bags of breast milk, couches, and even beanbag chairs. All that was missing were bongs and some

Jerry Garcia posters. How wonderful it would be to relax and pump at the office! My poor sister used to have to pump in the bathroom stall at her law office. Even female cows aren't milked where they sh*t.

My favorite pumping horror story is the one where a friend had dutifully gone back to work and left her eight-week-old with a nanny to whom she paid approximately 80 percent of her after-tax pay. Her boss called a meeting and would not let my friend skip the meeting to pump. (Pumping has to be done on a particular schedule or things become engorged.) Her boss—a woman, naturally—ordered her to pump *in the meeting*, while everyone sat around a conference table.

There I was, eyeballing the beanbag chair in the lactation room, secretly wishing I had a baby to nurse in it. I longed to go back to hanging out on a couch in my jammies, doing my freelance gigs on my own schedule. I prayed for a solution.

God swiftly intervened.

I soon found myself unexpectedly expecting at an advanced maternal age, which is the actual clinical term for a mother over thirty-five. When I went out on maternity (or in my case, grandma-ternity) leave, I knew I would never go back.

What imbecile pushed for more women in the workplace? Who can we drag before a tribunal for this crime against humanity? Who in their right mind wants to spend all their waking hours "in the workplace"?

Here's a dirty secret: the workplace *sucks*, from the dried-out granola bars, the dried-out HR ladies, the bad coffee, and the misery etched into everyone's faces as they log another eight hours in the cube—sober, lonely, and shivering under the cold fluorescent lights.

If you have any information leading to the arrest and prosecution of the bloodless ogres who devised this system, please let me know. No questions asked.

When I took my last baby home from the hospital, it was also a homecoming of sorts for me. My days in the salt mines were over for good.

"Arbeit Macht Frei"

Nazis and feminists can agree on at least one thing: "Work makes you free." The Nazis put those words—in the original German—above the gates of Auschwitz.

Feminists put those words into young girls' heads from an early age.

When you work, you are a free woman. You are an equal woman, just as important and valuable as a man. Think about it: feminists believe women are so pathetic that they need jobs to be equal in value to men!

Just sign the contract here, in blood if you please, and please initial where it says you promise to surrender your firstborn to the company daycare when it is two months old. Benefits include egg-freezing and embryo transfer until you turn sixty, thank you and welcome aboard. Welcome to Equality, Ladies!

Whenever I hear the word "equality," I think of the ancient Greek monster Procrustes. Procrustes was the son of Poseidon, and his hobby was inviting unsuspecting people to spend the night. He would tie them to the bed, and if their body didn't fit the bed, he would either stretch them on a rack or cut their legs off to make them fit properly. He was the Kathy Bates of Greek innkeepers.

Queen of the Sisterhood Sheryl Sandberg is a modern-day Procrustes, like all corporate feminists. "Equality" is the euphemism they use for forcing women to fit spaces not originally designed for their bodies. No nation on Earth can prosper with this many leaned-in feminists uncomfortably in charge. Just look around!

I was shocked to find out that there are an infinite number of non-governmental agencies, foundations, and charities whose shared mission is to "get women back to work" and to "make work *work* for women." Imagine wasting your charity dollars on this, instead of feeding barefoot orphans.

Catalyst is one such strange entity. A more opaque and terrifyingly sterile website you will never see. Here's some real copy from their website:

> Catalyst is a global nonprofit supported by many of the world's most powerful CEOs and leading companies to help build workplaces that work for women. Founded in 1962, Catalyst drives change . . . to accelerate and advance women into leadership—because progress for women is progress for everyone. . . . Now, corporate leaders have an unprecedented opportunity and challenge: to reimagine the workplace so that it is truly inclusive. Those who don't participate in The Great Reimagining will lose out on talent and may find themselves left behind. Only through more equitable and inclusive workplaces can we truly make work work for women—and for everyone.[5]

Oh cool, a Great Reimagining. Just what humanity needs!

If you dig into the Catalyst website (I did it so you don't have to, you're welcome), you learn how Catalyst helps CEOs become "C E-mpathy Os." L-O-L!

Aspiring CEmpathyOs can take a workshop on how to Demonstrate Empathy at Work. "Empathy is the skill of showing care, concern, and understanding to the life experiences of others." Imagine having to learn this. At work! It's like preschool again. "No hitting your neighbor, Avery. Share the cookies with your friend, Scout."

Of course, learning to "demonstrate" empathy is not quite the same as actually *being* empathetic. If you were not a corporatized, dehumanized robot, you would already possess a deep well of natural empathy. Instead, you were forced to cauterize that part of your operating system in order to live with yourself knowing you have forty-eight viable frozen embryos hibernating in a cryogenic lab in San Jose, none of whom you will ever meet.

What happens to men when the hard-charging, fully leaned-in career gals at Catalyst are put in charge? You get anti-men seminars, naturally. Catalyst offers an entire suite of "programming" (their word!) for this.[6]

> MARC, Men Advocating Real Change, is a Catalyst initiative that inspires men to leverage their unique opportunity and responsibility to be advocates for equity. Our research-based, experiential learning disrupts traditional DEI [diversity, equity, inclusion] approaches to enhance gender partnership and accelerate the creation of inclusive workplaces. We are proud to announce a $5 million grant from Chevron Corporation and a $2 million grant from P&G to support our breakthrough work.[7]

Funny that the oil and gas industry is considered super evil—unless it's dumping money into a feminist sinkhole. I guess the goal is to turn MEN into MARCs, which actually stands for "Male Asexuals Respecting Crude oil."

Obedient male feminists—MARCs—will become easy marks for the lady sharks prowling the boardroom waters. After all, how is a strong woman supposed to thrive in the workplace if her male coworkers exude powerful and threatening masculine confidence? For the empowered female to rise, it is necessary to surround her with nonthreatening pansies, spaghetti-armed zeroes who leap to put their pronouns in their bios.

Of course, male feminists *need* to have pronouns in their bios—how else are we supposed to know these boardroom eunuchs are still male? I call them MINOs: Men in Name Only.

Sure, Women Can Do Anything, but Why Would They?

We haven't discussed the most verboten topic of all: the fact that there are some jobs no woman should do. If your children were trapped in a burning apartment building, which fireman would you want to climb up the ladder to rescue them: a 200-pound former linebacker, or a five-foot-three former cheerleader? How do you feel when you get on a plane and see that both pilots in the cockpit are ladies?

I am willing to bet that almost everyone who gets a female pilot, even feminists, gets a tiny nervous flutter in their gut. I'm sure women make *excellent* pilots. But Chuck Yeager they aren't. Not to worry: the feminist sisterhood known as the U.S. Marine Corps introduced new maternity flight suits for pregnant pilots.[8] I couldn't ride Splash Mountain while I was pregnant, but you go, girl!

A press release about the new suits clarifies that pregnant pilots must be medically cleared before flying and *aren't allowed to sit in ejection seats*. True, blasting out of the cockpit going five hundred miles an hour while pregnant may get messy. Sorry, mom-to-be, if the plane starts to crash, you and the kid are both going down.

Don't Get a Job: Choose a Vocation

To those who say none of this applies to them, that they would never be able to get a high-paying job into which they could lean, even if they wanted to, I remind you that there is one career you are perfectly qualified for. And it earns you more dividends than the CEO of Facebook gets.

Once there was a young woman who never held a job, never got a promotion, or made a sale, or executed a trade in her life. She never even sent a single email. She lived and died in obscure poverty, content to raise her baby with her husband, a non-union carpenter. Instead of leaning in, she simply decided, "Let it be done to me according to your word."[9]

It is no coincidence that "lean in" is what the witch tells Gretel to do in front of the hot oven.

Speaking of leaning in, have you ever heard of Nell Scovell? No one ever talks about her. Who is Nell Scovell, you ask? She is Sheryl Sandberg's *ghostwriter*. It turns out that Sheryl—the former Facebook CEO who got every woman to *Lean In*—outsourced her leaning-in to Nell Scovell, the one who actually wrote her bestselling book but didn't get any of the credit. Irony of ironies!

Was anyone surprised to learn that Sheryl Sandberg was investigated ("stepped down," in the parlance of our times) in 2022 for misusing corporate funds for her own personal projects, including to help plan her wedding? She leaned in hard—to the office cookie jar. "The powerful executive also reportedly felt burned out after building Facebook into a global force and [the] scrutiny of her every move."[10]

Even the mighty Sheryl Sandberg couldn't, in the end, have it all. "Sandberg's personal and professional challenges occurred as Meta [Facebook] attempts to rebrand itself as a metaverse company following a series of scandals—including damning reports regarding the harmful effects that Instagram and other company-owned platforms have on the mental health of teenage girls."[11]

Oh, the irony. It's so meta.

Please note: No ghostwriter was used to write this book. I had to lean *all the way* in and write every damn word myself.

So go right ahead: give yourself permission to lean out, lean back, relax, and consider yourself absolved forever from seeking the slow-motion trainwreck of a Sandbergian corporate career.

Your true happy ending will never come from Human Resources. In the end, it can only come from actual humans.

CHAPTER 10

Your Parental Authority

Use It or Lose It

One way philosophers might think about solving the social justice problem would be by simply abolishing the family. If the family is this source of unfairness in society, then it looks plausible to think that if we abolished the family there would be a more level playing field.

— Adam Swift, professor, University of Warwick

We have to break through our kind of private idea that kids belong to their parents, or kids belong to their families, and recognize that kids belong to their communities.

—Melissa Harris-Perry, socialist feminist

What They Took:

☑ ~~Your Fleeting Fertility~~
☑ ~~Your Role~~
☑ ~~Your Gender~~
☑ ~~Your Virtues~~
☑ ~~Men~~

☑ A Soul Mate
☑ Your Unborn Children
☑ Your Maternal Instinct
☑ Your Real Job
☑ **Your Parental Authority**

Who's the Boss?

Y ou had a baby? Look at you—you're the captain now!
Or are you?

The words on a poster taped to a teacher's classroom door at a New Jersey public school expose the precarious corner American parents have been painted into. "If your parents aren't accepting of your identity, I'm your mom now."[1] The poster featured a drawing of a mama bear tending to her bear cubs, who are each painted the color of a different LGBTQ flag.

Parents, I have bad news. You've got competition. Someone posted a job listing looking for a new authority figure in your house, and they hired everyone who applied. Lots of other adults, most of them unpleasant strangers, would like to raise your children for you—or at least get your children to hate you.

This may already be happening—and you'll be the last to know! All your hard work to keep creeps, perverts, and kiddie-sniffers away from your kids may get reversed in an instant when you're not looking.

Some parents are okay with this. They can barely handle "adulting" themselves and are thrilled not to make any tough parental decisions. Abdicating their natural role as master and commander of the household is lazy, but it's a defensive posture. They live in terror of accusations from other parents of "closed-mindedness," or worse, being a prude.

American parents have either forgotten their innate, God-given authority over their household or surrendered it in the face of relentless pressure over many years from the outside. Just as millennia of trickling snowmelt can hollow out mighty granite mountains and turn them into canyons, a half-century of unchecked influence by feminists and far-left progressives have chipped away at the role of parents in their children's lives. What is left is a barren wasteland, a valley of shadows, where mothers and fathers have been reduced to nothing more than the oldest dependents in the house.

Your job as a parent is not easy, but it's simple: feed, nurture, love, and protect. In the face of life-and-death danger—say, an escaped tiger or an ax-wielding lunatic—probably 100 percent of parents would risk their lives for their children, even die, without hesitation. So why are so many reluctant to defend their children from less obvious, but equally dangerous, scenarios?

You can tell when you're about to be trampled by elephants. It's trickier when the trampling is invisible and being committed by a young teacher with peace stickers on xe/xer's car. I'll grant that having pronouns in your bio is not quite the same red flag as cruising a playground in a car with no door handles on the inside, but it's still a red flag parents need to fear.

People who manage to produce offspring are too often seduced into voluntarily surrendering their authority over them. They allow various "experts" to hold sway over their kids. Exhausted and confused, they willingly hand their kids off to the local public school teachers' unions, the DEI struggle-session facilitators, the storytelling drag queens, and the sex-education consultants who arrive at school with teaching props, including wholesome kid-friendly items like dildos and anal lube.

They all share a common goal: to dilute your authority and increase their own. They aim to groom America's children from birth to become compliant consumers of all they wish to sell them: bespoke genders, any-term abortion, strictly enforced racial hierarchies, a lifetime of therapy, prescription drugs, and whatever political and social ideology they choose to upload into their brains.

God forbid you are the only parent at your school who keeps your fifth grader home on Share Your Favorite Sex Toy day. What will people say?

Allow me to remind you gently: it's your job to steer the ship, avoid icebergs, prevent scurvy, and stave off mutinies. Parenting is not a game. There is no do-over. You are all that stands between your small charges and the roiling storms ahead—and the band of purple-haired nonbinary pirates that's about to storm the deck.

Coached to Hate

In the aftermath of 2020's Floyd riots, every school in the country doubled down on Critical Race Theory–infected lesson plans. You know what these are by now: "anti-racist" courses and lectures that describe the country as a bleak place where white children are irrevocably evil, black children are their helpless victims, and this condition is permanent and unsolvable.

Well, there is a solution, but they don't talk about this part much: it involves enforcing "equity" by "eradicating whiteness," which requires nonwhite children to browbeat classmates into submission and force white children to report on their own toxic and racist parents.

"You sit on a throne of lies," Will Ferrell says to the mall Santa in the movie *Elf*. These nefarious "teachers" are sitting on their own throne of lies and forcing impressionable young American schoolchildren to believe it unquestioningly.

A former math teacher at the progressive and expensive private Grace Church High School was one of the first to blow the whistle on the insanity. In an interview, Paul Rossi told the truth about what was really going on: "They're trying to carve out an intimacy with the child where they can foster a certain view of the world sheltered from what the parent thinks—and even turning the child against the parent and against the parents' values."[2]

Rossi found himself thrust into the spotlight after publishing an essay that exposed what was going on at his school. It was called "I Refuse to Stand By While My Students Are Indoctrinated."[3] For this thought crime, he was fired. Other journalists picked up the story and helped expose the shockingly invasive roots that CRT had already grown, in every school district in America.

Christopher Rufo, a writer at *City Journal* and perhaps the most essential man in America, had already taken notice of this toxic educational trend. He started exposing invasive CRT in our schools via eye-popping investigative journalism. An army of awakened, angry parents was shocked by his findings.

The media went to work. *New York Magazine* wrote a story called "How to Manufacture a Moral Panic: Christopher Rufo Helped Incite an Uproar over Racism Education with Dramatic, Dodgy Reporting."[4] The *New Yorker* tried to take him down with "How a Conservative Activist Invented the Conflict over Critical Race Theory."[5]

"Invented the conflict"? Oh, you mean exposed your bad ideas? All Rufo had done was publish the teachers' own curricula, their own lesson plans, and leaked videos of liberal teachers using their own words. He left it to parents to draw their own conclusions—and they did.

The panicked teacher's mafia union, one of the most corrupt organizations in America, didn't get the memo that CRT was just a right-wing plot and a conspiracy theory. Instead, they doubled down. The National Education Association, the nation's largest teachers' union, "approved a plan to implement Critical Race Theory (CRT) in 14,000 school districts across all 50 states."[6] You don't say!

I'm sure as I write this there is a plan to construct a time machine and send a Terminator T-1000 back in time to terminate young Christopher before he grows up to command the revolt against the Woke Machine.

How did parents, who are supposed to have the best interests of their children in mind, let it get this far? The answer is that they, too, are victims of sophisticated conditioning over many years to accept the idea that "the authorities" know best.

How'd those pandemic school lockdowns work out for you guys?

Sexualized Early and Often

Imagine being the only one at the PTA meeting who stands up and objects to your second grader studying detailed diagrams of adult genitalia, or your middle schoolers instructed on how to grant consent to anal sex.[7] (These are real sex ed guidelines introduced in New Jersey public schools in 2020.)

Your choices are stark: assert your authority over your children and get called a bigot, or go along with the madness and let them take your child to places you don't want them to go.

How bad is it? Bad enough that Tiara Mack, a "reproductive justice advocate" and "child sex educator" running for state senator in Rhode Island, tweeted this in 2021: "Really excited for the house sex ed bill hearing later today. Teaching comprehensive, queer inclusive, pleasure-based sex ed was a highlight of my time teaching."[8]

This is who wants to talk to your six-year-old about how to "pleasure" themselves and their partner!

Journalist James Lindsay made a video series called *Groomer Schools: The Long Cultural Marxist History of Sex Education.*[9] It exposes the method behind this madness, and you might be surprised to learn that their end goal is not to transform your children into sexually active gender-fluid furries. Their end goal is complete psychological ownership of your kids. It's not, in the end, about getting them to question their genders or their sexual orientations.

It's about getting them to question YOU, the parent. The first step in any cult, or any abusive relationship, is to get the victim to sever ties to their outside friends and family. Maybe you've seen this happen to people you know. They suddenly change their phone number, delete their social media, and have a new friend now—one that has them spellbound.

Once children come to believe their mom and dad are clueless bigots and racists who are holding them back from being who they are, the cult leaders own them. As Lindsay concludes in his *Groomer Schools* series, the entire project is based on the Marxist agenda of abolishing the family so they can produce an army of activists for the revolution.

Government-run public schools have accomplished "regime change" in America and transformed us, slowly, from a society centered around the family, where the schools work for the parent, into a society centered around government employees, where families are required to supply the raw goods for the teachers' unions to mold as they see fit.

Year after year, their assembly lines have been left unsupervised to churn out freshly minted graduates. These graduates move on to college, where their high school indoctrination is hardened and polished by professors. The end product is a citizen who will go to his grave believing a set of Ministry of Truth–approved lies: "whiteness" is intrinsically evil, abortion is health care, there are dozens of genders, America was founded on racism and must be dismantled, marriage is oppressive and bad for women, children hold you back, and unchecked sexual "exploration" with a variety of partners of every gender is the surest path to emotional happiness.

The gender wars in K–12 schools and inside the Walt Disney Company perfectly illustrated this. In 2022, Florida banned gender indoctrination and graphic sex education in schools up to third grade (the falsely nicknamed "Don't Say Gay" bill that doesn't say gay), and everyone lost their minds. Because Disney owns a large children's theme park in Florida, you'd think they would have sided with parents. Instead, after a bit of wavering, they took the side of their far-left employees.

"I apologize for not being the ally that you needed me to be," hapless Disney CEO Bob Chapek nervously groveled in an embarrassing hostage video to his employees.[10] In the video, you can practically see the imprint of a ball-gag harness on his pale jowls that his corporate captors just removed so he could make his public confession.

Showing no mercy, the Essential Mr. Rufo struck gold again, exposing stomach-churning internal Disney corporate HR sessions where higher-ups virtue-signal about their own "transgender" and "pansexual children," boast about their "not-so-secret gay agenda," and monologue their plot to insert sex-and-gender ideology into every piece of children's programming.[11]

Unfortunately for Disney, it turns out that most American parents aren't too interested in radical sex education, sexualized children's programs, or transgenderism in their kids' entertainment or in their elementary schools. Imagine that!

Sane people have a terrible choice to make: exercise parental authority over what their children are taught and risk financial ruin, social blackballing, and permanent cancellation—or allow their kids to be turned against them.

When a teacher or government official replaces the parent as the ultimate authority in the child's life, all bets are off. Educators know that any adult with the authority to influence a child has the power to expose said child to any radical or extreme ideas they want.

To them, *you* are the extremist if you don't think young children need to learn about sex and gender dysphoria yet. *You* are the extremist if you question a teacher or school administrator's choice of books to read or lessons to teach. You are an extremely *racist* extremist if you'd rather not force a five-year-old to feel bad about the color of his skin and apologize for it.

If you don't agree with this quote, you are a dangerous extremist: "It's normal and healthy to experiment with sexual activity, of any kind, starting at a young age. You may not be the gender you were told you were, because your parents are ignorant or transphobic. If you want to change your gender, you totally can, even in kindergarten, and you can always switch back later."

In California, students in middle school can ask their school to change their names and genders in the school computer system, and the school is not permitted to inform the parents. The school authorities and the teachers are legally allowed to conspire with eleven-year-olds in sixth grade to induct them into a cult and keep it secret. Literally "it'll be our secret," a classic groomer move.

These government educational bureaucrats may not drive windowless vans and carry dirty magazines and candy bars to lure young boys (although let's be honest, some do), but they are even more dangerous. Any parents who send a child into an environment like this, either knowingly or blindly, are forfeiting their authority over their kid.

How did this happen? Children have to ask permission to sleep over at a friend's house, but not . . . to become a totally different person? I remember being told as a child to always ask a parent for help making a big decision. I guess the Regime child-catchers prowl the locker rooms and cafeterias looking for lost, confused pre-teens to cart off to Pleasure Island, where they get transformed into donkeys without their parents' consent.

I wouldn't be surprised if Disney is working on a new version of *Pinocchio* where he asks the Blue Fairy to turn him into a real girl.

Parental Surrender

Too many sentient adults seem to simply wait for a new update to the operating system to decide what to do with their kids. They unquestioningly accept the Current Parenting Thing, the rancid gruel served up as "education" at the local public school.

They surrender their kids to the authorities, in all their forms: teachers, principals, pediatricians, drag queens reading stories, social media influencers, YouTubers, Disney, Netflix, TikTok, the Kardashians—anyone who is credentialed as a "kid expert" or "important" now holds more sway over American kids than their own mothers and fathers. "Who am I to tell my kids how to behave, or what to learn, or how to think about the world? I'm just a random person who had a baby. I made plenty of mistakes in my life. How can I possibly ask my children to obey me?"

This is why we can't have nice things. This is why healthy toddlers were kept in COVID masks for two years while they sat in sandboxes alone, outside, in rain or sleet. This is why you see massive brawls happening at middle schools, where kids punch their own teachers. This is why children are indoctrinated into the cult of trans, coached and groomed to say their pronouns, to switch genders, to explore various "sexualities" and "identities." This is why mothers pimp out their own children as "drag kids" and put little boys in princess dresses and post the photos on Instagram while thousands of likes wash over them.

This is what abdicating the parenting throne looks like. Childless weirdos have taken over every institution we look to for guidance on how to raise good citizens, and no, I'm not talking about Catholic priests.

In recent years, it has become only too clear what this absence of parental authority has wrought. Truly insane people have taken over the American education system, Big Pharma, and Big Tech. They know the best way to reach the Final Solution of the American family is to focus on young, impressionable minds.

We are enjoying the fruits of their labor now: an explosion of teen depression and suicide, an epidemic of children who are confused if they're boys or girls, and an incredible 40 percent of Gen Z reporting that they are some letter in the ever-expanding alphabet soup known as LGBTQ+.[12] Everywhere, in every way, the fertile, fallow minds of children are being terraformed by people who identify as "fur baby parents," i.e., pet owners.

I wouldn't let fur baby parents walk my dog, let alone educate my eight-year-old.

Authority Atrophied

Speaking of walking pets, getting children to do what you want can sometimes feel like trying to train a cat to walk on a leash. "The kid forgot to take out the trash again. That's it, I've failed as a parent, I might as well quit now." Then you step on a LEGO another kid "forgot" to put away, or in a pile of dog crap because none of the kids took the puppy outside on time. (This never happens to the fur baby parents—maybe because they don't have any non-furry babies to tend to.)

Then you get in your car and drive away to find a quiet place to contemplate the long series of choices you made that led you to this Land of Chaos. You imagine the voices of other, more capable parents—the real authorities, not pretenders like you, you know, the ones who fold their socks and iron their pillowcases—judging you. "Oh, your children don't always listen to you? Weird. What's that even like?"

Fortunately, this is not the type of parental authority I am talking about! It's not about getting the toys put away. It's about keeping *bad things* away from your children. When your kids are small, you are their only protection from ravenous wolves baying at the door. If the sitter you hired off Craigslist shows up and has neck tattoos and clammy hands and you have a really bad feeling but don't want to seem mean, and the tickets for the Radiohead reunion show are nonrefundable, so against your better judgement you leave your toddlers alone with the weird sitter—well, what's wrong with you?

The breakdown of parental authority leads to ten-year-old boys watching their first porn videos on their phones.[13] Most boys start watching porn on their phones in middle school, and I don't mean the barely masked porn on Netflix or the Prestige Rape Dramas on HBO.

It leads to stories like my friend who took his family on a nice vacation with another family. He reported that the other family had a little boy who thought he was a girl. The little boy wore bikinis and girl clothes, to the delight (naturally) of his mother. My friend told me that while the kid's mom was enthusiastic about her darling son's willingness to wear dresses, his father was not, "but had sort of given up."

This boy's father had been so beaten down by his woke wife, the school, and peer pressure to "affirm" his son—and thereby allow him to be pulled into a vortex of medicalized interventions and certain doom—that he was unable assert his parental authority. He'd probably never exercised it. It was a muscle he didn't know he had, and hadn't ever used. One day he will be forced to walk his "daughter" down the aisle at a wedding to they/them's nonbinary partner or partners.

To avoid his sad fate, *you* must exercise your parental authority early and often. You must speak up!

"No, I don't want you to ask my teenage son if he's comfortable with his gender during his doctor visit."

"No, you are forbidden from sleeping over at your friend's house where her mom's new boyfriend asks to take photos of you."

"No, you can't wear your sister's Elsa dress to school today, because boys don't wear dresses, now get in the car and never ask me that again."

"No, you can't buy those shorts that display the entire lower half of your rear end."

"No, you can't have a TikTok account, and if I find it on your phone, say goodbye to the phone."

Parental authority makes you the heavy in the house and the bouncer at the door. Pull on your big boy pants and lay down the law, or the law is going to lay down all over you.

CHAPTER 11

Your Happiness

A Not-So-Great Depression

A joyful heart is good medicine, but a crushed spirit
dries up the bones.

— *Proverbs 17:22*

What They Took:

☑ ~~Your Fleeting Fertility~~
☑ ~~Your Role~~
☑ ~~Your Gender~~
☑ ~~Your Virtues~~
☑ ~~Men~~
☑ ~~A Soul Mate~~
☑ ~~Your Unborn Children~~
☑ ~~Your Maternal Instinct~~
☑ ~~Your Real Job~~
☑ ~~Your Parental Authority~~
☑ **Your Happiness**

The Joy Gender Gap

Feminism was supposed to free women from the shackles of male oppression. It promised them a utopia of freedom and self-expression where they could finally be *happy*. They wouldn't be held back by husbands and children. They could finally achieve their dreams. Self-actualize! Be the mythical goddesses they were born to be!

After fifty years, the results of this long psychological mind experiment have just come in. Unfortunately, despite all the liberation feminism promised, women in all age groups report that they are unhappy. In fact, they are more depressed than ever before. In 2008, Wharton released a famous study called "The Paradox of Declining Female Happiness." They sought to understand why women are not happy despite all the "progress" on their behalf:

> By many objective measures the lives of women in the United States have improved over the past 35 years, yet we show that measures of subjective well-being indicate that women's happiness has declined. . . . Relative declines in female happiness have eroded a gender gap in happiness in which women in the 1970s typically reported higher subjective well-being than did men.[1]

Twenty-six pages later, the esteemed Wharton scholars conclude that

> the changes brought about through the women's movement may have decreased women's happiness. The increased opportunity to succeed in many dimensions may have led to an increased likelihood of believing that one's life is not measuring up. Women may now compare their lives to a

broader group including men and find their lives more likely to come up short in this assessment.[2]

The experts at Wharton have spoken, and they admit that the women's movement, in other words, second- and third-wave feminism, has ruined women's lives. Feminism has created a "gender gap in happiness." Enjoying guilt-free access to an infinite number of sterilized young women available for casual sex has, shockingly, made men happier than women. If I were a man, I'd laugh, too.

Feminism is the most incredible self-own of all time. Being used like a rented mule on the weekends and then having to compare your own career success to not just other women, but men, too, has created a mental health crisis among women of all ages. The rate of antidepressant use in older women is sky-high. "At age 60 and older, 24% of women used antidepressants compared with 13% of men."[3]

Young women are also in the grip of a mental health crisis. "Suicide is the second-leading cause of death among people age 15 to 24 in the U.S."[4] College freshmen are flinging themselves off parking garages left and right. What's going on? Could it be that true and lasting happiness does not, cannot, will never, emerge from ideas like "female empowerment" and "you can do anything"?

Female Liberation Theology was supposed to free us. Instead, we are more enslaved than ever. "Enslaved? To what? There are no metal shackles on our ankles!" Girl, look in your medicine cabinet. Slavery comes in a bottle these days. Big Pharma has created an entire army of medical slaves hooked on their "cures."

Tragically, the gaping shrapnel holes in their souls cannot be perfectly patched by Paxil or closed by Klonopin. Xannies, as the kids call the anti-anxiety drug Xanax, don't make you zen. In "Xanny," young Billie Eilish sings about seeing her friends on Xanax: "Too inebriated now to dance, Morning as they come down. Their pretty heads are hurting. They're awfully bad at learning. Make the same mistakes. Blame circumstance."[5]

The side effects of some of these pharmaceuticals are permanent and painful. Just ask anyone who's tried to quit cold turkey or had to microdose to wean off one of these "harmless" mood enhancers.

Real depression is no joke. It's debilitating and tragic. The national suicide rate is an absolute horror. There is a time and a place for appropriate pharmaceutical intervention.

But feminism has created a new mental illness: *situational* depression caused by poor life choices. What is making these women so unhappy? Is it lack of grandchildren? Comparing their lives to the life they were promised by their women's studies professors? Feeling something missing, like they forgot to do something before they turned forty? Did they leave the stove on when they went on another yoga retreat?

What is making them gobble mood-stabilizers like they're bonbons? I'm not a Scientologist, so I think there is a place for mood-stabilizing drugs, or psychotherapy, or other medical interventions for mental health issues.

It seems to me that the spike in cases of the sadz among women is not just some coincidental chemical thing happening for no reason just in the last few decades. If one of the causes is not biological but cultural, perhaps the cure then lies in changing the culture—not your prescription.

My Chemical Romance

Part of any perfectly happy, self-actualized woman's arsenal of wellness is a lifetime pharmaceutical dependence on artificial hormones. I don't think the fancy wellness resorts will actually insert your long-lasting birth control implant into your uterus for you, but I'm sure they'd be happy to mist it with your favorite Gwyneth Paltrow candle fragrance. For a special fee, they will even hire an authentic Native

American shaman to perform a smudge ceremony on your crotch with burning sage.

Birth control is marketed as medicine that's "for your health," but what does taking extra artificial hormones really do to the delicate natural balance of the female body? Hormonal birth control manufacturers claim their drugs prevent pregnancy by making it hard for an egg to be fertilized and implanted—but I suspect they really work by making patients too miserable to think about sex.

It's no laughing matter. A family friend, a devoted feminist and liberal, was rendered permanently infertile in the 1970s by the infamous Dalkon Shield IUD (intrauterine device). She trusted the experts who urged women like her to try out the new miracle birth control gadget. It was marketed as a safer alternative to pills. After all, it was invented by a Johns Hopkins doctor! What could go wrong?

In 1973, the CDC conducted a massive study and found that their IUD was causing thousands of serious complications. Nothing was done, and millions of women continued to use the IUD since it was the most popular one on the market. It wasn't until 1984 (!) that the manufacturer finally recommended patients remove their devices for good. Some three hundred thousand women suffered serious and sometimes lifelong side-effects, including sterilization and death.[6] The company went bankrupt, crushed by lawsuits and payouts.

Problem solved! Except . . . it's not. IUDs are common these days. They are "safer" now, so millions of women get them. At my six-week postpartum checkup, my OB practically begged me to let her give me an IUD. She had decided I'd had enough babies.

I turned down her offer. It sounded painful and horrible to have some weird object somewhere, doing whatever it does. Soon after this, I found out that lots of my old friends, the progressive ones with two kids each, had IUDs. They described the agony of the insertion process.

A small price to pay compared to the painful nightmare of having a third child!

The good news is that there's no other IUD on the market that harms women.

Except for all the other IUDs out there.

Joke's on you, ladies!

Say hello to the Mirena IUD. It's the kind that releases a hormone inside your uterus to prevent pregnancy. But what it really does to prevent pregnancy is turn you into a panicky, bloated, overweight wreck.

Do a Google search of Mirena IUD side effects, and you will see unending nightmare scenarios caused by this "safe and healthy" device.

One girl posted a heartbreaking before-and-after Mirena video on TikTok. The before video shows a beautiful young woman with a slender waist and a normal figure. The second video, taken six months after getting her Mirena IUD, documents her dramatic 50-pound weight gain and severe depression.[7] Her beauty is gone, replaced by a sexless, shapeless sad sack in a smock. She also looks about ten years older.

But she must be an outlier! You can't base this on anecdotal evidence! I found dozens of websites filled with horror story after horror story:

I hate the Mirena. I wish I would have known before what it does to some women.

Everything was fine at first until the rollercoaster to hell began! I normally suffer from migraines and have for about 10 years now. However, since Mirena they became excruciating. About a month after that I noticed extreme pain in my chest, shortness of breath, numbness etc., classic symptoms of a panic attack. I told the ER doctors that all this began since I started on Mirena. All thought I was being unreasonable except for one understanding nurse who said it was possible.

I try to tell my OBGYN what's happen [sic] to me and they want to put me on antidepressants. It's like they're not listening. It makes me so sad that women have to go through this and be told it's not the Mirena when obviously not all these women had it in for the same amount of time and are having the same exact symptoms as me. I just want my life back.

I too have been a victim of Mirena. I just got it out today, praise the [L]ord! I had mine in for 15 months. I had frequent cramping, back pain so bad that it has been debilitating, hair loss, and more UTIs than I have had my entire life prior to having this put in. I gained about 20 lbs and have not been able to lose any weight. When I first asked my doctor to remove it, she tried to talk me out of it and convinced me to give it more time. Finally I had had enough and months later I wouldn't take no for an answer. I had to push to have this thing removed. I've felt like a prisoner of Mirena.[8]

I was struck by how often doctors trained to care for women disregard these unpleasant side effects. IUD causing panic attacks? Here, have some more mood-stabilizers.

Are these doctors any better than the ones who wrote millions of unnecessary prescriptions for oxycontin and destroyed an entire region of the country with opioid addiction?

Is it a coincidence that these are the same doctors who think it's perfectly healthy to inject eight-year-olds with experimental puberty blockers that cause irreversible bone damage and infertility?

These are the same doctors who think children as young as three are psychologically capable of understanding concepts like gender and deciding if they're "born in the wrong body." These are the same doctors who prescribe castration and female genital mutilation for healthy organs in teenagers.

If you're looking for a prescription for happiness, it's probably not going to come from a doctor's pen.

Feminist Bingo

If you live in regular American society, read the news, or watch TV, you may come across the same terrifying women over and over again. Warning: you are advised to avoid these women at all costs. You can find them everywhere. They seem to congregate in offices, at preschool pickup, on college campuses, on crowded airplanes, on Instagram reels, and in the supermarket checkout line.

Here's a fun Bingo game you can play with your friends! See how many of these hellacious archetypes you can spot over the course of your week (game hack: it helps if you live in a liberal town):

❏ Women Who Hate Their Husbands

❏ Women Who Hate Your Husband

❏ Women Who Hate Their Children

❏ Women Who Hate Other People's Children, Including Yours

❏ Women Who Wish They'd Had That Abortion

❏ Women Who Can't Wait to Tell You about the Abortion They Had

❏ Women Who Love Being Child-Free

❏ Women Who Wish They Were Child-Free

❏ Women Who Ask You Why You Didn't Abort Your Last Baby

❏ Women Who Ask You If You Know How Babies Are Made When They Count Up Your Children in the Grocery Store

- ❏ Women Who Think Children Cause Climate Change
- ❏ Women Who Think Children Can Choose Their Gender
- ❏ Women Who Think a Baby's Body Parts Don't Tell You What Gender It Is
- ❏ Women Who Agree to Open Marriages
- ❏ Women Who Suggest Open Marriages
- ❏ Women Who Regret Nothing
- ❏ Women Who Regret Everything
- ❏ Women Who Call Themselves Dog Moms
- ❏ Women Who Call Themselves Drag Moms
- ❏ Women Who Use the Phrase "Girl Power"
- ❏ Women on Long-Term Antidepressants Who Think Their Lack of Libido Means They're Asexual
- ❏ Women Who Put "Immigrants Welcome" Signs on Their Front Lawns but You Never See Any Immigrants on Their Lawns
- ❏ Women Who Hang BLM, LGBTQ+, and Transgender Flags on Their Homes but You Never See an American Flag
- ❏ Women Who Donate to Planned Parenthood but Want To Tell You How to Parent
- ❏ Women Who Cheer When Biological Men Humiliate Biological Women in Competitive Sports
- ❏ Women Who Want to Surrender Their Hard-Won Rights to Anyone Who Says He's a Woman
- ❏ Women Who Divorce Good Men through No-Fault Divorce, Ruin Them Financially, and Take Their Kids Away
- ❏ Women Who Accuse Men of Rape after Having Drunken Consensual Sex They Later Regret
- ❏ Women Who Have "Live, Laugh, Love" Art on Their Walls

- ❏ Women Who Own Ruth Bader Ginsberg–Themed Accessories
- ❏ Women With Bettie Page Bangs
- ❏ Women Who Dye Their Hair Unnatural Colors
- ❏ Women Who Think They Can Slay the Patriarchy by Not Shaving Their Pits
- ❏ Women Who Think Full-Term Fetuses Are Not Alive
- ❏ Women Who Think Owning a Single-Family Home Is Racist
- ❏ Women Who Say "Love Wins" but Hate You

Because I live in Southern California, I'll always win this game.

The Top Ten Lies

1. Abortion is health care.
2. Marriage is unnecessary to a successful and happy family.
3. Children don't need a father.
4. Children don't need a mother, either.
5. The highest expression of female power comes from your career.
6. The more lifetime sex partners you have, the better.
7. All men are potential rapists unless proven otherwise. Believe all women.
8. If a man tells you he is a woman, ~~he~~ she is. Believe all women.
9. It's the government's job to provide childcare, and it's your job to use it.
10. Public schools know best when it comes to educating your children and would never indoctrinate them politically or groom them sexually.
11. The gender binary was invented by men in order to oppress us.

Even the name of this list is a lie, since these go up to eleven.

PART TWO

THE BATTLE PLAN:
HOW TO TAKE IT BACK

A Mostly Peaceful Movement

*War is the remedy that our enemies have chosen, and I
say let us give them all they want.*

— William Tecumseh Sherman

*One should always play fairly when one has
the winning cards.*

— Oscar Wilde

Become More Domestic—or Die

Not a joke, folks, as Joe Biden likes to say. We have painted ourselves into an existential corner, and the only way out is *my* way out, as the Ghost Host cackles on the Haunted Mansion ride at Disneyland. So please pay close attention to Part Two of this book. Our fate lies in your hands—and in your ovaries.

We can no longer outsource our God-given vitality, our identities, our children, and our one chance at family formation to institutions, media, political parties, trends, leaders, and corporations that hate us. "How does the government want me to live my life? What does my boss think about me having kids? Would my congressional representative be mad if I had another baby and stayed home to nurse her? Maybe I'll try a trendy open marriage! I read about those in the *New York Times*."

For many decades now, we have been listening to experts, academics, teachers, elected officials, celebrities, pop stars, Michelle Obama, and the pea-brained harpies on *The View* tell us how we should live our lives. We have allowed these nincompoops to strip us of our authority, our autonomy, and our ability to tell right from wrong.

The results are in: broken homes, aborted babies, unhappy people, an epidemic of loneliness, and population collapse—plus skyrocketing rates of drug abuse, alcoholism, pharmaceutical dependency, depression, suicide, child abuse, and wokeness, in all its unnatural ugliness.

It's time to try something new, folks.

And by new, I mean old.

To fight back, some of us are going to have to reorient ourselves. Shift our mindsets. We're going to have to become *ever so slightly* more domestic.

Normal: A Radical New Lifestyle!

The best part about becoming more domestic is that it's totally natural. It's organic. It's gluten-free! It's also a lot easier than you think. You were born to be a domestic extremist. You come from a long, unbroken line of hardcore domestic extremists. The domestic extremists in your family tree make me look like a total lightweight. Their extreme domesticity is the only reason you're here! Every single one of your ancestors, male and female (the only two kinds there were back then) were domestic extremists, stretching far back into the mists of time—every last prehistoric one of them.

Think about it: human beings only recently stopped being extremely domestic, just within the last couple of generations. Post-war modernity jettisoned domesticity, thinking it would switch our lives into Easy Mode.

Except it accidentally set the game to Impossible Mode.

In Impossible Mode, women walk around thinking, "I really can have it all, including a baby when I'm forty-eight!" In Impossible Mode, men walk around thinking, "I'll get married one day, when I'm ready. Don't want to rush into things, we've only been dating seven years. Any new porn on my phone today?"

When you become a domestic extremist, the game instantly resets back to Easy Mode.

Look, you and I both know you secretly *want* to be more domestic. It's what everyone would already be doing if they hadn't been bombarded with destructive anti-domestic messages their entire lives.

And don't worry: where we're going, we won't need butter churns.

CHAPTER 12

A Domestic Extremist's Origin Story

How I Became a Domestic Extremist: Slowly, Then All at Once

Those who leave the tradition of truth do not escape into something which we call Freedom. They only escape into something else, which we call Fashion.

— G. K. Chesterton

Domestic Extremists Are Made, Not Born

Y ou think I just woke up like this? Please. It took me many years to chew my way out of the web of lies smart, well-intentioned young women get caught in. We are raised blind, in the dark, and must feel our way out of the woods without even a trail of breadcrumbs to lead us.

Witches and wolves abound. Many end up in their cauldrons and ravenous clutches.

Some of us might be able to retrace an ancient pathway, or locate the faint traces of old ways, or retain faint memories of a long-dead ancestor's teachings. Some may already know how to follow the right sounds, understand which way shadows fall in the woods at twilight, trace the right tracks, and finally escape to a clearing, hungry and tired, where they glimpse the glowing hearths of a village off in the distance.

These days, most of us will spend our lives in these dark woods. Most of my former peers are there now, only they don't know it. Lost souls. They were born in the woods and will die there, as will any children that manage to survive the ejection seat installed inside their mothers' wombs. They will never know there is a better world—a world that is invisible to them. They've heard it's a bad place, filled with bad people and dangerous ideas.

Of course, you can't see mental freedom. It has no borders, fences, or visible markers of any kind. It only exists in the hearts and minds of those who have tasted it and made it their elixir of choice.

Sometimes the people stuck in the dark woods encounter one of these free men and women. They cautiously approach like one does a wild animal. "How can you live like that," they hiss, "in your terrible minivan and with those terrible mewling children, the ones who demand hugs at inconvenient moments and smear their peanut-butter-covered cheeks onto freshly washed pants?"

They run away, frightened but smug in their decision to only have as many children as can fit into the back seat of a Tesla Model 3.

So how did I find a way out? It was something of a miracle, frankly. I grew up in a secular, atheist household. I attended a progressive private school and a liberal arts university. My parents, however, were mainstream Reagan Republicans. *National Review* subscribers. Normiecons in every way. My mother was a classic boomer housewife and a traditional, feminine lady. She cooked every meal, took care of the kids, drove all the carpools, brushed all the tangles, made our Halloween costumes, and kept meticulous family tree records. She was also a staunch anti-feminist. She thought those hippie broads were nuts. She would tell me stories about going to "consciousness raising" get-togethers with her friends in the 1970s and getting shamed for choosing to stay home with her babies.

As a girl, I had all the basic ingredients to set me up for success, like a good maternal role model and a general sense of American patriotism and all that that entailed. But as a secular atheist, like most of the other moms in our leafy suburban neighborhood, it simply didn't occur to my mother to sit me down and fill me in on the fine print, like Judeo-Christian morality.

After all, her immigrant ancestors had left their various religions back in the old country, and that's where they'd stayed.

My childhood is proof that raising children illustrates British historian Robert Conquest's second law of politics: "Any organization not explicitly right-wing sooner or later becomes left-wing."[1]

This applies to families, too. Feminism, like nature, abhors a vacuum. If you forget or neglect to give a kid proper moral guidelines, bad ideas will fill the void. A child not taught the good rules will soon decide that he or she can make up the rules.

By the time I graduated from college, I was a full-blown feminist and a half-baked liberal. In other words, I knew nothing. For example, I believed abortion was always a woman's choice to make, and that only nerds would wait until marriage. I remember telling my mother that if my younger sister ever got pregnant, I would take her to get an abortion and never tell my mom.

Fortunately, my sister was a nerd, so I was off the hook.

I'm not ashamed to admit this. What did I know? What other message could I possibly have absorbed? I was a victim of omnipresent feminist brainwashing. Abortion was no big deal—*Mademoiselle* and *Newsweek* and my college roommates and the TV all told me so.

When I made my case about abortion to my mother, she surprised me by angrily snapping that under no circumstances would any of us get an abortion and she would happily raise her grandchildren for us.

It was the first time I can remember hearing her opinion on abortion. She was aces at cooking, homemaking, and lavishing us with affection. We came first and we knew it. But as a self-described devout atheist, she didn't provide any specific guidance about how to have a good life. Her natural identity was as a trad, but almost by accident. She somehow lived according to a strict set of traditional values (and still does), but it was tempered with the comfortable lifestyle of a highly educated member of the secular Southern California coastal bourgeoisie. I don't blame her; nobody's perfect.

Including me.

Raised by Wolves

Generation X remains the most together and stable of the post-boomer generations. We managed to put together lives that pretty much resemble our parents', only with smaller houses and a lot less dough. Until college, the only electronic gadgets we had access to were landline phones and VCRs. But despite our blissful lack of social media, we had our own issues. Baby boomers were the first wave of American parents who thought it would be cool to take their hands off the parental steering wheel. The repercussions were immediate.

I was lucky to have had a present and loving mother, but my father was a workaholic professional who had mostly checked out by the time I was twelve. My childhood was notable for his frequent absences. Without any rules in my life or a strong father figure, pop culture and media filled the gaps. Director John Hughes and late-night TV host David Letterman became my real dads.

I don't think I even met a devout member of any religion during my childhood; "religion" simply didn't exist in my world. Every bat mitzvah and WASP cotillion I attended was an ocean of secular atheists. Over time, like an anchor collecting rust, I collected every bad mainstream feminist rule of living. This received wisdom was uncontested; you didn't even think about it. You simply believed.

My peers and I had also grossly misunderstood the Thoreau we read and internalized in tenth-grade English class. When Thoreau wrote, "I went to the woods because I wished to live deliberately, to front only the essential facts of life, and see if I could not learn what it had to teach, and not when I came to die, discover that I had not lived. . . . I wanted to live deep and suck out all the marrow of life,"[2] we took this as a call to arms. We were going to the woods, too!

Instead of the woods, however (ew, bugs), we went to the clubs, the frat parties, and the big cities. We got fake IDs. We were going to live *deep*. That was our transcendentalism: to transcend the "boredom" of normal suburban childhood into rollicking young adulthoods.

Which meant that from age sixteen and up, my secular, "sophisticated," "educated" friends and I ran a terrifying gauntlet while our clueless, divorced parents left us completely alone. We had a lot of fun, yes, but all around me, people were getting hit with cultural shrapnel, their psyches shredded, medics choppering in to rescue them from themselves. Friends endured addiction, near-fatal ODs, date rape, repeated heartbreak, and attempted suicide. My younger siblings lost a handful of their classmates to fatal overdoses and actual suicides. I'm sure many people who have gone to progressive private schools—or any secular schools, for that matter—have similar stories. It was like the HBO show *Euphoria*, only without the cell phones.

No adults seemed to notice we were going a little wild. We whined about it less, I guess. Who would we have whined to? We didn't have the Internet or social media, and our parents were none the wiser. We just shrugged and shook it off—at the time, we thought we were cool.

Anyway, our grandparents had to deal with World War II. Who were we to complain?

What my generation of friends and the *Euphoria* generation have in common seems to be the total absence of any moral or religious underpinning. It's one of the reasons I was happy to raise my children as religious fundamentalists; how else to stave off the carnival of horrors ready to swamp them the moment they get a driver's license? I know what awaits young teenagers armed with nothing but their curiosity, their car keys, and their hormones. You can't keep them down on the farm once they've seen Karl Hungus; therefore, you must do all you can to keep them as far as possible from Karl Hungus and the nihilists.[3]

And yet, despite the decadent behavior around me during my college and post-college years, I never dove all the way to the bottom of the keg.

How did I dodge the cultural grenades long enough to become the domestic extremist I am today? After all, I listened to the same albums, read the same books, saw the same movies, went to the same parties, and survived the same boomer-parent divorce. Why was I relatively unscathed? (Or . . . am I?)

I attribute my ability to evade permanent disaster to the fact that I was raised by a proto-anti-feminist. Maybe the early, limited indoctrination I received from my mother proved to be just enough of a force field to offer me some protection.

Or maybe it's because I witnessed the toll that the Planned Parenthood industry took on young women I knew, tearing open unhealable wounds. It was a stark warning to young Peachy. An abortion? To paraphrase *When Harry Met Sally*, I *won't* have what she's having.

And so it came to pass that in the absence of any counter-liturgy, the Generation X female was forced to construct her own. Our liturgy did not allow for any reflection on future family creation. Are you kidding? Our first commandment was: thou shalt always be raging. As sophisticated college graduates, our plan was to enjoy life, work at some fake job, and then one day, inevitably, settle down.

The idea of finding a husband in our twenties was ridiculous to us. Sure, that was something we'd eventually track down, but there was no rush. Why bother with marriage when we were in our partying prime? Sometime around age thirty—when we got bored and started looking slightly less youthful—each of us would effortlessly conjure the perfect man for ourselves and live happily ever after. It was not something we worried about, ever.

Children, like the concept of a husband, remained a hazy mirage in my mind. I had nothing against kids, but no overwhelming maternal urge. Babies were foreigners, and I didn't speak their language. I had no young cousins and no family members with small children, so babies were scarce in my daily life.

Sometime down the road, I assumed offspring would simply materialize—sailing out of the clouds carried by a flock of storks—so why bother thinking about it? The main thing was to avoid children, at all costs—especially our own. And then, one day, everything would just magically fall into place at exactly the moment we wished.

Spoiler alert: our dumb plan worked. Most of my childhood friends got married right on schedule (i.e., right after turning thirty), had children, and remain married to this day.

Maybe our youthful excesses didn't ruin our chances at happiness because we were the last generation that still grasped the value of getting married *before* having kids. We were the last generation able to put together fairly normal adulthoods, even though we delayed it a few years too long.

The girls I went to college with made it through, too, for the most part. They are perfectly progressive liberals raising perfectly progressive children. Their youthful libertinism has evolved into magic mushroom microdosing parties for moms who could step smartly into *The Real*

Housewives of Beverly Hills. Their children go to expensive schools where kindergarteners announce their pronouns when they address their class; they're put on the pill the day they get their periods, no matter what gender they are.

These are your elite, America.

Nothing changes.

Not having access to dating apps, of course, was our superpower. We were the last generation forced to meet our spouses in meatspace.

Stranger in a Strange World

Cut to: me in my mid-twenties, single, miserable, living in a rotten apartment I hated and working for a string of overfunded, under-managed chaotic Silicon Valley media startups during the Dot Com boom. My jobs usually consisted of not offending the fabulously wealthy A-list actors who had sunk millions into the ventures and who would occasionally drop by to oversee us peasants for a few minutes. It sounds a lot more fun than it was.

I was in a rut, personally and professionally. All my good friends had moved to Manhattan, and they begged me to move across the country to join them.

I wanted a way out. I needed a change.

Then one day, fate took a hand—in the unlikely form of Osama bin Laden.

The TV show I had been working on abruptly got cancelled by the network as a direct result of 9/11. The entire creative team was laid off—with severance. The A-listers slunk back to their enclaves in the Hollywood Hills and their inpatient rehabs.

Severance check in hand, I did what any normal Generation X American female my age would do: move immediately to New York. Ground Zero was still a smoking pit of rubble, but that would not deter me.

This was during the peak era of the original *Sex and the City* television show, the most destructive—and wildly entertaining—social engineering propaganda ever created for impressionable young women. The streets of Manhattan were paved with Manolos and broken hearts! You get to live alone in the same walk-up apartment for years, crying over infinite breakups, having brunch with friends, while barely doing any real work!

Sounds good, we said. Where do we sign up?

When I told my mother my plans, she was thrilled. "It'll be just like *Sex and the City*!" she declared. Verbatim quote.

And oh, it almost was. I enjoyed nearly a full week of the carefree Manhattan single-girl life.

Then, plot twist: I met my future husband.

By this point, I was ripe for radicalization. Just months earlier, I had been politically radicalized (thanks again, Osama!). As of dinnertime on September 11, 2001, I had shed my libertarian-ish political apathy and become a newly minted neocon. Many such cases! Still, it's shameful to admit now. My Reagan Republican parents were relieved I had finally come around to their political ideology, as if by magic. All it took was a massive terrorist attack, four crashed passenger jets, the sight of office workers leaping to their deaths to escape an inferno, and the collapse of two one-hundred-story office buildings full of secretaries and heroic young firefighters to wake me up from my post-war Gen X slumber.

The final turning point came when I watched, live on CNN, a giant mob of proto-Antifa NYU students holding sit-ins and ranting against America in Union Square, just a few subway stops from Ground Zero, that very night. I was shocked to discover that the epicenter of the terrorist attack was also the epicenter of virulent anti-Americanism.

Despite my newfound partial political turn to the right, I clung bitterly to my no-guns, no-religion, pro-choice beliefs. Then, on my third date with the future Mr. Keenan, we got into a heated debate . . . about abortion. Like me, he had been raised by secular conservatives but formed by mainstream liberal culture He, too, had been a liberal Democrat until his own recent conversion.

He told me he used to be pro-choice until a Christian friend in grad school talked him out of it. I scoffed and thought, "Well, that's it, I can't date this pro-life fanatic. What will my girlfriends say?"

He presented this hypothetical. "A young couple gets pregnant after years of trying. They decorate the nursery, plan a baby shower. Then a mugger kicks the woman in the stomach while stealing her purse and she miscarries. Should he receive an elevated charge beyond theft?"

"Well, sure."

"But she could have walked into a clinic and legally had an abortion. Why is what the mugger did any different?"

I was forced to resort to arguing that it was about "the mother's intent. She's the only one allowed to . . ."

"To do what?" Backed into a corner, for a few desperate minutes I tried to argue that yes, abortion does, in fact, mean that you kill a baby, but hey, the mother's intent is all that matters. Women's rights . . . to, you know, kill!

I knew that if I budged from my precarious position on this moral precipice, I would be forced to rethink my entire lifestyle, everything my peers and I had believed for years, as not only wrong and misguided but willfully negligent and cold-blooded. Life would not remain a series of social events and parties that led nowhere. There might be real consequences to our actions. The stakes of our "choices" might be actual life and death.

I maintained my flimsy position as long as I could, but it couldn't hold the weight of my threadbare logic, and down it crashed. The feminism fell from my eyes, and I looked around, blinking in the bright sunlight. "Hey, where did this road to Damascus come from? I thought we were in the East Village!"

And just like that, as Carrie Bradshaw might have said if Aiden had successfully persuaded her to be a cabin-dwelling tradwife, I had found my way out of the darkness.

Defense of abortion is the last and most difficult barnacle to pry off a feminist, but this unusual new boyfriend had succeeded. I suddenly discovered that there is something very *attractive* about a man who wants to convince a young woman that babies—*her* future babies, perhaps even babies he wants to have *with* her—are precious and must be protected. It was a display of confident masculine energy I had rarely encountered among the skinny-jeans hipsters, waxed metrosexuals, and louche Ivy League grads I was used to dealing with.

This man wanted to protect children . . . *my* children . . . *our* children. Swoon!

Forget Mr. Big: here was my Mr. (Far) Right.

A man willing to risk his new chick walking out the door because he defended a child's right to live is a man who will defend his own child. By the time we got married the following year, I was already dabbling in domestic extremism and planning to have children as soon as we could.

These days, I don't understand how any woman could be attracted to a man who doesn't defend a baby's right to live. It was my husband's secret trick to getting my attention—and me. (It also helped that he was handsome and funny.) He'd cracked the code!

Postscript: My grandparents met while both served abroad during World War II; I met my husband thanks to 9/11. I sometimes remind my kids, "The only reason you're alive is because of Hitler and Osama."

Hey, always look on the bright side of life!

Men: You Can Fix Her

See how easy it was for my future husband to "red pill" me, in the parlance of our times? Gents, if she likes the cut of your jib, she will at least hear you out. Fellas, if she is into you, she won't run at the first sign of your own extremely domestic impulses. Besides, red pills go down much better when treated as aphrodisiacs. They are a magical elixir of romance! Many a progressive damsel who feels "oppressed" has been shown the light by the right man, and the right persuasion. It worked for me!

The pro-life man who wants to date you has an enormous advantage over other men: he is telling you, "If I get you pregnant, I would be a father to your child." If Timothée Chalamet (I'm guessing he's their type, but feel free to insert Pete Davidson into this hypothetical if you prefer; lots of women seem to not mind inserting him into *their* hypotheticals) walked up to one of the lumpy, shrieking fiends at the pro-abortion march and said, "Hey, beautiful, I want to have a baby with you," chances are she'd toss her protest sign and her diaphragm into the nearest recycling bin and run off with him.

Here are some easy conversation starters for men trying to woo woke women: "I take care of my body, and I can tell that you do, too." "Your name is [her name]? That's really pretty. I want to name my firstborn daughter that." "No, I don't use dating apps. Never had to." Drop subtle hints that you're not like other guys—you know, like their male feminist allies who rely on high-dose intravenous Viagra when it's their turn in the nonbinary polyamory house to service one of the housemates with a front hole.

Try it! Locate a fresh-faced lass who looks like she still identifies as female and has most of her original body parts intact. You might find her gawking at a campus Slutwalk, or parading in the nearest Women's March, or at a Lizzo concert. Approach her. Compliment her. Woo her.

If enough good guys deprogrammed enough fertile young feminists, I wouldn't have had to write this book. Would have saved me a lot of trouble, believe me.

Achieving My Final Form

It took a first pregnancy to transform me into my final domestically extreme form. At just seven weeks gestation, I was stunned to hear the galloping hooves of a tiny heart beating in the obstetrician's office. The little peanut on the ultrasound machine bounced and wriggled. Where was the "clump of cells" I'd been told about for years? How could a clump of cells have little arms and little legs and a heart—that beats!? What sorcery was this?

According to feminist hero Stacey Abrams, the "heartbeat" I heard was fake, a manufactured sound that was part of a hoax my evil doctor orchestrated to trick me into thinking the fetus was alive.[4]

By my 12-week ultrasound, we had a name picked out, and I'd started a baby scrapbook, filling it with every single one of the grainy black-and-white shots of the peanut. It was like being in a dream. Both of the peanut's grandmothers were already knitting outfits for what would be the first grandchild in the family.

The doctor fiddled with the knobs on the ultrasound machine. We waited to hear the now-familiar galloping hooves. I looked at my peanut, who had doubled in size since the last visit. I suddenly noticed its little heart was not pulsing like it did at all the earlier ultrasounds. Where were the galloping hooves?

The doctor kept fiddling with the knobs, but only tense silence filled the room.

Then I saw his face, and I knew it was over.

None of my friends had kids yet. No one had warned me this could happen. I was only on Chapter 1 of *What to Expect When You're Expecting*! I barely knew what a miscarriage was.

But I found out what it felt like on that ultrasound table. It feels exactly like getting a sledgehammer to the head. With dawning horror, I realized someone was going to have to get the dead peanut out. In total shock, I asked the doctor if I had to have an abortion . . . of my dead baby.

"We call it 'dilation and extraction,'" he explained.

They don't talk about that in Chapter 1 of *What to Expect When You're Expecting*, either.

Endgame

A few months after the miscarriage, I got lucky, literally and figuratively. This time the kid stuck, and we finally became parents. It was my first close encounter with a newborn since my little sister had been born decades earlier. No one had told me how magical newborns are—especially your own. Why had this been kept secret from me? I was instantly hooked.

We soon had three children, all under three years old. Three kids in diapers, folks. I (fortunately) don't remember much from this era, which is why, after a short break, we kept going and had even more of them, eventually requiring a car with three rows of car seats.

After baby number four, I finally converted to Catholicism. My husband, a fallen away Catholic, had gone back to the Church after the miscarriage. I waited a bit, but I eventually found my way there. I would have done it earlier if I'd been able to find matching shoes.

I admit that one of the reasons I was open to becoming Catholic after decades of bleak secular nothingness was my desire to rebel against the pushback I kept getting for daring to procreate. "Oh, you think I'm bad for having all these kids? That's nothing—just wait until I am a religious fundamentalist. You mad?"

With just three measly kids, I had already become the target of eye-rolling and public shaming for my unfashionable fecundity—at preschool pickup, at the store, in the mall, at kids' birthday parties—how dare I have more than two! Didn't I know the *rules*? Such is life in a deep-blue suburb. It's hard to lay low when the shameful evidence of your right-wing extremism is sitting smack in the grocery cart, staring at the other customers and drooling.

But as a Catholic, I could finally lean into my full rejection of anti-natalist social pressure. "Why yes, I am a fringe weirdo, now leave me alone and go feed your cat before you get a contact pregnancy from my powerfully fecund aura." Freedom, at last, was at hand.

A few years ago, I realized with shock and deep regret that I might have been able to request the remains of my tiny first child. I have Catholic friends who have had funerals for babies they miscarried at five or six months. One family I know requested the fallopian tube containing an ectopic pregnancy so they could baptize it.

But in my early non-religious days, I didn't know any of that stuff. None of it was explained or offered by the doctors, and I didn't think to ask. Request a medical waste bag containing bloody bits and pieces of whatever had been "extracted"?

That had *not* occurred to us, Dude.

I have since prayed for forgiveness for leaving the remains to be crudely disposed of and incinerated with the rest of the medical waste. Once I converted to Catholicism, it occurred to me that maybe I would actually meet this vanished child one day, in the beyond. After all, she or he had existed. That tiny heart had beat for three months. One day, will I get to solve the great mystery of whether it was a boy or a girl?

We foolishly named her when we found out I was pregnant, certain she was a girl. Will I greet her by name when we meet?

This kind of weird theological thinking gets you in big trouble. No wonder secular atheists can't spend too much time debating these issues rationally. Because if you believe in heaven, and that souls are formed at the moment of conception, and that innocent children who die become saints, then all aborted children must go to heaven, too.

Where do the souls of the mothers who killed them go? Is heaven filled with millions of orphans? Fifty million children a year are aborted worldwide. Oh dear.

And that, kids, is how your mother became a domestic extremist.

CHAPTER 13

Become an Anti-Feminist

Make Femininity Great Again

*Like a gold ring in a pig's snout is a beautiful woman
without discretion.*

— *Proverbs 11:22*

Beauty begins the moment you decide to be yourself.

— Coco Chanel

Beauty vs. the Beasts

"Anti-feminist" is a slur mainstream liberal feminists typically accuse conservatives of being when they resist the dominant narrative ("men are oppressors and misogynists, women are oppressed victims, all men secretly want to rape us, even though they won't propose to us or even return our calls, I've texted him ten times, I think he blocked my number"). Attempts have even been made to tie "anti-feminism" to white nationalist recruitment, the rise of mass shooters, and the terrifying online mystery group known as the "Manosphere." Helen Lewis wrote in *The Atlantic* about the dangerous groups who reject feminism and included this quote: "'Misogyny is used predominantly as the first outreach mechanism,' Ashley Mattheis, a researcher at the University of North Carolina who studies the far right online, told me. 'You were owed something, or your life should have been X, but because of the ridiculous things feminists are doing, you can't access them.'"[1]

(Helen, dear, kindly let Ms. Mattheis know that because of the ridiculous things feminists are doing, I, too, feel personally cheated out of what my life could have been. Thanks, girl!)

I didn't have time to write a 50-volume anti-feminist apologia, so I accept that various girl-hating Redditors and Manosphere[2] denizens have also called themselves "anti-feminists." But I propose reclaiming this phrase for our own purposes. By anti-feminist, I mean simply that more women must reject the entire feminist project, root and branch, as a destructive force that has not—sorry, Helen!—been good for women, on balance.

Sure, I like voting, I like being able to earn money, I like not getting forced to marry the randy, wart-covered elderly duke in the next castle over. But they've taken it too far. Feminism has jumped not just the shark, but the ocean. Their brand is no longer appealing or attractive. It sucks, frankly. Time to drive a stake through its bloodless heart and send it off to the mass grave holding all the other stupid, dead "-isms" humanity tried and rejected.

It is not enough to not be a feminist—you, men and women both, must become *anti-feminists*. I think of feminism, in its simplest form, as the opposite of femininity. Feminism convinces you that women are weak, and only the State can dispense and defend a woman's rights. Femininity is the deep confidence that you were born with innate power and don't need to rely on a faceless bureaucracy to grant you permission to wield it.

Feminism teaches you men are bad—they are your sworn opponents, competitors, and oppressors. Femininity reveals the truth: men are vital protectors, providers, partners, husbands, and fathers.

Anti-feminism does not mean men should suddenly revel in misogyny and start slapping their wives around. I'm pretty sure it's the staunch feminist men who are taking full advantage of sex-positive hussies looking to increase their body counts.

Anti-feminism requires everyone to stop pretending women are the same as men.

Anti-feminism requires women to stop sneering at men for being less like women.

Just because not all men are good guys, just because some of them ghosted you and broke your heart, doesn't mean masculinity itself should be treated like a disease. If an apple is rotten, you don't burn the entire orchard. We need them apples!

For a woman to be able to express her innate femininity, she needs some men around who are comfortable expressing their masculinity. When both femininity and masculinity are suppressed in favor of gender-neutral mush, both sexes suffer in the extreme.

The secret is that femininity, and not militant feminism, is where real power lies. This is a forgotten truth, one you can test out for yourself. Women can instantly regain their moral authority and their latent cultural and political clout by simply presenting themselves in public as, well, feminine. Practically, this means behaving and dressing in age-appropriate ways that involve a little more restraint. This idea triggers rage in many people; they accuse you of wanting to put women in burkas and robes.

That's silly—of course you don't need to wear a burka. But would it be too much to ask to not parade on stage in front of children waggling your giant green strap-on dildo, and allowing another nearly nude woman to simulate oral sex with it? Singer Christina Aguilera actually did this at a "family friendly" Pride Month concert in Los Angeles.[3] Christina, you're not beautiful to me anymore.

Feminism may be widespread and mainstream, but it still operates like a totalitarian cult. Step out of line, and you'll face the wrath of the cult leaders, who will excommunicate you from the sisterhood and banish you from the gender seminar. Deprogramming someone from feminism is tricky. It's like getting someone off drugs, or out of Scientology, or away from veganism. Your best defense is prevention. Just say no, kids: to cults, meth, plant-based meat, and yes, feminism.

If you are ready to reject it, the first task is perhaps the most difficult: you must accept natural femininity. Not by wearing high heels and push up bras or returning to the cartoon 1950s female stereotype that feminists always accuse traditionalists of fetishizing. I look terrible in poodle skirts, okay? Femininity is not about being "hyper" feminine or dressing like a nun. It's about—cue the outrage—dressing "normally."

The only women I see in full makeup, push-up bras, stripper heels, and skin-tight dresses these days fall into two categories: Caitlyn Jenner types and Kim Kardashian types. (I wonder if it's a coincidence they are related to each other?)

When I say, "Be feminine," I simply mean cling tightly to your innate femaleness, however it manifests itself in you, with your appearance and your behavior. Frilly dresses and fascinators? Great. Denim overalls and Doc Martens? Cool. Natural, long-buried reluctance to engage in meaningless sex with a string of strangers who don't like you? Good! Cling to that aspect of your feminine self as tightly as you can!

Just try looking like who you are and engaging in behavior that won't cause you decades of shame or trauma. At this point, that is an act of rebellion. To truly combat the plague of barren feminist ugliness, inside and out, we need more women of all ages to present themselves to the world with a bit more, well . . . I'm just going to say it: class. A bit of, yes, restraint.

There is a reason the Left embraces purposeful physical ugliness; we should reject it in favor of feminine normalness. No extraordinary beauty or "perfect" physique is required!

Instead, the shocking absence of nose rings, oversized gluteal implants, green hair, or baroque piercings anywhere on your body will immediately set you apart as a classy babe who positively exudes femininity. Pair that with a stubborn resistance to trendy "sex positivity," and you will be well on your way to domestic happiness.

Beauty Always Wins

Maybe you've noticed that most iconic women of the past share some aesthetic traits. There is a good reason Audrey Hepburn and Grace Kelly are still admired, while '80s sex symbol Madonna has descended into pure cautionary tale, posting stoned videos in which she displays her artificially enhanced geriatric rear end clothed in nothing but a G-string. Whatever the opposite of aging gracefully is, she is accomplishing it.

The great beauties celebrated in our culture were women blessed with excellent bone structure and flawless faces, but they also carefully enhanced their God-given blessings in *feminine*, i.e., non-extreme ways. It is easy to imagine that Sophia Loren and Raquel Welch looked a lot like themselves when they washed their makeup off.

By contrast, the Kardashian ladies' faces are worn mattresses upon which every plastic surgeon in Los Angeles has had his way numerous times. Their ultimate goal seems to be to look like high-end sex dolls. Looking at a Kardashian face gives me uncanny valley vibes. Where does Kim keep her semiconductor chip? Is she silicone or silicon? I understand the impulse to "look perfect," but unfortunately these women have used unlimited budgets to overshoot the beauty landing zone and crash in alien territory. When you mess with youthful good looks, your inborn feminine beauty can get effaced—literally.

Meanwhile, '80s supermodel Cindy Crawford, just seven years younger than Madonna, maintains strict age-appropriate outfit discipline. Cindy gets it.

We can see the trickle-down effects in their daughters. Madonna's daughter Lourdes Leon pouts angrily as she models outrageous BDSM lingerie in sickening, quasi-pornographic ad campaigns. Kaia Gerber, Cindy's daughter, has not yet descended to these depths, and still maintains a certain level of high-born grace. The warning lights are flashing, however: based on the number of tattoos she has and her tragic dating history (yes, I'm sorry to report it involves Pete Davidson), she may end up being the apple that falls far from the tree. I recently saw a magazine cover featuring a twenty-year-old Kaia posing nude, covered in faux tattoos.

If even Cindy Crawford's infinitely rich and beautiful Malibu princess is not safe from the ravages of contemporary feminist "beauty," what chance do regular American girls have? (Someone FedEx a copy of this book to Malibu Colony.)

There is a good reason the Left embraces ugliness, which manifests in young, pretty women as physical defacement: tattoos, piercings, brutalist clothing choices, and humiliating behavior. It imposes its ugliness harshly on the privileged daughters of the elite (Lourdes and Kaia) to bring them down to their level and immerse them in the muck.

Our cultural overlords subsume these girls' natural power as its own. It deforms them into potent weapons to use to trick other, non-elite girls into following suit. By stripping young women of the God-given gift of their own feminine gravitational force fields, they are rendered genderless, hollowed out of whatever made them fresh-faced innocents.

The process is virtually automated by now. The Ugliness Machine, via social media and peer pressure, chews up raw female material and spits out unrecognizable goblins. Best of all, they've convinced women to lower themselves into the machine *by choice*, actively stripping and subverting their natural beauty.

As you have probably observed many times, the most feminine women of all are imbued with a kind of superpower. Perhaps you have witnessed a crowded party's reaction to the entrance of a striking young woman. Or the barely contained hostility of childless boomers to a young mother out and about with a batch of young children, nursing an infant as she fills her cart. In both cases, these peak female archetypes exert immediate and instant gravitational effects on the people around them. This is peak feminine power, and it is an awesome thing to behold.

Most of us, of course, are not great beauties. Few are! Good news: you don't need to be one to have a wonderful romantic relationship and a happy life. Phew! Maybe you are well past youth and have no powerful beauty or blossoming maternal strength to wield. Fine! Accept this. A woman of *any* age can wield power with confidence, charm, and a proper outfit.

And now I must address a topic some readers must be wondering about: *But, Peachy, what about . . . the lesbians?* I happen to like lesbians. Old-school lesbians—you know, the gray-haired transphobes who aren't comfortable dating angry women with penises—are holding the battle lines for the rest of us hiding in the rear with the gear. They're fighting a hot culture war to defend women-only spaces and sports from other, more invasive genders.

We are going to *need* these trad lesbians on our side. Sadly, vanilla lesbians are going extinct because of the modern-day persecution of "tomboys" that induces many to undergo conversion therapy and become men. But that's a topic for a different book.

The good news for almost every young woman alive is that she is born with everything she needs to be fully female. You don't need to be a spectacular sex goddess or have any extraordinary gifts. Women like that intimidate most men. Simply existing, just being a *normal* young woman—imagine!—will put you far ahead of the feral pack of angry, nonbinary furries with shaved heads and chains through their noses that your former classmates transform into whenever there's a full moon.

Could it possibly be that embracing your natural femininity produces the confidence and self-acceptance that are prerequisites for happiness? Who knows? Real femininity has never been tried!

Hey, Not-So-Good Looking!

Of course, looking "sexy" is the only thing that's kept humanity from going extinct at every bottleneck. Youthful adults are designed by nature to look "sexy" for obvious biological reasons. It's the entire point of youth!

But now, even with the cursed COVID masks off, everyone just looks lumpy and disheveled, sporting random, haphazardly styled outfits, with the occasional shocking display of way too much rear end. You don't leave the house looking for a mate like that, do you?

The trouble seems to start with girls thinking that the *only* way to attract suitors is to display all their wares, all the time, in every situation. Maybe because their personalities and interests have been muted by too much time on social media or too many edibles. Maybe the only thing interesting left is whatever you've got to fill out those ripped cutoffs.

It would be an interesting theory to test out: As your vocabulary shrinks, does your bikini bottom shrink, too? That may explain why I have been forced to observe enormous hindquarters at the beach cleaved down the middle by a length of stretched-out dental floss hanging on for dear life. Crack is whack, okay? Also, this is poor salesmanship. You may get the customers you seek, but they will not be *return* customers.

Of course, there are times when a woman's goal is present herself in the most attractive and alluring way she can. Women understand the gravitational force field they can create when they choose to. But you must beware of your age and the context. Many forget this rule. Dress too sexy when you're too young, and you look like jailbait and will attract ex-felons. Dress too sexy when you're too old, and you enter *Whatever Happened to Baby Jane* territory. It's one thing to be a MILF; it's quite another to become a cougar.

Youth Privilege

The real privilege in America is not white privilege, or rich privilege, or college-degree privilege. It's youth. The wonderful thing about youth is that it makes almost everyone attractive in some way, if they are not grossly obese and have taken care of their skin. This treasure is a fleeting currency and should therefore be spent with great urgency. No amount of surgical intervention can make a fifty-year-old look like her twenty-five-year-old self.

Unfortunately, most women's prime beauty years are largely wasted. A girl in her mid-twenties will never have a better chance to attract a high-quality, long-term romantic partner. And what do they do with this gift? Burn through their beauty like a drunk burns cash at a strip club in Vegas.

A little more reflection would prevent a lot of wreckage—and regret—later.

"I'll settle down one day" means that you will, by definition, be working with material that has lost some of its shine, a knife that has dulled from use. A twenty-four-year-old who's ready for marriage represents a deadly threat to an unmarried thirty-six-year-old woman. No wonder these girls are told to embark on long and unproductive dating careers. "Go spend your twenties dating losers while you're young" is a nefarious plot hatched by miserable singles in their thirties to keep the marriage-minded men for themselves.

Note: I am not disparaging older women. I am a (slightly) older woman! Well, I'm not officially old, not yet, but I'm definitely older than I used to be, to my dismay. I'm stuck with my birthday, and my husband is stuck with me, but as my father-in-law says, God designed it so the wrinkles start to arrive just as the vision starts to go.

If I was divorced, or had never gotten married, I'd probably just lean into little-old-lady land. Besides, I don't have the energy to be a single MILF. It sounds like a lot of work, and I'd have to wear heels again. If I didn't want to die alone, I'd have to take up lawn bowling, attend erectile dysfunction seminars, or trawl the parking lot on Bingo Night at the nearest Shriners Lodge. I'd be lucky to attract a man with any of his own hair—or even his own toupee.

Some years ago, concerned that my divorced single mother would grow old alone, I helped her set up an online dating profile. I filled out her profile and got to the section that asked her to include important attributes she was looking for in a man.

"What do you want me to put, Mom?"

"Impotence a plus."

The truth is, I could swim in a vat of Botox and let a plastic surgeon iron my face with an anvil, and I still wouldn't recapture whatever youthful glow I may once have had. Not that there's anything wrong with that—I am totally fine with women doing reasonable maintenance they deem appropriate. This is a personal decision between a woman and her Botox professional.

Your wrinkles, your choice.

Maybe She's Born with It, Maybe It's Domesticity

Did swapping traditional feminine values for feminist values make young women happier? That was the promise, remember. Did it work? Let's check in with Gen Z and find out!

Ah, unfortunately, it looks like depression among Gen Z is sky-rocketing, and it's highest for young women.[4] Could there be a connection between all this summertime sadness and the feminist indoctrination they receive from birth? What is causing this *tsuris* in youthful women who should be at the peak of their nubile powers?

I'm not a scientist, but according to one survey, feminine women are scientifically proven to be happier.

> Elite culture most often celebrates women who embrace more masculine models of life, from the C-suite (think Sheryl Sandberg) to pop culture (think Captain Marvel). In fact, the message from the culture's commanding heights seems to be that there is no value for girls and women in embracing a distinctive and traditional feminine identity in the 21st century. But that message doesn't seem to be getting across to ordinary women across America, the majority of whom see themselves as "very feminine."[5]

According to the survey,

> women who described themselves as feminine were the most likely to marry and to say they have fulfilling marriages across various dimensions, including strong personal relationships and community involvement. High-femininity females were also, according to the study, more likely to describe themselves as able to take risks, manage uncertainty and self-regulate, which may help to explain lower rates of depression compared to other women.[6]

One of the nice things about marriage is that your husband ends up being one of the last people who knew you when you were relatively young and attractive, and when he looks at you years later, maybe he still can see the babe he proposed to in a fit of wild, passionate love. A long marriage is a powerful (and overlooked) hedge against the ravages of depression; the companionship of someone who still loves you can blunt the sting from the scythe of time.

In the end, being an anti-feminist is simply about recognizing—and accepting—that youth is your time to shine, and acting accordingly. It's when the courtship and mating process needs to begin. After that, your primary mission accomplished, you can sit back and relax, aging gracefully while you watch your single feminist friends grow more frantic. You know, the ones who will one day demand that their teenage step-grandchildren call them "Glamma."

When my grandmother was my age, to me she looked twenty years older than I do, with her tightly curled short hairdo, unchanged since World War II. But to my grandfather, she still closely resembled the young lass he'd whisked off to marriage, even though her hair had gone whiter.

Femininity is not just about looks or fashion. It is a mindset. It is a *lifestyle*. Adopting it early just might save your life.

CHAPTER 14

Explore Promiscuous Monogamy

Practice Radical Selectivity

I used to be Snow White, but I drifted.

— Mae West

*It's a male myth about feminists that we hate sex. It can
be a natural, zesty enterprise.*

— Maude Lebowski

The Dating-App Trap

Dating, at least until recently, was a good and normal thing to do.
But "dating" has now become a euphemism for performing what
can only be called unpaid sex work. How many Tinder dates end with
you on your knees—because you're praying you didn't get a disease?

Dating apps like Tinder seem to have taken romance out of the
picture completely. The only thing worse than a '90s-era singles bar is
an online meat market. It doesn't kick you out at 2:00 in the morning,
it never closes, there's no bouncer, and no drink minimum.

It's Amazon Flesh, delivered to your door in under an hour.

In our pleasure-on-demand, 24/7 culture, rejecting promiscuity and practicing chastity feels ridiculous, insane, and even impossible, for both genders. Why in the world would you stop at first, second, or third base unless you were a repressed prude or a crazy religious fundamentalist? Why *not* be promiscuous? How else are you supposed to find a boyfriend if you're the only one in the college dorm without a "Now Serving" sign posted on the door? Louise Perry observes that "when sex before marriage is expected, and when almost all of the other women participating in my particular sexual market are willing to 'put out' on a first or second date, then *not* being willing to do the same becomes a competitive disadvantage."[1]

Hooking up with anyone who'll have you is good for your ego, and it makes you temporarily happy. Plus, your antidepressants can pick up the broken pieces of your psyche after you're ghosted. "Hook-up culture is a terrible deal for women and yet has been presented by liberal feminism as a form of liberation," Perry notes. "A truly feminist project would demand that, in the straight dating world, it should be men, not women, who adjust their sexual appetites."[2]

But all the guardrails we used to have in place that prevented everyone from going buck wild have been abolished, so why resist? Modern, fully liberated uterus-havers have up-armored their innards to prevent unwanted IEDs (Intimately Exchanged DNA). Women have thrown off the shackles and the chastity belt forced upon them by a repressive Puritanical society and can finally live like eighteenth-century French aristocrats—with all the venereal diseases and alcoholism that go with it.

I'm not a psychologist, but it seems obvious that young women who seek out constant, low-stakes sexual encounters with people who don't love them are not actually doing it for the momentary sex act itself, which is unlikely to be a fond memory they recall wistfully on their deathbeds. So why do they do it? Why the race to increase your personal body count and beat your friends at the numbers game?

Maybe for the same reason they post cute selfies on Instagram. To feel good about themselves for once. To stop hating themselves for a few moments. To feel pretty, attractive, and desirable, in a real, tangible way. I was a young woman once. I remember the persistent feelings of self-hatred, of feeling not good enough or pretty enough. Is this a normal teenage thing, or was it exacerbated by not having a father in the home for all my teenage years? Is self-loathing common among young, fatherless young women? Huh, turns out it is!

"Countless studies have shown that fatherlessness has an extremely negative impact on daughters' self-esteem. . . . They may become promiscuous as a way of getting male attention without becoming too emotionally involved."[3]

Paging Dr. Freud! It is no surprise that girls ignored by absentee dads may seek out other forms of attention. A tale as old as time—many such cases. Radio DJ Howard Stern used to ask every stripper on his show if they'd ever met their fathers. But instead of seeing promiscuity as the obvious result of life-altering emotional and psychological trauma, the culture grotesquely *celebrates* it as "female sexual liberation." "He's just not that into you," only it's your dad, and you never get over it.

And just like all dopamine hits, the high from a brief encounter quickly fades. The next day, you are left with—what exactly? A slightly shameful memory, embarrassing bragging rights, and someone you hope either calls you immediately (he won't) or forgets you immediately (he will).

Meanwhile, each roundtrip takes its toll on your fuselage and your well-being. Years spent living like an unpaid escort are not healthy or beneficial to your fading youth. What young woman fantasizes about being used like a rented mule for a couple decades? Was that your plan all along, or did you start out seeking love and it just sort of snowballed into a weekend hustle as volunteer comfort woman for the neighborhood?

The tenth anniversary of the Tinder app launch triggered a spate of articles about women who had eagerly downloaded the app when it first appeared, and ten years later . . . are still using it. When your booming business model depends on keeping everyone single, you're going to do whatever you can to keep them that way. "We've Spent 10 Years on Tinder—Will We Spend Eternity?"[4] If the multibillion-dollar hookup technology industry has any say in it, yes, you will!

The illustration accompanying the article depicts a hand literally handcuffed to an iPhone displaying the Tinder logo. Handcuffed! "Sexual freedom is slavery" is the clear and obvious message to anyone who reads the article.

After ten years of Tinder hookups, some people decided that was too tame for them. Boring! Enter Feeld, one of the newest fringe sex apps on the scene, designed to help you plan your next threesome or group orgy. An unhappily single female journalist who wrote about Feeld, which she turned to after a painful breakup, described her state of mind: "Over and over in my adult life, despite being an introvert *with a preference for monogamy*, I have found myself in situations where I've had total sexual freedom."[5] When you can't get what you really want—monogamy—you will settle for a string of threesomes.

In the end, however, the infinite date horizon will drain your life force. "Most people are now meeting their partners through apps, meaning that even though a lot of women experience being sexualized and demeaned on a regular basis, they feel like they don't have a choice."[6]

You will end up with nothing to show for it but hardcore depression, hardened looks, and a hardened heart. Your dates may be paying for all those drinks, but you're the one who will be paying the tab in the end.

For people who claim to care so deeply about "women's health," feminists don't seem to care about the chronic sexually transmitted diseases and other health problems caused by having scads of sexual partners. Forget COVID—America has a chlamydia epidemic, a genital warts epidemic, and an epidemic of something called "super gonorrhea," which is antibiotic-resistant gonorrhea that you have *forever*. Like calls from people trying to sell you an extended warranty on your car, super gonorrhea never goes away.

Who is spreading all these STDs? I'm going to take a wild guess that it's mostly the people doing all the "dating." A truly feminist project, Perry notes, would be one that seeks a real solution to ending the casual sex supply chain imbalance between men and women.[7] Incredibly, such a system *already exists*. Imagine, if you will, a way for men to access a frequent and willing sexual partner whom they find attractive, and for women to enjoy sexual encounters *without* resorting to unsatisfying, soul-destroying sex with strangers?

Impossible, you say?

Brace yourself, friends, for we have a solution.

A Modest Monogamous Solution

Yes, friends, I'm talking about marriage. If that word triggers you, just focus on the monogamous part of it. I'm aware that lots of trendy progressives enjoy "open marriages" these days, which almost always end with one of them opening Yelp to find the nearest divorce lawyer. But real monogamy—practiced with someone you love, imagine—can instantly end the merry-go-round of trauma the app suckers are stuck on.

As inspiration, consider the tiny tribe of fringe radicals who somehow manage to—brace yourself, trigger warning—*wait until they are married* to sleep together. I'm fairly certain this is illegal in California.

I recently attended the lovely wedding of an attractive young Catholic couple who had met at college. They were obviously deeply in love, and most certainly both virgins. I have no doubt these wild rebels will enjoy a long, happy marriage rich in children. Watching them profess their vows to each other in the church brought a tear to my eye—not because of the ceremony itself, but because I was reminded that I was robbed of the chance to experience anything like that. The anticipation, the heady romance, the powerful and ancient cultural tradition they were choosing to continue—I'd never even been given the choice to seek out that kind of outrageously taboo lifestyle. In my young adulthood, anyone who talked about "waiting until marriage" would be laughed at, mocked, and dismissed as a hopeless loser and an undateable religious freak.

But maybe waiting until you're married to "do it" with the person you truly love is sort of like pitching a perfect game in baseball. Just because only a very few of us will ever accomplish this impressive feat doesn't mean it's not a good and worthy goal. Every time you give up a home run to a batter you don't love, your ERA goes up and your whole team loses. You become a less valuable trade in the future. You add one more L to your total lifetime weight of regret and loss.

Most will fail to achieve perfection, but it doesn't mean you can't at least try. For Catholics, you are supposed to avoid committing "a near occasion of sin." Since I'm a relative newbie, I asked some cradle Catholics to define it for me. It means avoiding doing anything that could make you "aroused." This is a high bar. Maybe the best approach is to decide ahead of time that before you get swept away by passion, you won't burn your limited capital on something fleeting. Maybe you should both, like, wait until you really like each other!

Will I be arrested for suggesting something so *obscene* when judged by contemporary values? And yet, I don't know anyone who thinks back fondly to their one-night stands and random drunken hookups. These things are usually recalled later with much eye-rolling and shudders of horror and shame. How many brides-to-be have informed their maids of honor that they are *absolutely not* to mention in their wedding speech *anything* that happened those last two years of college, or over spring break in South Beach, or backstage at the Backstreet Boys show, or at the afterparty for their friend's art opening?

When podcaster and author Bridget Phetasy published her now-famous essay, "I Regret Being a Slut," thousands of women responded—*agreeing* with her. The overall reaction was "Me too, girl, me too." Well, what do you know—a new #MeToo movement is born!

All the hookups, all the dates, all the people you are ghosting and who are ghosting you, are just detours and dead ends on your life journey.

We all make mistakes; maybe more of us should try to make *fewer.*

The brutal reality is that those fleeting, meaningless encounters build up, collecting like barnacles on the hull of a great ship. Over time, the barnacles create drag, slowing you down, marring your trim good looks, adding weight that will eventually, tragically, pull you straight down to the bottom of the sea.

Quitting Porn

Living a more chaste lifestyle does not just mean turning down dates. It also means doing two other things that blaspheme against the modern Church of 24/7 On-Demand Pleasure: abstaining from pornography and masturbation. (*But, Peachy, what will half the country do for entertainment? There are only so many* Friends *reruns one can watch!*)

It turns out that porn, or as I call it, eye meth, is epidemic, among men, women, young boys, and young girls. Most boys are exposed by age thirteen, some as young as seven.[8] By age eighteen, 84.4 percent of males and 57 percent of females have watched porn.

When they talk about drug addiction, liberals like to bring up "harm reduction." Harm reduction is accepting "for better or worse, that licit and illicit drug use is part of our world and choosing to work to minimize its harmful effects rather than simply ignore or condemn them."[9] Harm reduction is when you give someone dying of a heroin addiction an endless supply of free needles and a comfortable chair to sit in to shoot up where no one will bother them as they commit slow-motion suicide.

Making it easier for people to inject their brains with pornography by normalizing it as just another form of entertainment is causing untold harm—on both sides of the screen. Murder, bestiality, and child molestation also exist, but that doesn't make them healthy pastimes, either.

The damage pornography causes to the developing brain is by now well documented. It is highly addictive and deformative. It can incite people to seek out ever-more extreme videos as they chase an eye-meth high. Even worse, many of the young females in the videos are trafficked or enslaved in other ways to drugs and a vicious lifestyle that grinds their souls into dust. Suicide rates and drug addictions among porn performers are real boner-killers. There are a hundred reasons to avoid this mind poison, but because it has been normalized as "just another form of content," few resist the urge.

Sitting inside masturbating to broken, underage, bipolar child-abuse survivors humiliating each other for money is a terrible way to spend your days, especially if you are a young person. Focus your energy elsewhere: on improving your life, your health, your real relationships—and on saving your soul from demonic possession. There is *nothing* cool or fun about pornography. *Boogie Nights* was a horror movie with a great soundtrack.

The stakes are high. Porn addicts don't make good partners or parents. I'm one of those weirdos who think married men watching porn is cheating. No normal woman wants her soul mate spending his time abusing himself to images of naked drug addicts, and those who say they don't mind are lying, if only to themselves. What other form of "entertainment" exists that can potentially ruin your chances of having a family and a future? Therefore, you must resist!

Choose Wisely

To enable modern dating culture, lots of safety nets are required. Birth control and abortion are the key infrastructure that underpins the whole thing. Without them, people's sexual behavior might have to (gasp) change. Men and women would have to (faints) treat each other differently, with a little bit more (literally shaking) respect.

But are these safety nets actually safe? Do you really want to find out? Accidental pregnancies and sexually transmitted diseases are just the most feared dating hazards, but there are others. I'm talking about lifelong emotional consequences. Women who had abortions as young women must continue to support abortion rights to keep cognitive dissonance at bay. The moment they stop believing that abortion is morally okay, their house of cards will collapse. They will be forced to reconsider if their own abortion was a good thing, as simply a right they exercised, or the truth will crush them.

Maybe that's why they have to "shout" their abortions. If they shout loudly enough, they won't be able to hear the screaming of their own hearts—or the hearts they stopped. Do they dream about the children they erased from existence? Think about their birthdays every year around the phantom due date? I know some who do. I pray for these women.

It's one thing to make a mistake or two. It's another to make this your actual lifestyle, for years—decades even. It turns out that all their language around empowerment and confidence and equality is pure horse manure. Feminists and their male allies have turned several generations of young women into nothing more than budget sex slaves.

Women's studies professors are the real sex traffickers.

Here's an instant way to save yourself from this pain and suffering—delete your dating apps. Or at least, swipe much more carefully. Practice safer swiping!

Visualize not letting yourself be used as a human Fleshlight; a warm body to be discarded and forgotten in the cold light of day. Imagine not watching sex-trafficked women perform lewd acts onscreen for the momentary delight of strangers.

People fear and hate the concept of chastity. Mention it in public, and you are accused of being a backwards medieval peasant. Someone who wants to put women back in chains, or worse, back in the kitchen. Maybe the furious reaction to chastity is triggered because committing to it would mean missing out on promising Tinder dates.

Well, I am here to tell you that Tinder for women is a scam that could have been designed by a female-hating chauvinist pig. According to the candid reports of a few single, divorced male friends, heavy app users all, you should know that your new Tinder date is on his third date—that day. He has no desire for a girlfriend, and he certainly isn't going to tell you that. To the women he meets on the apps, "having sex is like brushing their teeth." He laughs at the women who put "absolutely no hookups!" in their bios (and he ignores them). He has zero desire for a relationship and just wants some, ahem, "company" for a few hours. He will excuse himself during dinner to go to the men's room to reply to the women he's already lined up for later, after he peaces out from your place.

In early 2022, a story broke that proves my friends were telling the truth. A young man named Caleb was exposed by his many, many Tinder matches as a serial dater.[10] Dozens of young women flocked to social media to report that he had also, ahem, "dated" them. He was a one-man #MeToo movement. He had, it turns out, burned through most of the female population of Brooklyn and the East Village. YouTube compilation videos featuring dozens of tearful Caleb dates appeared. It was like the final scene of *Spartacus*: "I dated him! I dated him!"

Some girls found out he had left their apartments in the morning and ended up on dates with one or two other women the same day.

Sorry, but the only shocking thing about the story was their shock. What did you think your Tinder date was going to do after you provided him with an hour-long party, gratis—propose? These poor girls didn't realize they were in an infinite open-casting call, and they'd all slept with the producer—except nobody told them there was no part, there was no movie, and he wasn't a producer.

I asked one prolific male app dater if he thought some of the women he meets who claimed to be cool with random hookups secretly wanted him to be their boyfriend. (This friend is what I'd call a "catch" for many women; successful, good looking, nice house, funny.) "Basically, all of them, and it's not so secret," he said, as he planned six new weekend dates with women twenty years his junior.

The lifestyle of the modern single woman is like being on *The Bachelor*—only the season lasts your entire life, you're competing with every other girl in the city, no one is there for the right reasons, the Fantasy Suite has another girl's bra draped over the shower door, no one puts a ring on it, and everyone goes home with genital warts.

Do you accept this rose?

An op-ed in the *New York Times* hints that some young people may be tiring of casual sex:

> The general outlook among heterosexual daters has come to take on a less playful, more depressive tone. This pessimism comes at a moment when we might expect the opposite. After all, one could say that we're living in a golden age of sexual freedom. The average age of first marriage is rising; it's more acceptable than ever to remain single or pursue a wide variety of relationship styles. [Open relationship, anyone?] Getting rid of the old rules and replacing them with the norm of consent was supposed to make us happy. Instead, *many people today feel a bit . . . lost.*[11] [Emphasis mine.]

It's always hilarious when a liberal writer rediscovers traditional values and thinks they're brand-new ideas. "Maybe we do have a duty to others, not just to our own desire," she concludes. Hmm, maybe. "We need norms more robust than 'anything between two consenting adults goes.' This might lead to less casual sex, at least in the short term. [Oh no, not that!] But, considering the clear dissatisfaction with the current landscape, that might not be so bad."

Incredible to witness someone's spiritual conversion in real time, in the pages of the *New York Times*, no less. What this writer stumbled onto was news to her, but not to us. What if I told you that if you were patient and discerning, you could uncover a third option for people stuck between Tinder and total abstinence? In the end, your best shot at lasting happiness is only going to be found in a fulfilling relationship based on mutual attraction, respect, and yes, love.

English poet Thomas Gray reminded us that "The paths of glory lead but to the grave." .

The path of horniness, coincidentally, leads there, too.

Meeting Cute in the Digital Age

You want practical advice on where to meet your mythical monogamous life partner? Unfortunately, meeting The One in real life is just as tricky today with all our technology as it was thirty years ago. Your choices are basically to meet in school, meet through friends, meet in church, or meet at a bar or club. Guess what? All of these traditional "meet" markets still exist! The most tried-and-true, of course, is the friend-group set up. If only people still had friends.

Some colleges are notorious places to get your Mrs. degree, as they say. Thomas Aquinas College in Ojai, California, is one such spot. The small size, the proximity to lots of other young, single people who share similar values, the gorgeous weather—it seems to have just the right magic formula to help graduates get engagement rings along with their diplomas. And if you fail to secure the bag on campus, you will have made enough friends to keep you supplied with potential life partners for the next few years.

Before you try to meet through friends, you must make sure you have the *right* friends. Or friends at all! What does your friend and acquaintance network look like? Is your Instagram feed a nonstop scroll of drunken debauchery and thirst traps? Maybe the reason you've never met anyone you could fall in love with through your friends is because your friends . . . are losers. If their lives are a mess, chances are they're not going to be any help to you on your search for a Trad Wife or a Chad Husband.

Clean up your network. Forge new connections with like-minded people who, like you, may have latent domestic tendencies, who aren't always trying to lure their married or committed friends to Girls Night Out or a strip club. The best way to form these connections is by attending a small religious college filled with people from large families who want large families of their own. If it's too late to do this, then the second-best way is to find them in any milieu where people like you may gather.

When I had my great religious awakening, I had exactly zero friends who shared my new belief system. Thanks to some dogged research and asking around, I soon found myself among a bunch of lovely California trad moms, who generously took me under their wing and showed me the ropes. Finding a cool mom group is not that different from finding any new network of friends. Once you locate your people, plug yourself into their world with all your heart. A religious network is obviously the quickest route to the altar, but it's certainly not the only route.

My husband and I met through mutual friends, so he came pre-vetted and from the same basic background as me. Politically we were far apart, but our interest in each other ironed out those differences fast.

And if those avenues don't work out, then go ahead and try some dating apps—but swipe carefully. Maybe the future of dating is inevitably on the apps, which are focusing on ever-narrower segments of the population. There are even apps just for young conservatives now. Of course, my ideal dating app would not be targeted at specific political demographics, since those labels no longer fit many Americans, especially the young and the fertile. Leave no young and fertile American behind, I say.

Besides, any app focused on "dating" can lead you astray. With a dating app, you can get tag teamed at NatCon or Turning Point USA just as easily as you can at the DNC or a Grammys afterparty. This is why my dream app would not be a dating app at all, since "dating" strangers is mostly a waste of time and will subject you to near occasions of sin. Instead, my app would be solely focused on finding a mate for life who wants to have children with you as quickly as possible. Paging Peter Thiel!

Try Radical Monogamy

If only someone could make monogamy into a sexual fetish, a kink practiced by super-progressive, sex-positive trendsetters, maybe it would catch on.

Plot twist: someone did!

They call it radical monogamy, and it's the new kink that's all the rage among polyamorous bisexual women. These intimacy pioneers have discovered a brand-new, revolutionary relationship choice: *only having sex with the one person you love.*

I'm pretty sure this earth-shattering discovery qualifies them for a Nobel Prize.

These women found out the hard way, so to speak, that the dreamy polyamorous lifestyle they were promised was not actually as fun as it sounded. After spending years rejecting old-fashioned monogamy as something only hidebound heterosexuals enjoy, these edgy radicals found it was the most promising path to meaningful love.

A Brooklyn-based (naturally) writer named Jericho Vincent (pronouns: they/them) confessed, "Radical monogamy works for me because I've always wanted a gigantic love. I wanted to be one person's joy and delight and I wanted them to be mine. Then I grew up and I was told that was ridiculous, unrealistic and unhealthy, so I gave up on monogamy and practiced polyamory. But now I've come around to believing that all those other people's messages were wrong."[12]

Life experience taught this individual (sorry, "them") that casual promiscuity depletes your soul with each temporary, loveless exchange of intimacy. For "gigantic love," as Mx. Vincent said, or what normies would call "true love," the only way forward is monogamy.

I told you there was hope!

Now all I have to do is get the radical monogamists to pair up with the breeding kink fetishists—maybe on my future marriage app—and my work here is done.

CHAPTER 15

Cultivate a Marriage Mindset

Become a Husbosexual

If I get married, I want to be very married.

— *Audrey Hepburn*

A Friend with Benefits—for Life

What do women want? Even the most cynical single forty-something can't deny the quiet dream she keeps locked away in her shrunken, wine-soaked heart: true love. Someone who *wants* to listen to her boring stories, who cares about that time in middle school she was bullied by the mean girls. Someone who knows what makes her happy, who is willing and able to be her ally and partner in all the things.

You're going to need more than ten cats in a trench coat to replace one good man in your life.

Let me put this in terms even a young feminist could understand: a loving husband is nothing more than the *ultimate* friend with benefits.

Imagine finding a best friend *and* a romantic partner—and it's the *same person.* Someone who wants to raise a child with you and support you both. Sound too good to be true? Ladies, it's called "marriage," and for a limited time you can lock it down at a low, low interest rate with no money down—while you both still have that new car smell. This deal won't last, folks. I'll even throw in a lifetime of devotion from a loyal partner. "Will you still love me when I'm no longer young and beautiful?" singer Lana Del Rey croons.[1] "I know you will, I know that you will," she answers. This impossible-sounding future is indeed possible—if you marry the right person.

I get it—after spending your twenties on the dating treadmill to nowhere, it can be tough to shift into marriage mindset. It was for me! As a spoiled and cynical Gen-Xer, I was not entirely prepared to find myself engaged some six months after falling in love with my then boyfriend. He was still my new boyfriend, only now I had to start calling him my fiancé. I was excited, but it all happened fast. The abstract event that would magically occur one day had actually, finally occurred. It was over. I'd done it. *He'd* done it, the madman.

I was in my late twenties, and I had a sparkly diamond ring on my finger, so I did the only thing I could do: go shopping for overpriced wedding dresses at Vera Wang. At Vera Wang, the first question the elegant salesgirl in the hushed atelier asks is what your budget is. When I told her mine, she grimaced and pointed me to a small rack of pauper gowns. "Those are from our Cinderella line—*before* her Fairy Godmother makeover."

Engagement for me was, as Aladdin sings, a whole new world. I'd entered the endgame, and I suddenly felt the full weight of all the time I'd wasted *not* making marriage a priority. Being engaged was awesome! Why hadn't I done it earlier?

The question is moot, of course. I'd met him when I'd met him, and I couldn't change a thing about that. But to this day, we both wish we could have met earlier in life. I got lucky and made it under the wire in time to have a plentiful crop of children, but . . . what if I'd said no?

What if, so used to my single ways, I hadn't been able to make a graceful transition to becoming part of a partnership?

Fortunately, the latent domestic extremist instincts I was born with finally kicked in. I threw myself joyfully into a marriage mindset and never looked back.

What is a marriage mindset? It's a mindset that allows you to commit to another person willingly and totally. If you've spent years treating relationships as temporary tattoos that can be scrubbed off with a bit of soap, it can be almost impossible for some to make the leap to permanence. It's ironic that so many men and women have no problem committing to ugly permanent tattoos—but can't seem to commit to another person.

It doesn't help that so many girls are coached their whole lives to believe marriage is oppressive, risky, holds you back, and is not required for raising children. I mean, it's true that it's not *required* for raising children—sort of like how an airplane pilot is not *required* for flying the plane. Yes, the plane will fly for a bit on autopilot, but your landing's gonna be pretty rough.

Getting married is just one more drop-down option among an infinite number of other "lifestyle choices." Another threesome, another piercing, and maybe, one day, a husband or two.

To end up in a successful relationship that can last as long as your newest tattoo, it's important to detach yourself from these marital myths. If you saunter down the aisle, hung over, telling yourself, "Well, if it doesn't work out, we can just get divorced," you are extremely likely to get divorced.

The odds of having a stable marriage go up considerably if both parties live more traditional (more *domestic*) lives before the wedding. If one or both of you squandered your youth sowing various oats, as my generation did and as many in subsequent generations have—each taking "partying" to a more extreme and degenerate level—then a healthy marriage is even less of a guarantee. It's not too late for you; there is always time to change direction, but the sooner you do that, the more likely you are to avoid lawyers. Before you ask someone to marry you, make sure the bouncers at the local dives have long since forgotten your face.

Here is the secret: a marriage mindset requires both of you to reject and disavow your old lifestyles—long *before* you say your vows. The safest path through the single 'hood is to make your singlehood *as short as possible.* The longer you are adrift in a sea of heartbreak and hookups, the less likely you are to find a safe harbor. The happiest couples I know are the ones who have the fewest ex-girlfriends and ex-boyfriends haunting their social media feeds.

How many Ghosts of Your Spouse's Relationship Past are you willing to tolerate jump-scaring you for the rest of your life? Sure, it's nice to know my husband was in demand as a young guy, but I'd rather not have those chicks request to follow me on Instagram. I don't exactly mind that they exist, but it *is* slightly awkward.

At least *my* ex-boyfriends had the good sense not to stalk me online after we broke up. The Two Genders!

Kick the Cohabitation Habit

Another way to develop a marriage mindset is to avoid cohabitating before the wedding. Yeah, I said it. Cats and dog living together, mass hysteria! But not only is living together *more* likely to make a wedding *less* likely (because why bother, you already live together), it is also more likely to lead to divorce.

Before you throw something at my head, brace yourself: on this one, the science is settled. The evidence proves marrying young before you start living together makes for the lowest divorce rates.

A study in the *Wall Street Journal* admits the following:

The research has generally backed up the belief that it's best to wait until around 30 to tie the knot. . . . Women who got married "too early" (mid-20s or earlier) were more likely to break up than their peers who married close to age 30. However, there is an interesting exception to the idea that waiting until 30 is best. In analyzing reports of marriage and divorce from more than 50,000 women . . . we found that there is a group of women for whom marriage before 30 is not risky: women who married directly, without ever cohabiting prior to marriage. In fact, women who married between 22 and 30, *without first living together, had some of the lowest rates of divorce.*[2] [Emphasis mine.]

It turns out that marrying young is safer than waiting until you've worn out your Tinder-swiping finger—as long as you don't live together first.

Living with one future spouse may be a marriage-killer, but having *lots* of live-in exes is a scientifically proven red flag:

We generally think that having more experience is better. But what we find for relationships is just the opposite. Having more experience is related to having a less happy marriage later. One reason . . . is that previous cohabitations may give husbands and wives experience with breaking up from serious co-residential relationships, making them more likely to head for the exit when the going gets tough. Having a history with other cohabiting partners may also make them compare their spouse critically to previous partners in ways that make them discount their husband or wife. Your husband David may be a responsible and reliable partner—but not as funny as Will or as good a lover as Nate, two other men you lived with prior to marriage. Keeping such critical comparisons in mind once you're married can be corrosive.[3]

Poor responsible, reliable David. Hope you found a good lawyer, pal!

Of course, women who marry a David after dumping a flaky alcoholic like Will and a cheating narcissist like Nate have learned the hard way that some qualities matter far more than others in a mate. After kissing—and cohabitating with—more than one frog in the swamp, you eventually figure out that what you really want is not a frog at all, but a much more pleasant, less slimy creature.

Acquire a Marriage Mindset—before the Wedding

Again, my equation for happiness is simple: you should maximize your number of children and minimize your number of spouses. Try to at least make the first number larger than the second!

If you have the chance to get married to someone you like, you should take it, but *choose wisely*. There are two ways to help make sure you are choosing wisely for your first marriage. First, if you can, choose *early*. It's always safer to acquire a life partner *before* ten (or even twenty) years of getting driven hard as a Budget rental has taken its inevitable toll under the hood and on the paint job.

Second, no matter what age you are, you must have The Conversation. The deeply religious will not need to have The Conversation, but everyone else should. This is a short discussion in which you both agree in advance, long before the wedding ceremony, that *divorce is not an option* unless things go catastrophically sideways. You both mutually agree to burn your boats when you reach Wedded Island. If you go into it thinking of divorce as a lifeboat, you are more likely to end up in that lifeboat.

Part of accepting the idea of a long marriage 'til death do you part is understanding what "'til death" means. It means confronting your own mortality to clinch the real prize: one of you must bear the burden of watching the other die. Hopefully after many happy years of bliss and companionship, and not after one of you stabs the other with one of the Wusthofs from your wedding registry.

Divorce doesn't really erase a bad marriage, either. After being divorced for longer than they'd been married, Lucille Ball called her ex-husband on his deathbed to say goodbye. "I put the phone up to Dad's ear in the bed," Lucie recalled of her mother's phone call. "I said, 'It's the redhead.' He just listened, and I heard what she said. She just said the same thing over and over again. . . . It was 'I love you. I love you. Desi, I love you.' You could even hear the intonations of the voice change, how she meant each one."[4]

It can be tricky to make such an enormous leap of faith like this, to see marriage as a forever proposition, especially when you're young. It was hard for me, and I was no spring chicken—I was more like a midsummer hen. Stuck with one solitary person for the rest of your entire life until you *die*? In a disposable world of ephemera, contemplating the long ribbon of time stretching out before you is daunting. *I mean, what if my husband eventually, you know, gets old? Loses his hair?*

I draw the line at losing the hair—luckily my husband is doing a pretty good job maintaining a healthy head of it. I keep a divorce lawyer on speed dial just in case I notice any more stray hairs on his pillow in the morning.

I'm kidding . . . mostly.

When you get married, yes, you must willingly give up some personal freedoms, like the freedom to blow your entire paycheck—or your boss—in Vegas. It's true: marriage is a trade off, but it's *almost always* a better deal. Take it if you can!

Identify as a Husbosexual

These days there are so many sexual orientations to choose from, there's truly one for each of us. When you pick a new sexual orientation, you get your own colorful flag and learn new lingo. It's like joining a club for cool kids, only everyone at the club is a pasty incel with dead eyes. Countless numbers of new orientations appeared suddenly in the last few years, like a cloud of locusts descending from the sky to devour everything in sight.

But honestly, some of the terms the cool kids have invented for their new sexual orientations sound like they're just repackaging traditional human relationships to make them seem edgy.

Maybe the new made-up words are how a basically "normal" straight person gets to claim a piece of the rainbow pie. Inventing a cool new word for your hopelessly lame heterosexuality lets you avoid an unforgivable taboo—being lame *and* heterosexual.

Let me give you an example. Some people (maybe four total nation-wide) claim they are something called "demisexual." Demisexual means you "feel romantic attraction to someone only after you've emotionally bonded."[5] Ooh, edgy! Liking someone you've bonded with, what will your priest say, you weirdo?

Then there's one called "allosexual," which refers to "people who do not identify as asexual—that is, people who regularly experience sexual attraction."[6] Imagine that!

I did some math and figured out that if you develop sexual attraction to someone you like, you get to be a demisexual allosexual! You can fly *two* of the special-people flags—even though you're just a straight normie with a crush on your own boyfriend. Hashtag winning! Congratulations to any king who gets into Harvard with an essay about the challenge and oppression he faced growing up as a demisexual allosexual in an oppressive society.

If you're having trouble getting a job as a heterosexual, feel free to add your fancy new identity-rebranding to your résumé. Maybe in the Miscellaneous section, or under Hobbies. "Kickboxing, microbreweries, exploring my demisexuality." The HR lady will be too scared to ask you what that word means, so she'll just check the LGBTQIA+++ box and hand you an employee parking pass. Welcome aboard, Chad!

I found out that anyone is allowed to invent a word to describe his or her sexual orientation. For example, I identify as a husbosexual. A husbosexual is only attracted to people who identify as my husband. If you're a married man, try putting "wifosexual" in your LinkedIn bio next time you're gunning for a promotion at work.

Luckily for my husband, there's just one person alive who fits the description (so far).

Becoming a husbosexual—or a wifosexual—also seems like a smart way to approach marriage. Might you meet good-looking and charming people during your marriage? You absolutely will. May all your friends be good-looking and charming! So how does a married person prevent a third party from interfering in your relationship with your spouse? What if you hit a rough patch and someone is flirty at work with you, or with your spouse?

I would sooner inject myself with bleach than contemplate a third party, but I recognize that for some, it may be an enticing fantasy. Let me offer you this short cautionary tale. Some years ago, I encountered an infamous essay in *Marie Claire* that "everyone" was talking about. American journalist Pamela Druckerman, a Paris-based columnist for the *New York Times*, had just published her 2012 bestseller on parenting called *Bringing Up Bébé*.

As soon as her book came out, an essay she had written even earlier was unearthed. It was about the time this bestselling parenting expert *arranged a threesome* with another woman for her

British husband's fortieth birthday.[7] The essay quickly disappeared from the *Marie Claire* website since it scandalized the mothers who were supposed to buy her book about how to bring up young children. Whoops!

Unfortunately, Druckerman's swinger essay was immediately reprinted everywhere. It went viral. When I read it, I found her matter-of-fact, jokey description of the threesome uniquely horrifying and vicariously humiliating. She locates a nice-looking single mother and sets up a rendezvous. She describes her surprise that the interaction between her husband and the other woman is "so, well, sexual."[8] She spends the time mostly watching her husband with their guest. Afterwards, she confesses that she is "left feeling unsettled. I can't wait to shower. Sadly, I'm more conventional than I'd thought. In theory, I didn't mind sharing my husband for an afternoon. In practice, I was shaken up. I wasn't bored; I was bothered."[9]

If you read the whole essay, you will need Dramamine to avoid throwing up. Poor Pamela hadn't realized it would *bother* her to watch her husband cheat on her, live and in person? It's like reading something written by an alien—or an American ex-pat living in Paris.

Maybe it's me; maybe I still have residual trauma from watching the key party scene in *The Ice Storm*. Maybe I reacted so viscerally to her swinger horror story because marital infidelity wrecked my childhood. I don't really understand what "open marriages" are, and I'd rather not, frankly. Why would you bother marrying another person only to immediately resume dating other people? If you're that bored with your life, you need to get some new hobbies.

Preferably hobbies that don't involve forcing your middle-aged carcass onto other middle-aged sad sacks.

Maybe if these people stopped thinking about their next illicit date, they could finally finish their novel or clean out their garage or do something better with all the energy they're wasting on planning sordid meetups. I doubt it, though.

Uninvited (or invited) marital guests are an invasive species you must defend against—or you risk losing your dignity, your mind, and your family. Decide in advance that you will do likewise, and your marriage will be much better off.

Being a devout Catholic doesn't hurt, either.

Therefore, I urge you to identify as husbosexuals and wifosexuals as soon as you are blissfully wed. Cut out the middlemen and never look back.

Once you are a fully formed domestic extremist, you will be impervious to the slings and arrows of unwelcome suitors.

And remember: cheating, like heroin, involves sticking something dangerous into your body—or sticking yourself into someone dangerous. Use extreme caution!

Endgame

Once the hot fires of youth and beauty are tempered with age, wisdom, and wrinkles, you are going to be left with a much older version of the man or woman you married. You get to exchange the most alluring, best-looking version of the person you married for a fatter, balder, more decrepit version. Yikes!

But you will gain by having a companion, maybe the only one you've got left, who remembers *you* when you were at your most sparkling and alive. They may not be much to look at anymore, but those old eyes are the only ones who might still see you in your prime. That is a priceless core memory only a longtime spouse can preserve for you. It also makes watching your own beauty fade easier to cope with. Imagine being eighty years old and still knowing the man who fell in love with you decades earlier!

My great-aunt once told me she missed her husband of seventy-something years "whenever he leaves the room." It's not a secret that life with a spouse and little kids can sometimes feel like you're trapped in a foxhole under heavy shelling. Like the time on Christmas Day when everyone in the house got Norovirus at the same time—that was a real "fire in the hole" moment. In sickness and in health, you want the person in the foxhole with you to be someone you really like, even as you shiver, curled up in the fetal position on the bathroom floor.

It can be hard when you're a newlywed to think about a spouse like that. After all, he's just some guy or girl you met at margarita night a few years ago! But if everything goes well, and you get lucky, he or she will be the one holding your hand on your deathbed.

Their forehead is the one you'll cool down with a wet washcloth when they're sick.

They are the one who will be present at your children's births, and all their other milestones.

They are the first person you will call when bad—or good—things happen. "He's my sun, he makes me shine like diamonds," Lana Del Rey sings, which I read as a plaintive ode to the romantic desire to be with your true love until death do you part—and beyond.

Not everyone will get to experience this type of relationship, but more of us should try.

CHAPTER 16

Have More Than Two Kids

The Case for Family-Maxxing

When the whole world is running towards a cliff, he who is running in the opposite direction appears to have lost his mind.

— C. S. Lewis

From Here to Maternity

Maybe it's too late. Maybe humanity is already in an irreversible population dive, and the computer cockpit is shrieking, "TERRAIN TERRAIN PULL UP PULL UP."

There is great strength in our numbers—but we need those numbers to increase, fast. I'd rather not see my grandchildren living in a *Children of Men* dystopia where there are no suitable mates their age and they are forced to marry AI-powered SpouseBots or digital nonbinary NPCs in a virtual reality hellscape. "Hey Alexa, our anniversary is coming up." "You're right, Jack. Would you like to hear about some new Amazon products you might like as my gift to you?"

The consistent message in the media is that you're much better off getting a pet than having a baby. A new kid? Great, one more mouth to starve in the coming food shortages.

In 2017, the supervillains at the World Economic Forum famously tweeted (and then deleted) this headline as part of their Great Reset publicity campaign: "Welcome to 2030. I own nothing, have no privacy, and life has never been better."[1] They even released a since-removed video called "8 Predictions for the World in 2030," which included a smiling young man and the caption "You'll Own Nothing and You'll Be Happy."[2]

The reaction was so bad to this that they quietly scrubbed all of it from the internet. Today, they claim it's a "far-right conspiracy theory." But the obvious result of owning nothing is having no children. It's tough to raise a family in the suburbs without possessions or property—which is the point. The chilling subtext is: you'll give birth to nothing, and *they'll* be happy. You'll be Doing Your Part for the Cause, and no one will remember your name.

Of course, as global economic conditions worsen and doomsday experts predict looming economic disaster—including a new Great Depression—it can seem foolish, risky even, to aim for more than one or two children. Could there be an ulterior motive to all their fearmongering? Why, it's almost as if they want to terrify humanity away from having children.

They forget that even in times of despair, a new child brings good tidings of great joy—or at least, it should—for everyone around it. The truth is, we need to massively increase our production of new domestic extremists—in other words, anyone who chooses not to partake in the sterilizing Regime-approved lifestyle. The more of us there are, the harder it will be for them to stuff us into gulags or subjugate us as serfs in the Great Global Reset. The only reason childlessness can be sold as a goal to so many is because the anti-natalists outnumber us at the highest echelons. We must, therefore, overwhelm them with our numbers.

After all, they can't round us all up. Right?

. . . Right?

I, too, want a Great Reset. I, too, want to Build Back Better. Only I'd prefer to do it using bouncing babies instead of bloodless bureaucrats. But before we can start cranking out the new humans we need, we're going to have to address the worst trend since the Tide Pod Challenge: delaying motherhood.

Wait at Your Own Risk

I understand delaying motherhood until you're married or have your life semi-together. The stars don't always align exactly when your ovaries need them to. I get it. But the problem is not the delay itself; it's the *length* of the delay. I also "delayed motherhood" until I was married and then, because of a miscarriage, I didn't have my first baby until I was in my early thirties. (Of course, I made up for this "delay" by having children into my early forties.) I was extremely lucky I didn't suffer from fertility issues. I also had the benefit of marrying someone with powerful Mediterranean blood.

You may not be so lucky. You never know what will happen once you decide to "start trying," which is the wholesome euphemism couples use to describe, the, uh, baby-creating process.

That's why I encourage young, healthy couples to exercise their fertility early and often. It's a societal imperative. You want to save the planet? Forget driving a Chevy Volt; produce a new person! You care about the ice caps melting? There won't be anyone left to care once we're all gone, dear. Meanwhile, the cultural pressure to delay adulthood means that the average age at which an American woman has her first baby has risen to twenty-eight. Warning: if you tell your obstetrician you are thirty-five or over, he or she will write "advanced maternal age" or the even more accurate clinical term, "elderly primipara," in your file and hand you a pamphlet explaining all the IVF options available for old crones like you.

What I didn't know was that babies are, like, great. I had no idea how awesome they are! I had some hazy memories of younger siblings coming home from the hospital and helping take care of them, but after that, there were exactly zero babies in my life. I didn't hold a single baby for at least twenty years before I had my own! Maternity was a totally alien culture to me. Like RVing or quilting, parenthood was a hobby *other* people enjoyed. One day maybe I'd give it a whirl, but I was in no rush.

I was fortunate to have a husband who *was* in a rush. He Persisted. Four months after that first awful miscarriage, we found ourselves expecting again. In a bit of infamous family lore, I was long overdue with this first baby and refused to get in the car to go to the hospital for my induction. I was well over forty-one weeks, but still not quite ready. Apparently, you can't delay parenthood any longer at that point.

My husband and my mother cajoled me into the car. I realized with a shock there was no getting out of it—the only way out was through. Through *me*. Would it hurt? What would an IV full of Pitocin do? What if I had to get cut open? "Having a baby" had been an abstract notion, a far-off dream. But there I was, climbing into the space capsule, about to be launched on a one-way trip to an unknown planet populated by one tiny bald fellow who pooped his pants and screamed.

I was so clueless I brought a giant yoga ball to the hospital with me, complete with a fancy felt cover. The pregnancy books told me to take it, and they're never wrong! "But honey, the book said if you sit on it, it thins the cervix." Also, what was a cervix? I'd forgotten to ask.

It took two days for the OB to trigger any signs of labor. I begged them to let me go home, to no avail. I had plenty of time lying in that bed watching the baby's heartbeat monitor to ponder the end of my nulliparity. On my final childless night, the baby's oxygen dropped, and I had to sleep with a mask strapped to my face. At that moment, I would have sacrificed anything for the baby's health. I was ready to do what was necessary. The only way out was through, and I was finally ready.

I wasn't religious at the time, but I prayed to God to let my baby be born alive and healthy. I had never wanted anything more. The eventual arrival of the mythical, magical creature occurred with no further complications, and was nothing short of earth-shattering. If you've been there, you know.

(That mythical creature, the Firstborn, drove me and some of his siblings to Sunday Mass the other day, so it all worked out fine.)

Podcaster Alex Kaschuta has written eloquently about how her first baby transformed her, in ways every new mother can relate to:

> My relationship with my husband is transformed by the fact that we're now also co-conspirators in the creation of "most precious, most important being" and even though we were "family" before this—actually, this is family. Moving from a life where "who am I?" has been the center of my preoccupations for decades, with all the incessant burdens of becoming this or that, to one where he's so clearly more important was an immense spiritual transformation.[3]

Yes. You become who you were meant to be—when you become a parent. It's the truest, most human experience there is.

Once you have a kid, their happiness is instantly more important than yours. One of the gifts you will want to give them is a sibling. More than one, ideally. Siblings mean they will never be totally alone. They may *wish* they were alone sometimes, especially when you have teens sharing rooms with younger kids, but in my case, my siblings eventually became my closest friends. Without them, I don't know if I would have made it through the minefield of our childhood.

Develop a Baby-Maxxing Mindset

To paraphrase Conan the Barbarian, what is best in life? May I suggest this: to outnumber your enemies, to watch their genetic lines go extinct before you, and to hear the lamentations of their unborn descendants, who never even got a shot.

When I lived among libs with small families and small minds, I was exposed as a dangerous extremist early on. I was visibly pregnant with my third baby when a neighbor spotted me and my belly. "Are you pregnant—again?" the Mercedes-driving mother of two sneered.

"Yep."

"Is this your third?"

"Yep."

"What are you, Mormon?!" She practically hissed the words. I hadn't even converted to Catholicism yet, and already a third pregnancy flagged me as a dangerous religious fundamentalist. Ah, the tolerance, the acceptance. I still remember when having three children was the norm; now it's a shocking taboo.

If having three children makes you a radical in America, then having more than three is like getting a face tattoo—you're outed as an extremist in public instantly.

We once attended a friend's birthday bash at a lovely home near the beach. At the time, we were up to four children. The couple hosting had two kids. So did every other couple at the party. Two kids, two kids, two kids, two kids, two kids. "And now we're done." "Done." "Totally done." "*So* done." "Stick a fork in me." When party guests asked me how many *I* had, I almost had to defibrillate them when I told them.

These aging hype dads—so cool, so iconoclastic, so *unique*—all wore identical fedoras, sported identical goatees, and had created identical families. It turns out that certain brands of iconoclasm—like mine—are very uncool. Does having four children make you racist? Because once the party guests realized some real freaks (us) had shown up, people started looking at me like I was wearing a Klan hood.

I enjoyed the experience. It is great fun horrifying people who think of themselves as open-minded and tolerant! I decided I enjoyed out-radicaling those who style themselves as radicals but are actually strict conformists. Instead of feeling ashamed and embarrassed at my reproductive output (at least compared to theirs), I started *not caring what anyone thought.*

This was an important step in my domestic transformation. You, too, must learn not to care. You must learn to love their scorn. Lean into it. Feel their hatred flow through you!

Nowadays, of course, I love getting asked how many kids I have. I like to see the whites of their eyes when I tell them casually like it's no big deal. Sometimes I even add, "Only wish I'd had a few more."

I didn't start out like this. I didn't always want a big family. I didn't plan on a specific number. Fortunately, nature is designed to seek its own opportunities.

There I was, six months into my first motherhood, still nursing my firstborn on demand around the clock, both shoulders draped in spit-up-encrusted burp cloths, when my husband came home from work. He looked at me from a safe distance and said, "You seem grumpy. Are you pregnant?"

Grumpy? Was he kidding? I hadn't slept more than an hour straight in months. Besides, how could I be pregnant? My pregnancy books said that breastfeeding was foolproof birth control! How could I be pregnant? I had no memory of doing anything that could cause a pregnancy, if you know what I mean. Had I sat in something at the park? Was it an immaculate conception?

Plus, I had birth control pills! I mean, I hadn't *taken* any of them. But they were still in my purse—my OB had handed them to me at my postpartum checkup and ordered me to "wait two years" until I got pregnant again.

I'd shrugged, dropped the pills into my bag, and forgotten about them.

I was so excited to prove my husband wrong that I ran upstairs, dug through a drawer in the bathroom, and located a leftover pregnancy test. They weren't even expired, because I'd literally just had a friggin' baby!

Turns out that the pregnancy books are fake news. It was his turn to laugh when he saw the positive results. Six months of sleeplessness makes your wife a cheap date, fellas.

Smash cut to: We are home from the hospital with our second newborn. There is a fifteen-month-old in a crib in the next room. We have two babies in diapers. We have fled our impractical condo and moved into a slightly larger house with a yard, *seven days* before the new baby arrived. We didn't even have the beds set up. We'd built the crib for the toddler and thrown a mattress down for ourselves.

I woke up in the middle of the night in a Vicodin-induced stupor, looked down at the new baby, and asked my husband, "Which one is this?"

Once you have two kids close together in age and you experience the practical convenience of having "twins" that are slightly different sizes but have the same basic needs, the idea of having a third doesn't seem so insane. Adding one more kid is practical! How else are you going to amortize all the useless baby gear? You're going to have a whole baby shower and only use the big, expensive stuff once or twice? We already had car seats. We'd already built the cribs. I no longer screamed in pain when I nursed.

Why go to all the trouble of learning how to get a hungry, tongue-tied baby to nurse properly if you are going to stop after just two lousy infants? That's like spending a year training to climb Mount Everest and calling it quits at Basecamp 2. You gotta at least make it to the Khumbu icefall!

I did allow myself the luxury of spacing baby number three out a bit. In my case, the third child arrived twenty months after the second. For a few white-knuckled months, we had three under the age of three. All in different-sized diapers.

But once you have done that, you are immortal. You are omnipotent. You are the Lord of the Crib. The God-Emperor of the Diaper Genie. You have *become* the Diaper Genie. If the baby rubs your tummy three times, you grant your baby a wish. (And the wish is: a sister, please.)

You do stick out at the playground with a two-year-old, a one-year-old, and a newborn. Other moms would stare at me. They'd sweat their only child. "I can barely handle one! How do you do it?" I'd nod my head and pretend to commiserate. "Yeah, one is really hard. Gets much easier when you have a few more."

And in many ways, it does. They play with each other, yes. But when you don't have the time to focus obsessively on one child's every move and utterance, you realize *you don't have to.* You can relax, let them be, even let them play in the other room!

Once you crack the seal of "just two kids" and break the sound-mind barrier, the vastness of time and space and possibility opens up. Wait . . . you mean I can have three, four, or however many I want? I can just, like, *keep going?*

For now, at least. I'm sure our government overlords will outlaw having three children soon. Do it while it's still legal!

Bottom line: three children is my *minimum* recommended number of children, if you can swing it. *"But, but,"* my hate readers will sputter, "some people can't *have* children, some people have chronic diseases, some people get divorced, some spouses die, some people never find anyone who wants kids, some people get hit by a bus! What about them, huh? Not everyone can just have whatever number *you* think they should!"

Exactly. Not everyone makes it to the summit.

Which is why more of you need to try.

The Case for More Kids

I have childless friends. Sometimes I wonder what their weekends must be like. No frantic racing around town to multiple activities or hellacious toddler birthday parties. They get to enjoy the life-changing magic of tidying up the house, and somehow it stays tidy. Marie Kondo only works if children don't exist or you keep them in cages.

You will have plenty of time for tidiness in your dotage. Once the ship sails, it sails. You can't go back in time and be a parent. It's a lifestyle choice you can only make for a relatively short time. If there is time to squeeze in an extra child, if you are even considering it for a second, go for it. Older couples lament to me that they wish they'd had one more. Allow your children to come, and I promise you won't regret it.

If there is any doubt, there is no doubt, as Robert De Niro says in *Ronin.* Don't leave money—or progeny—on the table.

But to be clear, I do not ever suggest parenthood to people who are not suited for it. Deranged progressives, for example, seem to have chosen childlessness, and who am I to argue? When you see these people in public, you would agree with me that, yes, they should absolutely *not* reproduce themselves. I must reluctantly agree with the life choice they've made. Anyway, they've made their twin bed; now they must lie in it. They've chosen self-sterilization. We should calmly accept the terms of their genetic surrender and not high-five each other until they are out of sight.

If the child-haters wish to go extinct, I say we let them. Never interrupt your enemy when she is making a mistake!

While it is true that not everyone has what it takes to be a parent of three or more, a large cohort of childbearing Americans has been tricked into thinking they are not suited for parenthood at all. They have been lied to by people they trust. Get this: they think children harm the environment.

Millennials now report they're terrified to have children because of climate change. "Polls suggest that a third or more of Americans younger than 45 either don't have children or expect to have fewer than they might otherwise because they are worried about climate change."[4] Thirty years of public school and media propaganda are working exactly as intended on their brains. They never seem to mind that Nancy Pelosi emits more carbon in a single month of roundtrip private jet flights from D.C. to San Francisco than a baby could produce in five years.

One kid is probably okay. Two may turn their lives upside down. But a third? End up outnumbered, broke, and overwhelmed? Three kids might even trigger hurricanes, tsunamis, volcanos, and worldwide drought!

I know—when you factor in the cost of childcare and college and health insurance, even the smallest "big" family can seem like an unimaginable luxury. Three kids will really cut into your gaming time, your Instagram time, and yes, your free time.

And yet . . . one of the only things you may regret on your deathbed is the child you refused to let in the door. You were the scowling club bouncer, and they were not on the list.

Size Matters

Family size, that is. Our kids get to have something I never did: a big, close family. There is a wonderful Yiddish word for this: *mishpocha* (pronounced "mish-pukka.") It means "the entire family network of relatives by blood or marriage." Not just your own kids and their cousins, but also the aunts and uncles and their parents and in-laws and cousins' cousins, and so on. Not only do my children have brothers and sisters, but because I married into a big family, they get to enjoy a cornucopia of cousins, too.

My favorite reason to have more than two children is to have them *for each other.* "You guys hate each other now, but I promise—in ten years, you'll be each other's BFF."

Plus, don't you want to establish your own mini-dynasty? Wouldn't you like to die knowing hundreds, maybe even thousands, of other human beings owe their existence to you? That is real power. It accrues over the course of multiple fruitful generations until, one day, someone counts up all the great-great-grandchildren and builds a shrine to the long-dead couple who made it happen.

Big families are the greatest and only real protection you have against the tightening cultural onslaught. They are the best hedge against disaster. If you didn't grow up in one and didn't marry into one, that's okay—you can start your own!

When people tell me they wish they'd had one more baby, I want to say, well? Why didn't you? You had your chance, and you blew it.

Newsflash: Life is hard *with or without children.* But most people (there are some sociopaths out there) agree it's infinitely better *with* them. Children do not guarantee happiness, of course—that's not their job. The baby is not there to make you happy! It is *your* job to make *it* happy.

The only reason humanity perseveres is because children keep showing up. They have bad timing, good timing, and comical timing.

They rudely arrive during wars and plagues, aboard sinking ships and on wagon trains in winter, and in caves surrounded by baying wolves.

The best things in life are these small people who look like you—and some of the only things you can look back on in your final days with pride and deep joy.

Fortunately, for the vast majority of us, children *do* bring immense joy! Not every single second of every day, but even on the blackest days when you feel like you're drowning, you are buoyed by a bottomless ocean of eternal love.

But that's not even the best reason you should spawn. One does not simply have a child for one's personal gratification. Only reality TV stars and pedophiles do that! Kids are not lifestyle props or fashion accessories or therapists or antidepressants in diapers. No—they are the promise of human continuity. One is not going to be enough. Two will barely cover it. You're going to need an ace in the hole, and that's the third kid and beyond.

But don't you worry your pretty little head about all that just yet, darlin'! Go on and light a few candles, slip into something more comfortable, and invite your very special friend to join you for a very special benefit. You can start tonight!

(Put this book down first, so you don't muss the pages.)

Writer Tom Scocca wrote a beautiful essay about forgetting to have kids when you're young. In "Your Real Biological Clock Is You're Going to Die," he writes, "If you intend to have children, but you don't intend to have them just yet, you are not banking extra years as a person who is still too young to have children. You are subtracting years from the time you will share the world with your children."[5]

To anyone waiting for the perfect time: you will die waiting for the perfect time. You might as well do it while you have the most energy. While your body can still spring back from pregnancy. The baby won't notice how old the car is or how many square feet it lives in.

Here's a secret: newborns don't cost that much, especially if you resist the urge to splash out on unnecessary baby gear (and it's all mostly unnecessary). They're even cheaper when you choose to breastfeed. (Now you know why Big Formula doesn't want you to breastfeed.)

Yes, older kids cost more, but if you don't screw it up too badly, they'll be taking care of you when you most need it. Tiny babies are small financial investments with absolutely massive payoffs.

Meanwhile, your future awaits. Your descendants and your future *mishpocha* lie just beyond your reach, trapped in hazy mists of possibility. Until they invent synthetic wombs (and let's hope they don't), you're still their only portal to the world of the living.

Unlock the door and let them in—before you're too old to remember where you put the key.

CHAPTER 17

Lean In—to Parenthood

Surrender, Dorothy

But still I hadn't dreamt nothing about me and Ed until the end. And this was cloudier, 'cause it was years, years away. But I saw an old couple being visited by their children, and all their grandchildren, too. The old couple weren't screwed up. And neither were their kids or their grandkids. And I don't know, you tell me. This whole dream, was it wishful thinking? Was I just fleeing reality like I know I'm liable to do? But me and Ed, we can be good, too. And it seemed real. It seemed like us and it seemed like, well, our home. If not Arizona, then a land not too far away. Where all parents are strong and wise and capable and all children are happy and beloved. I don't know. Maybe it was Utah.

— Raising Arizona

Just Do It

The Coen Brothers aren't known for their wholesome sweetness, but that final scene in *Raising Arizona* gets me every time. In it, the bitterly childless couple played by Nicolas Cage and Holly Hunter dream that they are old. Their front door swings open, and a huge crowd of mythical children and grandchildren pour into their living room and embrace them. It's the happy ending they didn't get in life.

Many people urgently desire a family. Then why do so many, once they get one, act like their family is just an annoying burden? As soon as they have children, their parental mission is to create as much child-free time for themselves as possible. Summer vacation looms like an adult prison sentence. Each school holiday requires a scramble for camps and all-day childcare. Homeschooling? Are you on crack?

Here is a secret: the easiest way to deal with the change, sacrifice, and hardship that has always come with raising children is to thank your pre-parenthood life for getting you this far, say goodbye to it, and let it drift back into the past. You must burn all your ships, as Cortés did after landing in Mexico in 1519 on his way to conquer the Aztecs. How else to motivate his exhausted men to continue their dangerous mission?

There can be no going back. Better to dive in headfirst. *Lean in* to parenthood, in all its glories and defeats. You must surrender! You must submit!

The good news is that your family is going to be the source of your real happiness—not another girls' night out. "In 14 of the 17 nations surveyed, more people mentioned their family as a source of meaning than anything else. Respondents highlighted their relationships with parents, siblings, children, and grandchildren; quality time spent with their relatives; and the pride they get from family members' accomplishments."[1]

Let your new baby be the excuse you needed to pull the rip cord on the lifestyle you forgot to give up when you got married.

Housewives in Control

A woman's natural, inborn maternal instinct is now treated as a virulent disease. It's a syndrome to be eradicated, an outdated, socially constructed lie women must fight against. To surrender to it means you have failed to live up to the expectations laid out for you by feminist doctrine. Don't make us de-person you!

Women with more than a couple of kids are routinely disparaged as "breeders" by young feminists, like they're braying farm animals. Everywhere you look, the deep human longing for family is mocked, since it is a betrayal of the "promise" of feminism. "You don't need a family," they lie. "A husband and a bunch of kids will crush your spirit. We fought too hard for you to be barefoot and pregnant now! You don't need them—you just need us, your sisterhood of traveling wine aunts."

If you do rebel against Planned Parenthood's panning of parenthood and create your own family, you are still required to signal that it is, in fact, crushing your spirit. "Yes, I had kids, and yes, you were right—it sucks." You must constantly virtue-signal your way out of the taboo of parental devotion. God forbid you enjoy it, or worse, are secretly glad you got to quit your job so you could spend all day cuddling your newborn. Don't tell the junior girlbosses at work! (*"Conceal, don't feel, don't let them know. . . ."*[2]) "Yeah, the baby's cute, but I can't wait to get back to work—are there any good emails I missed? Funny Slack chats? I can't wait to catch up!"

To compensate for your betrayal to the sisterhood, you will have to learn to complain publicly about your kids and spouse. You will fill your Instagram and TikTok pages with posts about how your messy brats and slob husband are making you miserable. You will confide over drinks that you envy your single friends' clean, husband-free one-bedroom apartments. "It's really hard," you tell them. "I mean, I can't imagine my life without them, but. . . ."

That phrase. "I love them, but...." But ... what? Are you looking to hire a hitman? Are you trying to make your child-free friends feel better? Or do you truly regret your decision to become a parent?

I have met many mothers of one or two children who really are totally overwhelmed, exhausted, frazzled. Their life has two gears: stuck at home with the kids and miserable, or free of kids and happy. They confuse "postpartum" with "post-party." They live every moment with one foot still in child-free land, one hand still clutching a cocktail. If your parenting mindset is stuck in a loop where all you do is compare it to the relative ease of your former life, then yes, you are doomed. "Remember when I could just leave the house alone?" "Remember when I didn't have to wipe someone's butt ten times a day?" "Remember when we could just sleep in?"

That is the path to insanity. Let me break some more bad news to you: avoiding children does not guarantee you a life of leisure. Far from it!

I remember my single, pre-family days well. My kid-free lifestyle gave me complete and total freedom! I could do whatever I wanted! My time was my own. My complete and total freedom included forty or fifty hours in an office wishing I were somewhere else. On a typical weekend, I'd spend Saturday morning enjoying the pure freedom of a nasty hangover from karaoke the night before. I'd spend Sunday dreading commuting to work the next day. Ah ... freedom!

If the only metrics you use to measure the quality of your life are sleep, tidiness, and free time, then your life will be objectively worse after having a few kids. Why would *anyone* do such an unpleasant thing to themselves?

Because this is the prevailing mentality, many don't.

And yet, some parents don't live in this state of constant mental distress. Most of the women I know with four or more children are calmer than the ones who have one or two. Mothers of seven or more (yes, I know some of these rare creatures) achieve a sort of Zen-like serenity. They have made it to light speed and gone to plaid. They have reached Total Enlightenment and get to sit back and watch as armies of children complete their to-do lists for them.

Why are they so calm? Because: they have shifted their pre-baby mindset to a post-baby mindset. Each day is not a grim reminder of the peace they left behind or the "freedoms" they gave up. Instead, they focus on the nature of the sacrifice. They see motherhood as a natural, time-honored calling that brings out their inner heroic female. Every day is another step forward in shaping a new human being who repays you with a million joys, a million delightful giggles, and profound love. From the outside, an infinity of mundane moments—wiping a tear, cutting up grapes, pushing a swing—looks like nothing. But each throwaway gesture is another stone in the monument to you that slowly rises unseen deep in your child's heart.

"Women, by creating new life, bear witness to the possibility that body and soul can in fact be reconciled: in childbirth, human flesh becomes the medium of the divine," Spencer Klavan poignantly writes.[3]

Parenthood, in the end, is a largely selfless act. It is a vocation best suited for those able to set aside their own immediate and grubby gratification for the long, slow process of unfurling a new human being for the world.

Then again, nearly everyone can do a decent job of it. No special skills are required. You don't need to know big words or do any math. But it's a lot easier if you surrender to it, just a little.

Good-Enough Parenting

My amazing mother-in-law, who has more children and more energy than I do, says that every time one of her friends would ask her how she handled life with so many small children, she would reply, "You just do it." That was her entire parenting survival philosophy.

"You just do it." Why sit around missing the past? You're too busy to worry about that, so get on with it. Just do it!

The struggle is real, but it brings real rewards. These kinds of mothers know there is no going back. They have *willingly* torched their own ships. They don't look at their lives before kids and wish they'd made a different choice. To them, there is no "but" after "I can't imagine my life without them."

On my worst days as a parent, after losing my temper and yelling at someone younger than me, I suffer feelings of guilt and remorse. I'll call my perfect sister for moral support. She'll usually say something comforting like, "Really? Wow, I've never had to yell at my kids." Or my favorite: "What's all that noise in the background?" "They're fighting." "Yikes! My boys never fight."

Thanks, Sis! (Although recently she told me her boys *have* started fighting, and I had to try to hide my relief. "Oh no! That's too bad.") I try to remember a few things to comfort myself during the bad days at the Peachy Corral. Compared to most children who have ever lived, my children are in the top echelon of loved and cared-for kids. They've never known hunger, thirst, or parental neglect. God willing, they're going to make it to adulthood without experiencing anything that causes severe trauma, like a drag queen show or a Harry Styles concert (but I repeat myself).

Of course, they are not being raised with anything close to the level of material privilege my siblings and I enjoyed (at least, until my parents' marriage imploded), but they're vastly richer in family, friends, and faith. They get to enjoy one special privilege I didn't: life in a stable home with married parents who love each other.

What I'm trying to say is, I may know a lot about taking care of babies, but I can't claim to know much about "parenting." I have recently begun on-the-job training for parenting teenagers. So far, it's a lot like parenting toddlers. They're moody, messy, stubborn, and sometimes they smell bad.

I don't read any parenting books. I hate parenting books! By page three, I start to panic that I ruined someone's childhood ten years ago because instead of spending the recommended fifteen minutes calmly negotiating a tussle over a dinosaur toy, I hid the toy and promptly forgot where.

(I once tossed my daughter's Nintendo Switch into the kitchen garbage can as a bluff because she would not stop playing on it. I forgot all about it, and it got thrown away that evening. She is learning this now for the first time. Sorry, honey!).

I just hope I figure parenting out in time to give my future daughters-in-law my expert unwanted advice. But—here are a few of the big lessons I've learned, and none of them involve memorizing a 75-point conflict mediation script.

Embrace the Sacrifice

What is parenting if not the ultimate form of sacrificial love? There is no greater sacrifice and no quicker way to enter the gates of heaven than offering your time, your youth, and your best efforts to create, form, and launch wonderful new people into the world.

Express Unconditional Love

I'm not the best at plenty of things, but we really tried to get a few big things right for our children. Like not making our love conditional. If somebody failed Algebra or didn't make the varsity scuba diving team, well, that's a shame, but it has no effect on how I feel about you, kid. To some parents, certain disappointments may not mean you love them less, but the child might perceive that you do.

I'm sure you've heard some dads talk about how the son they schlepped to Little League for ten years failed to get on a college team and then quit playing. It does sound like maybe you'd love that kid just a little bit more if he was wearing Yankee pinstripes by the time he turned twenty-three.

Luckily for me, thanks to those powerful Mediterranean genes, I have no future professional athletes to worry about!

Instead, I have faith that if they remember we love them unconditionally, no strings attached, my many shortcomings as a parent will be forgotten (please, Lord) over the span of their lives.

What I mean by unconditional love is: It is immutable. It can never be diminished. They'll sometimes test this idea. "What if I killed someone, Mom? Would you still love me the same?" I reassure them I would, but I would be extremely disappointed.

Never Leave Your Wingman

A good rule—it worked for Maverick. While lots of good people end up parenting alone, and may God bless them for parenting through difficult circumstances, I think we can all agree that two married parents who still like each other is the Platonic ideal. My darling husband and I are committed to the idea that beyond the romantic, religious, and legal nature of marriage, we're family. I spent my entire childhood living in fear that my parents would get divorced, and my worst fears eventually came true. I saw the trainwreck coming towards us for years beforehand. You can always tell when you have built your house on quicksand. Sure, the Big One may eventually hit California and shake our old house off its rickety foundation, but at least I'm not going to be the force that does it.

Time > Quality Time

My legendary father-in-law once told me before I had any kids, "There's no such thing as quality time with your children. There's just *time*." I didn't believe him at first, but it's true. When my kids were all small, my "office" was a desk in the corner of my bedroom. They often sat in my lap as I worked. Did you know you can minimize Elmo videos on YouTube and let them play in a tiny corner of your computer screen while you send emails to clients? It might not be a fancy enrichment class where they are crafting butterfly puppets out of organic yarn and snacking on heirloom nuts and twigs, but still, I was hanging out with my toddler.

For my oldest kids, their childhood is swiftly—too swiftly—drawing to a close. We're about to wrap this project. Nerf guns and LEGOs have been replaced with car keys and weight plates. Whatever time we spent together cannot be increased or modified in any way. It's set in stone now. Hope your childhood was good, kid, because you're not getting any more of it.

The heartbreaking reality is that one day, much sooner than you think, your impossibly cuddly, eternally two-year-old son will be waving goodbye to you in the doorway of his college dorm room. *I can't believe they let a two-year-old go to college*, you'll think. You notice that his new roommate's mother looks like she's *also* wondering where her two-year-old is. You'll stand there and watch the baby you just brought home from the hospital last Tuesday stretch out on his extra-long twin bed, his feet hanging off the end of it.

Then you'll go home, unable to shake the feeling that you left something important behind. Oh, the baby! You'll check his silent bedroom, since maybe *that's* where you left the baby . . . only there hasn't been a crib in there in ages. What happened to his crib? You don't remember throwing it out. How could you have just thrown it out like that? You will sit on his bed in a vague panic and wonder where your sweet baby has gone, and who that strange young man in the dorm room who kept calling you Mom was.

CHAPTER 18

Respect Domestic Life

Be a Rebel, Stay Home

*What can you do to promote world peace? Go home
and love your family.*

— *Saint Teresa of Calcutta (Mother Teresa)*

*Teach the older women to be reverent in the way they
live, not to be slanderers or addicted to much wine, but
to teach what is good. Then they can urge the younger
women to love their husbands and children, to be self-
controlled and pure, to be busy at home, to be kind,
and to be subject to their husbands, so that no one will
malign the word of God.*

— *Titus 2:3–5*

Homebound

The housewife is the most hated figure in America. Does she remind
the others what they gave up when they got psy-oped into sen-
tencing their newborns to five years hard time in daycare and heading
back to their soul-sucking, underpaid jobs? Sorry for your loss!

The existence of the stay-at-home mother triggers feminists like nothing else. They shriek about respecting women's choices, but staying home to raise your own child is a "choice" they cannot allow you to make. They call for more paid maternity leave while condemning anyone who chooses to stay home for longer—without pay. Imagine doing something without being paid? Why would you do that, you idiot?! Only single girls on hookup apps are allowed to perform unpaid labor!

The best thing about the COVID pandemic was how it freed all the tiny prisoners from their miserable jailcares. I understand that many of the working women of America were not amused by having their kids home all day, but for the toddlers who were sprung from their full-time daycare facilities, it must have been sweet relief to wake up and remember that they would not be dragged to the horrible place anymore and could just play with their own damn toys for once, if you please. If you're going to be semi-ignored anyway, better to experience that at home than in the care of minimum-wage childcare workers who film toddler fight clubs for TikTok during snack time.

Staying home, especially when you have very young children, is a priceless gift. If you choose to stay home instead of rushing back to work while your episiotomy stitches are still healing and you're still wearing that big ol' postpartum diaper, you are committing a radical act of domestic extremism. For it is only at home that your latent domestic extremism can blossom. The State's overreach naturally has to stop at your front door. Inside, it is still legal (as of this writing) to maintain parental control over your children's minds, lives, and education. This is much harder to do when you are absent from them for forty-plus hours a week.

Carrie Gress and Noelle Mering write in their book *Theology of Home*, "Ironically, despite the innate human desire that there is for home, the notion that someone would want to make a home, providing a place of safety, love, order, education, and hospitality, has fallen out of favor. Could there be, in the minds of millions of women today, anything worse than being a 'homemaker'?"[1]

As you have probably deduced by now, I work. I am a working mother! I left a not-so-glorious career as an in-house creative at a TV network when I had my first baby and became a freelance writer so I could stay home. I got my next office job almost ten years later at a giant globo-corporation when my then youngest was in preschool. I trudged back to a new, higher-paying, "exciting" career with lots of "perks," where I toiled for a couple of years until a surprise pregnancy sent me back home for good.

Like the shark in *Jaws*, I could stay underwater with a few barrels harpooned to my back, but add one more and I was forced back to the surface for good.

These days, I still try to earn some dough while working from home. But this is not just luck—I designed my life so I could be around my children as much as possible. Trust me—I would make way more money and enjoy better, cheaper health insurance if I had remained a W-2 employee at a big company.

But it's just fine with me. It's my *choice* to do school drop-offs and afternoon pickups. I *choose* to be as present as possible during their fleeting childhoods, even if I'm on a work deadline (like I am as I type these words). Even the most domestically extreme women I know—the ones who effortlessly manage their households while tending multiple young children—understand and respect the value of work of some sort. No one, least of all me, thinks women should be prevented from working or earning a living. I worked full-time until I had my first child!

The trick is figuring out how to avoid too much work when your kids are small—and need you much more than your boss does. Our broken economy is no longer able to support many families on a single income, especially in overpriced cities. (This must change before my army of domestic extremists can take over the world, but that's a different discussion.) Your task is to find a way around this eternal conundrum if you can: to be able to 1) not starve and 2) stay home with little kids.

I'll just say it (I can't get in any more trouble than I'm already in): becoming a stay-at-home mother should be every woman's ultimate career goal. (Cue the no-knock raid!)

Go ahead and argue that truth. Could there be anything more important than managing your household and its inhabitants? Is your fake email job going to make as much difference to the salvation of humanity as raising good kids will?

Living the housewife life, at least while your babies are small, is a glorious aspiration to have, even if you are not able to do it yet. The joke about "stay-at-home mothers" is that they aren't home very much, especially when kids go to school and need rides everywhere constantly. Sometimes I wonder why I pay a mortgage when I spend most of my waking hours in my car shuttling various people around. I don't even get good tips. More unpaid labor!

I have also lived the other side of this. I have watched the clock and longed to head to the office exit, take the elevator down to the parking lot, and go the hell home. Trust me: staying home is so much better. I'll never swipe a corporate ID badge again.

Now let's check in with America's favorite feminist, Jill Filipovic, and see what she has to say about stay-at-home moms:

> Lots of super-ambitious people marry other super-ambitious people because they're attracted to ambition. I would have a really, really hard time being married to a spouse who chose not to work. If I came to my husband and said I am going to quit my job and dedicate all my time to keeping our household, now I need your income, I think he's in his rights to

say, uh, no. What example are you setting when dad works for pay and mom does the care work at home? Lots of reasons not to want to set that example for a child. Among them: Girls with working moms do better in school. Men with stay-at-home wives are less likely to promote & support women in their workplace.[2]

Let us remember to pray for Mr. Filipovic.

Crumbling to Crumbs

It's true, taking care of a house and family does require work. Apparently this comes as an unpleasant surprise to many women. *The Feminist Handbook* (an actual book[3]) doesn't include a chapter on homemaking. The drudgery of basic housework, it turns out, is one of the driving forces behind the exodus of mothers from their country homes to four-floor walkups in Brooklyn. Honor Jones admits as much in her infamous *Atlantic* essay, in which she describes housewife life in gulag-esque terms.[3] She's been sentenced to a real-life *Midnight Express* prison, only it's a spacious farmhouse in the picturesque countryside. She laments,

> Our kitchen became a murder scene, a forensic investigator could have told the story of my days with those crumbs. Three percent blue Play-Doh; 10 percent toast; 87 percent Honey Nut Cheerios dust: This was who I was. But the crumbs got me down. I sometimes felt that they were a metaphor, that as I got older I was being ground down under the heel of my own life. All I could do was settle into the carpet.[4]

To think that the entire tragedy could have been avoided if she'd simply purchased a broom. Won't someone please send Ms. Jones a Roomba?

My low-tech solution to the problem of crumbs was to get a dog. Dogs are happy to gobble up all the crumbs you can make, even Play-Doh crumbs. We once owned an old black Labrador who would "clean" the litter box for us by devouring whatever the cat produced. He kept that thing spotless. Truly, we don't deserve dogs.

As a bonus, dogs even lick the floor clean for you, for free! Try finding a Roomba that can do that.

Ms. Jones's solution was a bit more complicated. Instead of cleaning her kitchen, she decided her family and their crumby ways were in the way of her Living, Laughing, and Loving like she used to. So she skipped out and moved to a one-bedroom apartment (can you guess where?) where she could finally *be herself.* Crumb-free at last!

I'm obviously not advocating for anyone to stay in a cruel, neglectful, or abusive marriage. But in situations involving children, ditching a decent dad for a fourth-floor walkup in Bed-Stuy because the vacuuming's got you down doesn't seem like the healthiest choice for anyone involved.

Poor Ms. Jones. No one tell her that there are by now at least fifty thousand other middle-aged white feminists exactly like her who live in Brooklyn—and they have each written the exact same plaintive essay.

Let us remember to pray for poor ex–Mr. Jones.

You Only Have to Be Domestic Enough

I have a good friend with grown kids whose house is spotless, and her secret is: she cleans it all day long. *I could be just like her,* I think, driving home from her house in awe. Imagine: pretty vases with real flowers on the mantle, a fingerprint-free picture window, no backpacks spilling papers out on the family room floor. One day, I will triumphantly declare, like the great Zelda Rubinstein after clearing messy spirits from the house in *Poltergeist*: "This house is *clean.*"

The problem with cleaning your house, of course, is that it gets dirty again *immediately.* Do child-free women think we domestic people *like* housework? Housework *sucks,* okay? Honor Jones was right—I just think she *way* overreacted, okay? But yes, clipping gooey play slime out of the dog's fur, fishing Hot Wheels cars out of *unflushed* toilets—no one signs up for that. I mean, I have done all those things, but I don't derive deep personal satisfaction from doing them. Because... *shhh*...you're not supposed to! Anyone who gets a tingle every time they have to use a Magic Eraser to scrub mystery stains off the walls behind a commode frequented by small boys is a real sicko.

Just between us, I am not what you would call a natural home-maker. I do not own a sewing machine. I have never baked a pie from scratch or knitted anything other than one absolutely wretched scarf. I despise doing dishes. One day, I plan to patent disposable boys' socks that I can throw away instead of washing. Every day I wish I owned a robot maid like they had on *The Jetsons.* When I watch British period movies, I don't covet the fabulous country homes or the gardens—I covet the scullery maids and cooks that everyone has. (When we stopped being British, couldn't we at *least* have kept scullery maids?)

My plight is that I was not *raised* to be a charwoman or a scullery maid. Growing up, we had a housekeeper who came at least twice a week! I admit I am somewhat domestically deficient because of this. But a good domestic extremist is one who trains her *children* to wield brooms and vacuums.

Like my mother before me, I simply outsource the housework to impoverished live-ins.

As mothers of large families can confirm, laundry is the real cru-cible. I do so much laundry that I consider it my main hobby now. I've even started a Reddit support group for other laundry hobbyists: r/emptyhampers. I plan to set up a Laundry Fantasy League where my friends and I compete in tournaments to see how many loads we can push in a single day. We'll get cute (dry-clean-only!) shirts made with our names embroidered on them in cursive. At the end of each laundry season, we'll exchange large golden trophies in the shape of Tide bottles.

I get a little too excited when I see the bottom of one of our two deep laundry hampers. It's like striking gold. One of my fondest wishes is to depart the Earth with all my dirty laundry hampers empty. *Mission accomplished*, I will whisper to my loved ones as my eyes shut and I shuffle off this mortal coil, my soul as clean as my bleached and dried dish towels.

Here is my dirty secret to doing laundry at scale: fold nothing! *Je ne fold rien*! Here's a World Economic Forum slogan I could get behind: "You'll Fold Nothing, and You'll Be Happy." Folding is for chumps, and mothers with two or fewer children, or people who employ washer-women. Plus, have you ever *seen* a little boy searching a neatly folded drawer for his favorite T-shirt? Kiss your precious folding efforts goodbye, sucker!

It's not that I'm lazy (well, maybe it is), it's just that I have a machine that washes, a machine that dries, but for some reason there is no machine that folds. Because: *you* are the machine that folds.

And truthfully, if I did fold all the clothes, socks, towels, and sheets I wash in a single day, it would fill 100 percent of my waking hours and some of my sleeping hours, too. Folding nothing is a shortcut I take out of sheer necessity.

Once I tried explaining my anti-folding strategy to a folder. She was appalled. "But you *have* to fold the children's clothes!" No, you really don't. Nice baskets full of fresh clean clothes tossed (lovingly) into them will do for now—until they start folding their own. Until then, I hereby *absolve* you of folding. I'm *reclaiming* your time, as Maxine Waters likes to say in congressional hearings. You gotta know when to fold 'em!

Reclaim your time from the folding vortex! Or else it will suck you in and you may never emerge from its infinite, cottony depths.

A quick word on laundry's ugly stepsister—ironing. Any attempts I made at ironing before my marriage always ended in disaster. The iron's Permanent Press setting permanently pressed wrinkles into whatever I ironed. Then I married a man who, for some reason, absolutely *loves* to iron. Maybe in a world where men no longer wield spears or swords, the iron fills some deep, primal need of his to handle hot, shiny steel.

My solution is this: instead of ironing things, I stuff wrinkled unwashables into the dry-cleaning bag, which usually gets shoved to the back of the closet by accident. Then you can happily forget about it and move on with your life.

Here's some good news for lazy people who aspire to domesticity: you can be a domestic *extremist* without being a domestic *expert*! You don't have to enjoy or be good at housework, chores, crafts, cooking, or the other "traditional" tasks of homemaking. You can easily get enough of them done *well enough* to keep everyone alive, clean, relatively happy, and fed. Remember, cooking, cleaning, and laundry are going to be part of life no matter who you are, no matter how many children you don't have. That is, unless you employ full-time servants—or live in a tent under the freeway. Whenever I drive past a tent encampment under the freeway, I wistfully think, "I bet *those* guys don't worry about laundry." The grass is always greener, folks.

Becoming more domestic also doesn't mean strapping scrub brushes to your knees to get your kitchen floor clean enough to eat off (as my peasant-stock great-grandmother did, even after emigrating to New York City). She would roll in her grave if she saw my kitchen floor, which tends to be covered in dog hair, despite my best efforts. (Hm, maybe a fourth-floor walkup in Bed-Stuy wouldn't be so bad.) I'm gonna need a bigger Roomba.

I may be a domestic extremist, but I concede I am not yet a domestic *goddess*. My bathroom is not beach-themed. My kitchen is not farm-themed. One day, I plan to spend long, luxurious hours cooking the recipes from one of Gwyneth Paltrow's cookbooks—a recipe that gives you a flatter stomach as you eat it and requires eighty ingredients and rare spices you need to source from obscure websites and pay for with currencies you didn't know existed—chopping exquisite organic farm produce on my honed Carrera countertops as tasteful jazz music plays.

But not this day!

"Well, I tried" is my home décor motto, after I see yet another new throw blanket covered in crushed Cheetos or appropriated by the old mutt as her bed.

One day, I will buy cute knickknacks and arrange them there, I think when I see my lovely fireplace mantel stacked with school papers and children's art projects.

"One day," I whisper, "I, too, will have a curated wall of framed family photos."

"Maybe no one will notice," I mutter after a toddler uses a Sharpie to redecorate the living room and his baby sister.

I find myself following Instagram interior design accounts and marveling at the women who can transform dark and dingy spaces into dream designer rooms with nothing more than a nail gun and a cute tool belt.

Sounds impressive, but have they ever had to get Sharpie ink off a baby using nothing but a Magic Eraser? I didn't think so.

You don't need to wax your floors or iron your husband's socks. Please *don't* do those things. Wearing socks on waxed floors will send your husband to the ER anyway. Instead, leaning into domestic life simply means reclaiming your God-given authority as master and mistress of yourself, your home, and your family.

A few cute throw pillows wouldn't hurt, though.

Home Fires

"Home is the place where, when you have to go there, they have to let you in," is how Robert Frost put it. Home may not perfect, but it's where our children are safe, loved, warm, and fed. One or both of their parents are almost always in the house, somewhere. There are places to play and sleep, to eat and cuddle.

I hope when my children are grown, they come home frequently. I will have taken care of the dog hair issue, I promise. My plan for this involves outliving all the dogs and resisting the urge to adopt a new puppy. Perhaps some grandchildren will arrive around the time our last pet heads up to that big dog run in the sky.

From my lips to God's ears!

CHAPTER 19

Have Faith

Become a Domestic Extremist—with This One Neat Trick!

*Conversion is not only changing the faith. Conversion is
changing the heart, and working over there is the grace
of God. Then only comes the question of change of faith.
Nobody can force you, not even the holy prophets.*

— *Saint Teresa of Calcutta (Mother Teresa)*

*O Holy Spirit, descend plentifully into my heart.
Enlighten the dark corners of this neglected dwelling and
scatter there Thy cheerful beams.*

— *Saint Augustine*

In Case of Emergency, Break for Mass

What if I told you there was a quick shortcut to living the domestically extreme life? A lifestyle plan that's been in use for, like, two thousand years. A plan already designed for you that can help you navigate the culture and its land mines. A program for the whole family that encourages a happy marriage, children, and inspires you to strive towards goodness, kindness, and loyalty. When you mess up, they even offer a generous forgiveness benefit. It's even got a nifty rewards program that pays out some cool death benefits (eternal life, etc.).

Such a shortcut exists, folks. Religion—a real one—gives you the cheat codes for life. When you become a "person of faith," like I did years ago, you get to jump ahead of all the laborious steps involved in becoming extremely domestic. It's like playing Candyland and picking the card to go straight to the Candy Castle on your first turn. Game over—you win.

Sadly, the ranks of fellow believers grow thin. Pews in some parishes are as empty as the banal homilies droned by the pastors. Noelle Mering writes, "[T]he promise that we can cut ourselves off from the Almighty and have no master has been disproven time and again, but still it is seeded and shown in new generations."[1]

When you raise children with a strong belief system, you are giving them a powerful force field against the most depraved ideas of mainstream culture. It isn't foolproof, but it's still the best we've got. Religion can offer them a solid scaffolding on which to construct their worldview—and give them a better chance of avoiding the pitfalls of modern American life.

And these days, it's all pitfalls.

I chose Roman Catholicism. Or maybe it chose me. I didn't convert until well into my marriage, but I made it in.

You don't need to be Catholic to be a domestic extremist, of course. There are other attractive religions that offer their own radically domestic guides to living. Although many self-professed "devout" people ignore the tenets of their faith, if you try to follow the rules, you're going to be in the top percentile of domestic extremists nationwide—even in the running for most domestic worldwide. Like magic, you will gain robust natural immunity to the worst excesses of the prevailing culture.

Just make sure to avoid cults, like Scientology and veganism. Stay away from cringe parishes that feature rock bands and middle-aged women doing interpretive dances during the Mass. And always reject any house of God that has tossed the Ten Commandments aside for "In This House We Believe" rules.

Catholics and Protestants especially are always complaining about the ridiculous "woke" elements ruining an experience that is supposed to be reverent. Progressive Christianity has successfully turned many parishes and their associated schools into little activist academies. Rainbow flags commonly adorn the front lawns of churches of every denomination. The Floyd Wars of 2020 (result: we all lost) unleashed busybody church ladies everywhere who set about stitching giant "Black Lives Matter" banners to cover up images of that less popular dead martyr you usually see in Christian churches.

When choosing a parish, pay careful attention to the tagline they use on their website. Avoid churches that greet you with statements like: "Welcoming All to Believe, Belong, Become, and Be the Difference," "Radical Inclusion: Whoever you are and wherever you find yourself on the journey of faith, you are welcome at our table," "We are black, brown, white, yellow, women, men, heterosexual, gay, lesbian, bisexual, single, married, divorced, widowed, rich, poor, disabled, homebound, unemployed, working people."

These were all actual statements I found on some local church websites. The funny thing is that every Catholic church I've ever attended, including the conservative ones, has been incredibly welcoming. A parish we used to go to in the heart of West Hollywood offered wonderfully reverent Masses free of all the bullshit, and the pews always had a few men in leather fetish gear who looked like they'd had to shoulder aside the heavy iron door to their gimp dungeons to make it to the noon service.

If you can, try your best to choose an attractive place to worship. This may be a tall order, unless you live in Italy or France. Don't get me started on contemporary church architecture. As the great art historian Kenneth Clark put it, when trying to decide whether you can learn more about a society from its buildings or from its leader's speeches, "Believe the buildings."[2]

You want a vaccine against the culture? Choose one that works.

Warning: this vaccine's side effects may include the sudden appearance of grandchildren. Another nice side effect of joining a "religious community," as they say, is that your children will have "radical" (i.e., traditional) beliefs that will forever keep them at arm's length from their secular peers. This is a great advantage! Wearing a scapular, praying regularly, and keeping a Bible or two around will warn progressives to stay far away from your children. It's like red spots on a tree frog—keeps the dangerous predators at bay.

Children raised to be, for example, devout Roman Catholics, will grow up with a deep understanding of the value of chastity, monogamy, marriage, and protecting the unborn. Boys will not shy away from embracing their innate masculinity. Girls will embrace the gifts of their natural femininity. Young couples will value each other as equals and partners, while also recognizing how their differences complement each other. Beauty, health, tradition, and history will be revered. And babies: babies will be welcomed and cherished, the more the better.

I'm not saying your children can't achieve all this as secular atheists. I'm sure some do. I'm just saying it makes your job a lot harder. Switching from a mainstream, pro-choice, God-free lifestyle to a pro-life, big family, trad-Cath (or whatever old-fashioned faith you prefer) lifestyle is like switching your diet from McDonalds to Whole Foods. It's a major upgrade. You're adding years to your life, reversing decades of free-radical damage to your spiritual telomeres.

I can't even imagine trying to fight the woke tsunami as a secular parent. Would I have given in by now? Surrendered to the peer pressure? Would I have attended White Trans Allies Zoom parent meetings and clapped as yet another mom announced her child's transition? Would I have told a daughter who complained about the hairy dude with a stiffie in the girls' locker room to shut up and accept her new six-foot-four lacrosse teammate?

I'm grateful I was saved from this dystopian hellworld, and I cannot believe millions of families are mired in it, helpless victims with no hope of escape.

God remains the one guy who can lead you out.

Atheism: At Least It's an Ethos

I never, *ever* dreamed I would become a "person of faith," as they say. My secular atheist childhood offered me no God, no church, no temple, no prayers, no heaven, no hell. It was like living in the song "Imagine," but without Yoko Ono. We had lovely Christmas trees and all the trimmings, but it was a purely consumerist bacchanal. In my childhood, there was no God but Santa, and Rudolph was his messenger.

When I say we were atheists, I mean it. My mother kept a folder in her desk labeled "Religion." She used it to store newspaper articles about church buses filled with pilgrims plummeting off cliffs. She would shake her head as she filed yet another clipping about missionaries raped and murdered by the natives.

The "why do bad things happen to good people" argument was her bedrock belief, and who was I to argue? "Why do little kids get brain cancer? What kind of God lets that happen? He wants it to?" Impossible questions to answer, and I still don't have the answers.

Don't get me wrong: my childhood was great in many crucial areas, but I could have avoided many loitering munitions if I'd had a more religious underpinning. *Any* underpinning, frankly; some infrastructure on which to scaffold my somewhat chaotic early life.

It wasn't my parents' fault, really. Both my mother and father were raised in the happy afterglow of post-war America in middle-class households that considered religion a dirty word. It was a backwards thing their first-generation ancestors had shucked off as soon as they made it off the boat at Ellis Island. The ones back in the old country, well, just look what happened to them: mowed down by Cossacks, chased by Vikings, persecuted by Anglicans, pogromed out of their villages, strafed by Germans—where was God then, huh?

Like many Americans, my ancestors are a melting pot of persecuted European races and religions, which is why they crossed the pond in the first place. They were so busy trying not to get murdered for their religion, ethnicity, tribe, or clan that they had no time or desire to impart said traditions onto their children.

Religion, to quote my Eastern European great-grandmother (who lived until she was well over one hundred years old), was "a big vaste of time." Better to leave those superstitions behind in the old country where they belonged, where they had caused her nothing but grief. When, newly widowed and grieving the death of her first child, she spotted the Statue of Liberty as she sailed into New York Harbor, she said she "threw religion into the vater. You don't need it in de new country." When asked her opinion of the afterlife, she would always say, "Ven you die, dey bury you and your body rrrrots!"

My mother still quotes this whenever the subject of religion comes up.

I should note that my great-grandmother and the other non-religious matriarchs in my family led daily lives of extreme domesticity, at advanced expert levels that no longer exist in our era.

They were "scrub the floor with sponges strapped to your knees"–level domestic. "Three days making homemade dough for one thousand dumplings"–level domestic. They were unimaginably domestic in the extreme.

Even my mother, despite her complete lack of faith, was a domestic extremist in every other way. She tried her best to teach me to make her grandmother's famous chicken soup, and I shamefully resisted. (I once had to call her to walk me through the recipe when I was taking care of a sick boyfriend.)

Because my European-American female ancestors overwhelmingly rejected traditional religion, within three generations their culture of extreme female domesticity was lost. When you look at grainy videos of European immigrants arriving at Ellis Island, hope shining on their faces, remember that every single one of them has an unmarried bisexual great-great-granddaughter on long-term birth control and SSRIs.

Tragically, for many of these immigrants, coming to America also meant coming to the end of their genetic line—especially if they forgot to bring their religion with them.

But sometimes, what is lost and forgotten can be discovered again.

I had to do it the hard way. Thanks for nothing, Grandma!

(But thank you for getting on that boat.)

Finding My Religion

As a child, my secularized and sanitized household left me to grope my way in darkness. I was baptized in the Church of MTV. Pop culture was my religion, and I dutifully prayed the Gospel According to Matthew, Mark, Luke, and John—that is, Matthew Broderick, Mark Wahlberg, Luke Perry, and John Taylor from Duran Duran. We revered Madonna—not the virgin, the one like a virgin.

In the great black vacuum of emptiness left by the absence of religion, a child will fill it with whatever cultural detritus is lying around.

Maybe you're a staunch nonbeliever, but you're politically conservative, so you think that's enough, right? Maybe you think that if you just teach your kids to reject contemporary feminism and vote Republican, all will be well.

I know a lot of right-wing nonbelievers, and it's true, some have successfully indoctrinated their kids to mostly reject woke culture. But what happens in high school when their kids are invited to the polyamorous clothing-optional BDSM-themed prom? What page in the MAGA handbook tells you how to handle this? Will your subscription to Fox Nation be enough to guide your children through the minefield? Pure politics is no substitute for a powerful religious antidote.

And at the end of the day, politics, even the "correct" politics, is not going to be enough to entice children to reject the seductions of modern culture. It won't keep your kids off the pole, so to speak. The other side is offering your children a lifetime supply of guilt-free promiscuity, 24/7 on-demand porn, and abortion safety nets. That's a tough offer to top. "Because I said so!" may not be enough to get them to delete Pornhub and Tinder off their phones—or never download them in the first place.

Besides, I don't favor politicizing kids. I'd be happy if my children had no idea who the president was. Even our current president doesn't know!

So what can you as a parent offer a kid that the culture can't?

Nothing.

Plot twist: I know someone who can!

What can you, a mere mortal, do to give your children the best chance at a satisfying and happy life? Simply raise them to know they are not alone in the darkest times, that it's not just you and your spouse, alone in a house. There are guardian angels and saints to pray to, and bedtime prayers, and stories to learn and read together. There is an ocean of comfort and resilience built into children who grow up knowing God loves them.

I didn't have this opportunity, and folks, I made it through by the skin of my teeth. My more fortunate children will not have to cling to the sheer cliff walls above the abyss for as long as I had to.

Sometimes I wonder what my life would be like now if I had been raised with any religion. I mean, I did fine, I have a nice life, I'm not on drugs or in jail or a Democrat, but maybe I could have had ten more children by now, or written ten more books! Instead of sitting inside on a glorious sunny day, my aching fingers bleeding into the keyboard, I'd be dictating these words from a sumptuous private jet headed to my family compound on the shores of some blue tropical water somewhere. The mind reels!

Fortunately, I found God while there was still just enough time for me to execute Operation Extremely Domestic, punch in the cheat codes, respawn a few more times, and win the game with a life to spare.

Please check back later to see how my dozens of grandchildren and hundreds of great-grandchildren are doing.

Conquering Your Fears

It's remarkable, even to me, that the Ten Commandments pretty much sum up the rules for a happy life. Amazing that God's chiseler managed to get them all on just two little stone tablets. Imagine if he'd had to tweet it out in 280 characters or less. You know what the commandments are, right? No killing, no cheating, no stealing, no blasphemy, no lying, love God, love your neighbor, don't love his wife or his donkey or his ox too much, and listen to your parents.

Another nice feature of Catholicism is how you can make a mistake, even a *really* bad one, and instead of filming a confessional TikTok, you can just go to confession and get absolved—by God himself!

The Seven Deadly Sins pretty much cover the rest: pride, greed, lust, anger, gluttony, envy, and sloth.

Too many people these days mistake the Seven Deadly Sins for a bucket list. Like you, I'm guilty of all of them, frequently, but at least now I feel bad about it.

One thing faith gives you that I didn't learn until recently is: confidence. Mainly, the confidence to live and to *be happy*—despite the ever-present shadow of death. How can you even get through life without this safety net? Nearly every day, I receive an email or see a news story announcing another innocent person afflicted with a terrible disease or injury, or a miscarriage, or a sudden death. Death permeates daily life; the trick is learning to accept it.

In *Hannah and Her Sisters*, Woody Allen's character (a neurotic, hypochondriac writer, nothing like me) spends the entire film trying to find a reason not to kill himself. "Do you realize what a *thread* we're all hanging on?" he mournfully intones after finding out the scary ringing in his ears is not cancer, but then immediately realizing that despite the temporary reprieve, he will die one day *no matter what*.

His struggle to accept mortality sends him on a spiritual quest to find meaning in his life. We see Woody meet with a Catholic priest and chat with Hare Krishnas in Central Park. But it's no use, he just can't find a reason to keep living. Then, in a movie theater watching the Marx Brothers classic *Duck Soup*, he suddenly finds joy again and gives this little speech:

> What if the worst is true? What if there's no God, and you only go around once, and that's it? Don't you want to be a part of the experience? You know, what the hell? It's not all a drag, and I'm thinking to myself: Geez! I should stop ruining my life searching for answers I'm never gonna get and just enjoy it while it lasts. And after—who knows?

Maybe there is something, nobody really knows. I know that maybe is a very slim reed to hang your whole life on, but that's the best we have.[3]

When I first watched this scene as a devout atheist, I was deeply moved. If even *Woody Allen* could acknowledge there may be mysterious forces beyond our reach, maybe I could, too!

The world is full of terrors. The main terror is knowing that one day, when you least expect it, all the other terrors will suddenly end. Faith is the only thing I have found that gives me the courage to accept my own certain death. Suffering, instead of driving me away from my faith, has only brought me closer to it.

The grand finale of your life, and the lives of your children, looms. It's a mystery why we don't spend all day screaming. We worry instead about the color we chose for the guest bathroom and why our phone isn't charging fast enough. But you *should* spend a little more time thinking about your grand finale. Someone once told me that as a Catholic, your entire life becomes preparation for your death. Maybe he was stoned, I don't know, but it's a pretty good way to approach things.

As a world-class hypochondriac who also gets sick sometimes, I have stared into the imagined abyss lots of times. I *do* realize what a thread we're all hanging on. The older you get, the crisper the dimensions of your own Act Three get. The whole thing begins to emerge out of the mists of time and come into sharp focus on the horizon.

Probably because you are quickly *approaching* the horizon!

Revelation

"Men have forgotten God; that's why all this has happened," Alexander Solzhenitsyn famously said about why there has been so much human-caused calamity.[4] It should be self-evident that becoming authentically domestic almost *requires* you to believe in a higher authority. How else to accomplish the grand task ahead: to save ourselves, our families, and our civilization from the clutches of an oppressive, anti-human, nihilistic tyranny?

There are other good reasons to have faith, of course. You know, like getting yourself and your children into heaven. While writing this book, a true miracle actually occurred in my family. My sister, a devout secular atheist her entire life, suddenly decided to convert to Catholicism. This was a woman who rolled her eyes when I told her years ago that I was converting. "Really? *You?* You actually *believe* that stuff?" She reacted to my announcement like I'd told her I was selling my worldly possessions to join Heaven's Gate and hitch a ride on the Hale-Bopp Comet (look it up, kids).

And yet here she was, a pagan, a religion-scorning modern woman, telling me she had started reading the *Bible* with her children at night—and was planning to start the conversion process immediately. What!?

For my sister, faith had appeared as a lifeline after two horrid years living under COVID restrictions in a dark blue state. Several years before the pandemic, she had suffered a catastrophic medical injury caused by a rare severe reaction to a commonly prescribed medicine. It caused life-altering, permanent side effects. One side effect is that she must avoid many other medications, including COVID vaccines. She's mostly okay now and lives a mostly normal and happy life—but it shook her to her core. For a while, she fell into a deep depression and started having dark thoughts about how she was supposed to live with a nonfatal, but still difficult, new condition. Maybe because of that, and because of the two long years she was treated like an "anti-vax" pariah by her liberal "friends" and neighbors, her suffering finally delivered salvation—in the form of a sudden and overwhelming belief in God.

I can't take credit for her revelation. Her *children* were the ones who first suggested their whole family convert. I was as shocked by this as she was when I dropped my own Jesus bomb on her. Now her kids, along with mine, will be raised with the great gift of faith.

When you raise children to believe in God, they have a final authority to answer to. Not you, not the president, not even their favorite YouTube personality, can fully control them. No politician or government official can ever gain complete power over their hearts and minds.

This is why the people in charge bleat so loudly about the dangers of "Christian nationalism" and "religious fundamentalism." They are *afraid* of you laughing in their faces when they attempt to impose their dumb rules on you. Children raised to believe in God just wave these haters away, like Glinda waves away the Wicked Witch. "Begone! You have no power here!"

Even in the depths of a gulag, no human authority holds sway over a human spirit that is one with God. An elderly man in a concentration camp was ordered to dig a deep ditch under the watchful eye of a Nazi guard. "Where is your God now, Jew?" the guard sneered at the prisoner. The old man looked up from the hole he had dug and answered, "Here in the ditch with me."

When your values, morals, and rights come from the divine, they are not up for discussion or debate. They cannot be repealed or replaced. God cannot be canceled.

Children who believe this will naturally be skeptical of politicians who make dumb decisions. They will intuitively understand that unborn children deserve to live. They will seek to live by a powerful moral code that cannot be legislated, repealed, modernized, or overturned. They will be forces for good in a world breaking bad. They will be better able to resist the urge to join the mind-flayed lemmings flinging themselves by the thousands into the Trans Canyon. They will have more willpower to refuse the first offer of a dangerous drug. They will be better prepared to resist the temptation to indulge in harmful sexual behaviors. They will value their own lives, knowing they are much more than just a clump of disposable cells without a soul.

Faith gives children ballast. Faith gives them confidence that even while suffering, even after they *die*, they will be okay. Best of all, children who believe in God are much more likely to raise their *own* children to believe in God, thus perpetuating goodness and decency—and grandchildren for you.

Nothing is foolproof, of course. There is no guarantee that a devout child will thrive.

But it's the best we've got.

CHAPTER 20

Reclaim Your Parental Authority

Defend Girls and Boys

Long periods of peace foster certain optical illusions:
one is the conviction that the inviolability of the home is
grounded in the constitution, which should guarantee it.
In reality, it is grounded in the family father, who, sons
at his side, fills the doorway with an axe in his hand.

— *Ernst Jünger*, The Forest Passage

A man and a woman had a little baby.
Yes, they did.
They had three in the family, and that's a magic number.

— *Schoolhouse Rock*, "Three Is a Magic Number"

No One Is Coming to Save You

On May 24, 2022, a lunatic barricaded himself inside a Uvalde, Texas, elementary school and began executing children. For nearly an hour, tough men wearing body armor and holding high-powered rifles stood outside the school, inadvertently protecting . . . the shooter. He was able to kill nineteen children while armed law enforcement stopped Good Samaritans from entering to begin a rescue operation. Desperate parents screamed for them to go in and save their kids. In response, the police began arresting . . . the parents.

Angeli Gomez was among the mothers and fathers begging the police to rescue their kids. Her two little boys were trapped inside the school. She was handcuffed, then freed, but detained. She somehow managed to bolt out of police custody, jump a fence, and run right into the school where a live shooter roamed. Inside, she reported that there was not a cop in sight. Alone, as shots rang out nearby, she retrieved her boys from their classrooms and got them out safely.

Instead of awarding her the Mother of the Year medal, the police threatened to charge her for speaking to the media.[1]

We may not all be faced with situations like this, but Angeli Gomez's heroic efforts illustrate the stakes at play for all of us. Whose job *is* it to protect our children? Who has final authority over them, the parent or the State? Who is in charge? Is *anyone* in charge?

Deranged shooters are not the only lunatics loose on our campuses. A school counselor at Richards Middle School in Fraser, Michigan, sent an email to a student's teachers warning them not to reveal during the upcoming parent-teacher conferences that the student had decided to become a girl. The email warned teachers "to only use the student's birth name and refer to the pronoun 'he' when talking to the child's mother."[2] When confronted, the school—like all public schools that think they're the boss of your kids—cited Title IX, which prohibits sexual harassment or sex-based discrimination at schools and universities that receive federal funding.

To the school, telling a child's parent about a secret sex change constitutes harassment—of the child. Facilitating a life-altering decision behind the parents' back is therefore the lawful and proper thing to do.

They are just following the legal code, after all. They are just following orders!

It sounded better in the original German.

Who do you think you are, parents? You think you know better than a school's cock-a-maiming interpretation of a law written to give girls a chance to play sports?

After decades of dismantling parental authority and handing it over to faceless bureaucrats, we are now trapped inside a circus where *no one* has full authority over our children—and the clowns have become the ringmasters.

No one is coming to save our kids. It's all up to us now.

Waking a Sleeping Tiger Mom

The secret is out: degenerates are in charge of all the public schools and pretty much everything else these days. The best thing about COVID was that it revealed this truth—and awakened a sleeping giant. Millions of outraged parents suddenly woke up to the reality that their school hated them and their kids. They endured a year or more of learning-free "remote school" because teachers didn't want to be exposed to germ-riddled young disease vectors. They forced little kids to wear masks, even outside, for over a year. They demanded that kids receive experimental vaccines—for an illness that barely affects them.

Once kids got back to "normal" school (LOL), parents had to run a new gauntlet: race and sex reeducation. The kids are back in person, so cue the dismantling of their white privilege and their genders! They can take off the surgical mask, but only if they put on this dental dam!

Libs of TikTok meticulously documents and exposes the insanity taking place inside America's schools. Thousands of public school teachers, it turns out, are disturbed weirdos who don't know their own genders—or in some cases, what species they are—and are fully committed to making little kids as confused as they are. They boast about this on camera, and the clips find their way to the internet.

Parents have gotten a look at the garbage taught at their local elementary school—and at the circus sideshow freaks pretending to be teachers. Normal people are expected to cede authority over their children to twenty-seven-year-old nonbinary furries with made-up pronouns and more piercings in their faces than Pinhead from *Hellraiser*. Libs of TikTok is doing the Lord's work exposing the undoctored videos that America's early childhood educators post online.

I concede that not all teachers are like this. There are probably still some normal ones out there. Good luck finding them!

In early 2022, the Regime was so furious about unionized government teachers' own words being used against them in the court of parental opinion that the Jeff Bezos–owned *Washington Post* tried to silence the person behind Libs of TikTok via harassment, doxxing, and intimidation.[3]

Curious about your own kid's teacher? Wondering what kind of sexual fetishes or kinks the preschool aide is into? My longtime rule is to assume *any* given adult is questionable until proven otherwise over time. Priest, teacher, coach, other parents—I'm watching you. On the first day of kindergarten, take a good look at the teacher. Would you let this person walk your dog? Babysit your toddler? What do you think their internet search history looks like?

Trust your instincts, and remember: *if there is any doubt, there is no doubt.* Take your kid and run!

You should not avoid weird teachers just because they may be slightly creepy or demand the children call them by different pronouns depending on the day of the week. You should avoid them because a weird teacher means you'll also contend with a weird school administration on high alert searching for the Holy Grail of Wokeness: a kid questioning their gender. A student who drops the slightest hint that they may have gender dysphoria is like blood in the water to the woke school staff.

Instead of using metal detectors, they employ their "mental" detectors, which sound the alarm every time some little boy does something like use a pink crayon once. Every new trans kid they can mint is another pliant soldier in the obedient, fully medicalized Orc army they are methodically constructing. They are hungry for recruits, and each new kindergarten class means one thing: fresh meat. Mm, they look tasty. Meat's back on the menu, boys!

You may be certain your son is a boy, but social justice activist teachers are skilled in detecting the slightest whiff of "queerness." They're like truffle pigs—and your clueless kid who likes the wrong color shirt is the delicacy they hunt.

Teacher: "Do you feel like a boy, Peter?"

Kid: "I mean, I guess I do. I don't know?"

Teacher (heart beating faster): "You're not sure? You don't know? Peter, step into my office so I can present you with a new name, new pronouns, a multi-decade irreversible medical treatment plan, and your new foster parents. They will help you with this transition, unlike your bigoted biological parents, who have been remanded into federal custody. Patricia might make a lovely name for a pretty girl like you!"

I wish I was exaggerating. A mother in California sued her district for grooming her seventh grader and convincing her she was a boy.

> In one of her shocking claims, Konen [the girl's mother] said the two teachers actively sought out students who they thought were struggling with their identities and invited them to the school's Equality Club. At the Equality Club meetings, Ms. Caldiera and Ms. Baraki would coach students on LGBT+ identities, such as homosexuality,

bisexuality, transgenderism, gender non-conformity, etc., and how to express those identities.[4]

In state after state, teachers are not required to inform parents when a child presents with gender dysphoria. "Washington state requires teachers to conceal students' gender transitions from their parents unless the student gives the green light for their parents to know."[5] Living in a "red" state will not offer you any protection. Some obvious states committed to the "it'll be our little secret" student policy include groomer sanctuary states New Jersey and California, but your kids aren't safe in Idaho, Virginia, North Carolina, or Kansas, either.

In Loudoun County—ground-zero of the 2020 Parent Rebellion that saw Glenn Youngkin upset Democrat Terry McAuliffe for Virginia governor by running on an anti-Critical-Race-Theory agenda—has fallen to the more powerful transgender lobby. "Loudoun County School District officials instructed staff to avoid informing a transgender student's parents about their child's gender identity unless the student gives the school express permission, according to materials from the training."[6]

In Kansas, a retired teacher won a lawsuit she filed after refusing to go along with her district's policy on concealing a student's transgender identity from their parents.[7]

Parents of these children are often the last to know. By the time they find out and try to wrest control back, it's too late: child protective services are called in and the parent-child bond is quickly severed. God help you if your child casually tells a teacher or a doctor that they aren't sure how they feel about their gender. Your parental rights can be terminated with the stroke of a school psychologist's pen. Maybe your child will want to see you again after completing their medical transition, maybe not. They're not your concern anymore, lady—the State will take it from here!

Incredibly, this has already happened several times in the United States. In 2018, an Ohio judge removed a female teenager from her religious parents because they wouldn't allow her to undergo hormone treatments and "become male."[8]

In 2020, a Muslim family in Washington State was informed by Seattle Children's Hospital that their suicidal, autistic son was now a girl. The boy's father was smart and sensed disaster looming:

> Believing he might be walking into a trap, Ahmed reached out to both a lawyer and a psychiatrist friend he trusted. The psychiatrist gave him advice that he believes saved his son, saying, in Ahmed's words: "You must be very, very careful, because if you come across as just even a little bit anti-trans or anything, they're going to call the Child Protective Services on you and take custody of your kid." Ahmed assured Seattle Children's Hospital that he would take his son to a gender clinic and commence his son's transition. Instead, he collected his son, quit his job, and moved his family of four out of Washington.[9]

The family later reported that their son was happy, not depressed—and no longer thought he was a girl.

In an especially heartbreaking case, a California school district removed a fifteen-year-old girl from her mother's home and sent her to a group home because her mother didn't always use the right pronouns. The mother could only talk to her daughter through glass, like in a prison. After four years in foster care, with no contact allowed with her "obstructive" mother and lots of testosterone injections, Yaeli Martinez stepped in front of a train and died.[10] It's hard for them to keep arguing that kids *need* to transition to prevent suicide when they kill themselves years after their State-ordered transition.

Public schools are now no-go zones for normal families. Classrooms have become creepy, windowless basements where teachers form "special bonds" with their young charges and ask them to share all their "secrets" with them. Los Angeles Unified School District is taking radical gender theory to the next level. They bragged online about a charity called Gender Nation that is helping them share the good news about irreversible bottom surgery with kindergarteners. "Gender Nation empowers and validates children through access to uplifting, inclusive stories that demonstrate the full spectrum of sexuality and gender identity. LAUSD is excited to receive an emormous [*sic*] donation of LGBTQIA-themed books that are developmentally appropriate for elementary and span [*sic*] schools."[11]

Based on just the number of typos on their website, you should avoid every single trash book on their list. Better yet, use their reading list as a list of what *not* to read in your house. Thanks, Gender Nation!

We are now living through an age where parents are threatened for refusing to "affirm" their own child's new gender—by local bureaucrats who hate them. Parents are losing custody of their children for not using the pronouns *their teacher taught them to use*. The American public education system, along with its enthusiastic employees, has undergone a silent transition—into Groomer Ed. It is quickly asserting total authority over your children, and there is no one left to stop it. The Department of Re-Education has plans for your family.

It's not just the gender indoctrination that's gone too far—it's the explicit sexual content being taught. Literal pornography, in some cases, with illustrations depicting sex acts and language that would make Larry Flynt blush. Child pornography, graphic descriptions of sex acts between middle schoolers, pedophilia—this is not your grandfather's reading list.

Acclaimed kiddie porn bestsellers like *Gender Queer* and *Lawn Boy* can be found in nearly every public library in the country, including in "safe" red states like Texas, Wyoming, and Kentucky. *Lawn Boy* is written from the point of view of a gay man fantasizing about early sexual encounters, including oral sex, between fourth-grade boys.[12]

Gender Queer, an award-winning graphic novel described lovingly as "frank" and "honest" by the teachers who assign it, was written by Maia Kobabe, a "nonbinary" biological female who uses e/em/eir pronouns. It contains, among other gems, X-rated drawings of a ten-year-old performing oral sex on another kid wearing a strap-on dildo.[13] Although the book listing page on Amazon says it's for "18 and up," the author "recognizes the importance eir [*sic*] book has to queer audiences, particularly younger, questioning ones."[14] How young, exactly? The younger the better, right?

But school officials, whose job it is to know best how to teach our children, are not interested in parental concerns. If you complain, you might be a literal Nazi. Dr. Lynn Reynolds, the pea-brained executive director of Library Media Services at Jefferson County Public Schools in Kentucky, defended *Gender Queer* by comparing the parents who wanted it removed to book-burning Nazis. "Dr. Reynolds argued that *Gender Queer* has literary value and is aligned with Common Core standards." This "child expert" Lynn Reynolds (she's a doctor, remember) explained that "*Gender Queer* impacts readers and allows them to feel those that are marginalized. When books explore ideological and literary elements, educators are better equipped to lead social and cultural conversation. It disrupts norms, and it allows them to examine text for different conceptualizations."[15]

Thank God people like Dr. Reynolds are out there, disrupting norms, making the world a safe space for fourth graders who like to blow each other after school.

We're Not Gonna Take It

Parents—at least the sane ones—have begun demanding changes. A group called Moms for Liberty went to war with some particularly nasty local school boards—and they're winning. "Our mission is to save America by empowering parents to stand up for their parental rights," one of their leaders said in an interview.[16] After being ignored by politicians for decades in favor of school boards and teachers' unions, parents are suddenly the hottest new political bloc in America.

The Battle Moms of the Republic have finally tapped into their innate power as parents, and they aren't gonna take it anymore. Recent developments have offered a glimmer of hope that parental authority is on the verge of making a roaring comeback. Outraged parents have stood their ground against craven school board cronies and demanded the end of mask mandates in schools, the end of teaching everything through the lens of racism, and the end of gender ideology introduced to very young children.[17]

In Virginia in 2020, so many parents woke up to the reality of Critical Race Theory taught in schools that they turned the state's school board meetings into rallies. The Battle of the School Board kicked off, and the parents beat the establishment by electing a new governor who vowed to eliminate CRT.

In response, parents were literally smeared as "domestic terrorists" in the media and even by the United States Department of Justice.[18]

Some parents wore the slur as a badge of honor, putting it in their Twitter bios. The woke school board members felt "terrorized"—by parents attempting to assert their authority over their own kids!

My fellow domestic extremists: welcome to the fight. This time, I know our side will win.

Five Ways to Reclaim Your Parental Authority

How do we begin the process of reclaiming authority over our own children? If you've ever had to comb head lice out of a child's hair, you will understand just what it's like to get the government out of your children's lives. It's a task that is messy and unpleasant, but it's vital to their health and well-being. This is not a parenting how-to book, but I thought it might be a good idea to articulate a few simple ways you can begin to comb other unwelcome parasites out of your child's life.

Exit Government Schools

I saw a *Babylon Bee* headline recently that pretty much summed up the state of American public education: "Study Shows Kids Who Are Homeschooled Could Miss Out On Opportunity to Be a Gay Communist."[19]

K–12 schools want your kids: body, mind, and soul. Unless your particular campus is staffed with people who agree that the child's primary authority and educator is the *parent*, your family is in grave danger. Many public school employees and school union members would love nothing more than to sever your bond with your child in order to assert *themselves* as primary caregiver in your place. Want proof? Ninety-four percent of political donations by teachers' unions go to liberal politicians who believe that kindergarteners can choose their own genders.[20]

Think your kids are safe if you pay for a fancy private school? Think again. The only difference between public and private schools is that the drag queens who perform at private schools wear *real* Christian Louboutin heels, not the cheap knockoffs public school drag queens wear. You get the same grotesquerie, only at a much higher price.

Good news: there are alternatives. Find one, or the convenience of a free local school will prove inconvenient in the extreme over time. I always tell people to look for a school with the word "classical" in the name or description: it's a dog whistle for anti-wokeness. I've found the map of schools on the Institute for Catholic Classical Liberal Arts Schools[21] to be an excellent resource. Hillsdale College also runs a network of classical K–12 schools[22] that seem like welcome refuges where your little public school escapees may have a better chance to thrive. New schools are being founded all over the country. Do your best to find an alternative!

And for colleges, I have finally accepted that I can never send a child to a "top" university. This is hard pill for a meritocratic Gen X academic striver to absorb, but those schools are not what they used to be. If you like your child's gender, you can't keep your child's gender once he or she has been put through the elite college meat grinder. The good news is that none of mine would get in anyway: they're white cisgender religious fundamentalists. Instant rejection! Instead, I plan to start with the list of colleges the Cardinal Newman Society publishes.[23]

That is, *if* we send them to college. By the time my firstborn is in college, any college savings we had will be requisitioned by the IRS to fund gender education camps for Ukrainian orphans.

If you don't want or need to put your kids in school, homeschooling is the answer. It's the hottest trend in America, mostly because it's affordable, convenient, and kids generally prefer it to getting assaulted in the bathroom by mean girls with gonads.

Millions of parents fled their schools during the pandemic and took refuge in homeschooling. There are tons of wonderful homeschool curricula out there; I've used several. You can get an entire school day done in a few hours or less. No bullies, no bizarro teachers trying to groom your child, no transgender students raping your daughter in the bathroom,[24] no political brainwashing, no new pronouns, and no racial struggle sessions. You are firmly in control!

There are too many resources for me to list here, but you could start with the Homeschool Legal Defense Association website[25] to learn more, or check out Cathy Duffy's reviews of various homeschool programs.[26] Find a homeschooling friend to help get you started. Do what you must to keep your children out of the system!

Delete TikTok from Their Phones

Unless you are living in an Amish community or are going to dedicate most of your time to overseeing screen use, you are eventually going to contend with unwanted content in your house. Kids have phones and iPads and laptops. That toothpaste is out of the tube. But there are a few simple guidelines we try to enforce in a house full of teens and preteens—and it starts with banning TikTok. For some reason, that app has become a portal to hell, and children (and adults) fall right into it.

Raising teenagers who are devout Catholics—the kind who kneel by their beds to say their prayers at night and scold me when I don't go to confession regularly—is my secret weapon. Strong morals can't always be imposed on a child; not when there's a good Wi-Fi connection. Instead, good judgment must come from within. I won't be there telling them "no" when they're out of the house, so the best I can do now is inoculate them as much as I can against internet cesspools.

Thank you, Lord, for the assist here.

I know many parents who are much stricter than I am about computers and phones. I know kids who enter high school and still don't know how to type, which is a sure sign of a child with healthy screen limits. So far, our house rules are working pretty well, but the worst offender is the littlest one, who still thinks the rules don't apply. The kid's in for a rude awakening one of these days.

Keep Your Boys Male and Your Girls Female

Children should be dressed and presented according to their God-given genders. Nightmarish drag shows—you know, for kids!— are all the rage among progressive parents. Boys wearing skirts have become trendy among the idiot celebrity class. Popular children's enter-tainers Harry Styles and Lil Nas X appear in magazines wearing ball gowns. Madonna's adopted African son has taken to wearing her dresses. The singer Adele puts her son in princess dresses, as do about a dozen other celebrities, including Charlize Theron, Naomi Watts, Jamie Lee Curtis, and Megan Fox.[27]

Hmm, could little boys wearing dresses be . . . a *trend*? Whatever would make you think *that*? We are dealing with celebrity-influenced parenting lifestyles that exceed the wildest dreams of those who warn us about a rampant "Hollywood child-grooming cult." How are all these young boys acquiring princess dresses in their sizes? Are they taking their money to the Disney store and buying them? Could it be that their parents are steering them?

Raising a little boy these days is like the wedding gown reality show *Say Yes to the Dress*, only your job as a parent is to say NO to the dress. The only acceptable answer to a boy under the age of eighteen who asks if he can wear a dress is, "No, dear, boys don't wear dresses. Now get in the car." If he asks you for a cigarette, would you give it to him? (A dress, friends, is more dangerous than a cigarette.)

In a world where masculinity is going extinct, we need all the human male children we can get. Reclaim your authority over how you present boys and girls to the world. Instead of Cinderella dresses, nail polish, long hair, and glitter, get your sons a weightlifting bar, a bas-ketball, or boxing gloves.

I have encountered pediatricians who told me my eight-year-old boy was "hyper" and urged me to put him on ADHD medication. No thanks! Normal boys have much more energy than middle-aged female physicians who think medicine is the "cure" for boyish energy. I am not a doctor or an anti-vaxxer, but I am *never, ever* going to give an otherwise normal and healthy child a drug that changes behavior typical for their gender and age.

Young girls are a little trickier. Girls can wear boy clothes without trying to dress as though they *are* boys. The sweet spot is to encourage them to be girly and modest without veering into *Little House* prairie skirts or hooker outfits. The key is to get them to remain *female*, and not get tricked into thinking they are somehow bisexual (they're not). As I mentioned in Part One, over 40 percent of Gen Z kids now identify as LGBTQ+![28]

A large percentage of this group are teenage girls who either say they're bisexual or just claim to be "queer" so they aren't shunned at school. Just being a straight female, especially a *white* straight female, is the social equivalent in woke high schools of wearing a MAGA hat or a pro-life T-shirt.

As many as 23 percent of teens with gender dysphoria are autistic.[29]

Your best bet is to get them away from toxic friend groups, peers, Discord chat rooms, and classrooms where this contagion is spreading. Just like with COVID, masks won't help with this virus. Social distancing, however, works great. Find some distance, fast.

It doesn't help that the beauty industry has started using male models in advertisements for women's cosmetics. Or that clothing for young girls looks like it was designed by porn stars. I took my daughter shopping for a new dress, and all the dresses at the mall were ultra-short, had cut-out backs, and holes where the pockets should be. They looked like they came with their own morning-after pills.

American culture wants your precious daughter to grow up to be a hooker or a dude, and there is no middle ground. You must help her rediscover the forgotten middle path: a "regular girl."

Hold Fast to the Truth

A boy at my friend's son's elementary school in Oregon claims to be "gender fluid." Some days he feels mostly like a girl, and other days he only feels a little like a girl, according to the boy's mother. In an absolutely amazing coincidence, his mother gave him a strange, gender-neutral name at birth, almost as if she knew he wouldn't grow up to be a "normal" boy. For his ninth birthday, his parents invited the entire class to his party, which featured the birthday boy walking a runway in full drag. His mother, you will be shocked to learn, is a pediatrician.

Out of an estimated 8,700,000 animal species on earth, biologists have so far identified a grand total of two genders.[30] Two! So go ahead and teach your children the immutable truth: men cannot transform into women, no matter how many people in positions of influence say otherwise. Girls cannot turn into boys, though some of them may wish they could. No one can be both genders, or neither gender, or several genders, or change genders depending on the day of the week or their horoscope.

What's going on? Well, it's very simple: it's all bullshit. Refuse to give this nonsense any chance to ferment in your children's minds. It's the equivalent of teaching them the Earth is flat and is at the center of the solar system. Some people feel like they are a different gender, that's true, but that is a feeling, not a biological fact.

It makes me laugh that this even has to be stated, and it also makes me cry.

You are the last line of defense here—your children's (and grand-children's) future fertility, mental well-being, intact body parts, and ability to live normal lives free of unnecessary and dangerous medical intervention are defenseless to this highly contagious virus. You have to hold the line on their behalf.

Any fully grown adult can live as they choose. Go for it, fully grown adults! Transgender adults have the right to life, liberty, and the pursuit of happiness—just like every other human being on earth. Live whatever way you like. I don't really care. Just please—leave the kids out of it.

Does this make me "transphobic"? Please—I don't hate trans people; hate is against my religion. However, based on the vicious aggression towards normal people by angry transgender people, you're damn right I'm scared of they/them!

Become the Domestic Extremist Your Family Needs

In the end, you must claim the mantle of domestic extremism yourself. Dig down deep, throw away old ideas, and become the domestic extremist you were always meant to be. The real key to authentic domesticity is having the *courage* to take control of your family and rediscovering the magical power of saying "no."

The children most likely to seek authority elsewhere—online, their friends, at school—are, obviously, those without strong influences at home. It's your job to be the strong influence at home. The rate of gender dysphoria and trans identity among teenage foster children is, not surprisingly, much higher than that of children raised in intact two-parent homes. "Studies have found that about 30 percent of youth in foster care identify as LGBTQ+ and 5 percent as transgender, in comparison to 11 percent and 1 percent of youth not in foster care."[31]

It should be obvious why that is. With no buffers and no strong parental authority to pump the brakes, foster kids get the full firehose-in-the-face blast of bad cultural influences. Like other dysfunctions and mental illnesses, these ideas find their way to the most susceptible among us. Like water, this poison flows into voids and seeks the lowest ground. Children with weak, woke adults in their lives are going to have a hard time escaping the maw of the ravenous trans machine, staying off drugs, and forming stable adult relationships.

Be *parents* to the children you brought into this world. Relinquishing your parental authority is a cowardly surrender that will echo long into the future. It is also a self-perpetuating cycle. Weak parents produce weak children, who themselves will not be able to assert their authority over their kids. Show your kids that their parents are forces for good, and they'll do the same for theirs. Develop in them a healthy, natural skepticism of officials, institutions, and malignant cultural influencers. Remember when "questioning authority" and "speaking truth to power" used to be progressive buzz words? It's time to reclaim those for ourselves.

Who's the boss? You are, if you want to live.

Reclaiming your parental authority is the only way you can usher your family across the dangerous cultural minefield unscathed. Succeed, or face your own personal extinction bottleneck.

CHAPTER 21

Live Happily Ever After

Make America Normal Again

*Courage! Do not fall back; in a little the place will be
yours. Watch! When the wind blows my banner against
the bulwark, you shall take it.*

— *Saint Joan of Arc*

All about the Numbers

I may be a domestic extremist, but I am also a realist. I have seen some
stuff, okay? My friends, my family, and I have, *gasp*, done plenty of
the stuff I recommend you avoid doing.

I know people for whom divorce was the only possible option. For
example, my own mother. I know people who ended up with zero or
one child, not out of choice but because of a million life circumstances.
Spouses change. Spouses die. Accidents, abuse, addictions, and overdoses thin the precious herd; many young men and women get sidelined
by real tragedy over time. My heart aches for people who are not able
to achieve the baby numbers they desire: those afflicted with chronic
infertility, repeated miscarriage, domestic problems, inability to find a
spouse, inability to maintain a marriage, and all the rest. Life can

absolutely *suck*. We all contend with unfair circumstances, and every one of us makes bad choices and stupid mistakes. Yes, yes, yes.

That's precisely why *the more warm bodies we can throw at this problem, the higher our chance of success!*

Not all baby sea turtles make it to the sea; many hatchlings in each clutch of eggs become lunch for hungry seagulls and crabs. Only one in a thousand baby sea turtles survives into adulthood. Does the mama turtle quit, hang up her turtle ovaries (if they even have those; I'm not a marine biologist), and retire to Boca? No. She simply lays a ton of eggs—up to two hundred a season. She is hedging her bets!

I am not telling you to lay eggs. If only it were that easy! (I'm sure America's scientists are already working on artificial egg-laying technology for transgender women down at the bio-labs. They've got 'em working in shifts!)

But this is a numbers game. As of this writing, the total number of Americans who can achieve their desired level of domestic extremism—in the form of lasting happiness and a solid family with their ideal number of children—is much, much lower than it needs to be. These are rookie numbers; we've got to get these numbers up.

How? First, we have to increase the number of people who are *able* to achieve true domestic extremism, and second, we need more people to *attempt* to do so. Maybe you know someone in college who isn't sure what to do with her life—if she should get married, or even have kids at all—but hasn't been fully terraformed yet by the Marxist strip mines masquerading as gender studies courses. "Excuse me young lady, you there, in line for a venti pumpkin spice latte! You look reasonably fertile. Have you ever considered a life of domestic extremism?"

It's a radical alternative lifestyle, after all, so there's no reason why young people *wouldn't* embrace it. They've embraced plenty of others, am I right? America's got room for Juggalos, Beliebers, Swifties,

Cottagecorers, gamers, incels, gymcels, Redditors, streamers, e-girls, punks, goths, dorks, stoners, ravers, art hoes, Marxists, tattoo fiends, cosplayers, crypto bros, furries, and the Faction of Truth—there is no end to the list of fringe aesthetic movements they build their lives around.

Even better, the domestic extremist lifestyle is one of the only aesthetics left that's *still* fringe, radical, and far outside the mainstream. Want to be a true counterculture rebel? Looking for a lifestyle that signals to your friends that you are truly punk rock? Get married young, raise your own kids, and have more than three of them. Imagine their shock!

It's time to flip this around. If the Earth's magnetic poles can flip, we can flip domestic extremism. Just think: if only two or three more seniors in each high school graduating class could be diverted from a lifetime of parenting fur babies towards one parenting human babies, we could take back the country and rescue civilization.

Do they still read the 1915 poem "The Road Not Taken" at every high school graduation? I'm guessing no, since Robert Frost has been canceled and replaced with America's new poet laureate, the unintentionally hilarious Amanda Gorman. But our teachers always used the poem as a metaphor exhorting us to take "the road less traveled," i.e., the lesser-worn path of two going through the woods. The message they sent to generations of kids was: be a nonconformist, don't follow the pack, and choose your own less-traveled way through the woods of life.

Kids, have I got a less-traveled path for you!

Here in the third decade of the twenty-first century, you would do well to avoid the well-worn path. Yes, it leads you through some pretty scenery, but without warning, it suddenly veers off a cliff.

With apologies to Robert Frost, here's my updated version of the poem:

Two roads diverged in a rainbow wood,
And sorry I could not travel both
And keep my gender, long I stood
And looked down one as far as I could
To where it bent in the undergrowth;

And saw depression, despair, and dying alone
In a State-run nursing home.
Then took the other, as just as fair,
And having perhaps a more hopeful vibe,
Because it would lead to multiple generations
Of non-feline descendants from my tribe.

Not everyone will be able to choose the domestic extremist option. Which is why more of you must try.

Welcome to the Party, Pal!

Are you ready? Becoming a domestic extremist may change your life, rescue your children from a terrible fate, and even, yes, save the country. (At least, the parts that are still worth saving. The list grows shorter by the day.)

Imagine a world where adults are empowered to make choices that put their families and well-being first. This world *already exists*, only it's invisible. You won't see people like this celebrated on social media or in fawning *People* magazine stories. Why? Because they are defeating the nihilism of modern life—by completely *ignoring* it and refusing to let contemporary trends derail what they know to be true. They are living extremely domestic lives that are centered around home and family formation.

To the average modern first-world family, domestic extremists may indeed look extreme: they tend to have at least three kids, they may homeschool their young children, and they may dress their children in clothes that affirm their birth gender. If you live in a progressive town, you can usually spot these dangerous extremists in your midst. Their house may be the only one on the block that doesn't have a Trans Lives Matter sign on the front lawn, but in the backyard, you'll hear the happy shouts of children playing.

We live in an upside-down world where "normal" people minding their own beeswax, just going about their lives, represent an existential threat to the ruling class. By rejecting contemporary morals and values in favor of old, out-of-favor *human* values (the ones that worked pretty well for thousands of years), these families are powerful rebukes to the shrieking elites who are trying to bring them to heel.

They hate us 'cause they ain't us.

Extremely domestic families make extremely hardened targets. Fake news, false narratives, dangerous social trends, and poisonous mainstream beliefs cannot easily penetrate their defensive shield. It's not foolproof, of course—nothing is—but extreme domesticity offers you the best possible way to survive and yes, thrive, in such bleak cultural conditions.

Families raising children who consider God and their parents the final authority are a grave and growing threat to progressive elites. In a way, families like this are THE existential threat to the status quo. Families who don't mindlessly buy the products in the commercials, who don't mindlessly watch whatever's streaming on Netflix, who do their best to dam the flood of race, gender, and porn-infused contemporary school curricula from swamping their children's minds—these families are incubating a new generation of normal people.

Choosing to live the way American families lived for decades is unfashionable today and, yes: extreme. Ideas once widely acknowledged as the best things in life by your great-grandmothers—finding true love, getting married young, having babies—are suddenly taboo and hopelessly cringe. They are things young women are taught to avoid and delay at all costs.

Except there *is* a cost. Walk into any fertility clinic and look at the tear-streaked faces of the couples desperate to conceive. Read the stories of women who feel duped and deceived by the "reproductive choice" industry and the dating industry. If you somehow manage to defeat the odds and slap together a family, you are forced to cynically hold your husband and children at arm's length, complain about them to your friends, and shudder at the very *idea* of having more kids.

You may have achieved a family, but the current ideology maintains an iron grip on your heart and can't allow you to lean into it fully. To celebrate it. To be proud of the legacy you are building. "Legacy? The climate is going to kill us all in a few years! We're all gonna die!"

It's true, we will eventually die. But I'd bet you a million bucks that the climate *isn't* what's going to kill you.

Becoming more domestic is organic. It's all-natural. It's the biological equivalent of not eating GMO foods. It's what you are meant to be doing. Young women grow up knowing what they want, but they soon get caught in a vicious cycle of peer pressure, to "never settle" and to "find themselves."

There is no more dangerous terror group in modern American society than a self-sufficient, loving family *who has no need for the people in charge*. Even worse, these families *dare* to reject mainstream culture and the toxic nihilism it manufactures and then sells back to you as "progress." That makes them—you!—difficult to control.

Never forget: the powers that be *want* broken families.

They *require* children to hate their parents and to look instead to the "experts" and "officials" for love and affirmation.

They have convinced legions of young women to self-sterilize, run out the clock on their fertility, and exterminate their own children.

They have reduced masculinity to a disease and seduced young men into lifelong pornography addictions.

They have methodically and deliberately sown confusion and psychological trauma in young children by brainwashing them to doubt something as obvious and innate as their own gender.

They are grooming students with X-rated "sex education" that renders them unfit for healthy relationships and parenthood but perfectly equipped for lucrative careers as sex workers.

They have debased and demoralized the value of fidelity and loyalty in a mating pair, replacing it with more "liberating" trends like polyamory, open marriage, and multi-parent children.

Now you tell me: Who are the real extremists?

Courage!

Only normal people can win the culture back and save our civilization. The more domestic you are, the more power you will have to thwart their plans. They have a vested interest in you owning nothing, marrying nobody, and giving birth to no one. Do not forget this as you forge ahead! Why else do you think they work so hard to get you to reject wholesome domestic traditions in favor of brand-new globo-corp fake holidays like "Pride Month"? Why else are they so desperate to get nursing mothers back to work and away from their children as quickly as possible?

Sack the normies and you sack humanity. Today the nursing mothers, tomorrow the world. But the key to our victory is clear. It is simple, but not easy. Nothing worthwhile ever is. If you have gotten this far, you know what you have to do: you're going to have to claw back your God-given purpose in the Current Era. Be brave! Ladies, refuse to let them strip you of your ancient, profoundly female, wondrous superpowers.

To achieve your full domestic form, go ahead, make their day: unleash your femininity. Your inborn, self-evident gifts cannot be taken away from you so easily—which is why they want them so badly.

As we joyfully, confidently take the fight to our enemies, rejoice! You will know we are winning when you hear, echoing across the great plains, the lamentations of our spayed enemies and see them driven before us hauling bags filled with their fur babies. Recall the other famous words of Joan of Arc: "I am not afraid. I was born to do this."

Now go—and do likewise.

Be fruitful, and multiply.

And may you live happily ever after.

PART THREE

WHAT WINNING
LOOKS LIKE

Ten ~~Commandments~~ Life Hacks

*I have given you power to tread underfoot serpents
and scorpions and the whole strength of the enemy;
nothing shall ever hurt you. Yet do not rejoice that the
spirits submit to you; rejoice rather that your names are
written in heaven.*

— *Luke 10:18–20*

"Conan, what is best in life?"

*"To crush your enemies, see them driven before you, and
to hear the lamentation of their women!"*

— *Conan the Barbarian*

At Least It's an Ethos

For a muscular fantasy-world steppe barbarian, that's a pretty good
rule for living well.

For you and me, we need some simple rules that are just as specific
for what we want out of life. I'm going to go out on a limb and assume
you want the same thing I want: a basically happy, healthy life, a nice
family, plenty of children and grandchildren to warm me in my old age,
a loving spouse, and as few deathbed regrets as possible.

I thought I'd try to distill this book's worth of ideas into a short, simple list of helpful recommendations. Simple, but not easy!

Note: this list is aspirational. Few people will be able to check every box. That's okay. Most us fail to follow the actual Ten Commandments, and those were written on stone tablets and carried by Charlton Heston! Just do your best. Even a small change in a few areas can change your life over time.

But just imagine thousands—millions, even—of Americans, picking a few to try for themselves.

Would you, your family, and our country be better off?

My Ten Favorite Life Hacks

1. Have at least three children, if you can, and you don't have to stop there.
2. Marry young, try to stay married, and don't cheat.
3. Shun government-run schools and most colleges.
4. Avoid daycare like the plague (because it is a plague).
5. Don't rely on birth control or abortion to underwrite a destructive and unhealthy lifestyle.
6. Aim for femininity (or masculinity, if you are male) in your presentation and restraint in your behavior. In other words, no more Instagram selfies.
7. Don't "date" too much.
8. Stay home with your babies as long as you can.
9. Assert your authority over all matters related to your home and family.
10. Life is much too short. Live in such a way that at the end, you are at peace.

In other words, trust what you already know to be best in life!

CHAPTER 22

The Nuclear Option

Point of No Return

The old that is strong does not wither,
Deep roots are not reached by the frost.
From the ashes a fire shall be woken,
A light from the shadows shall spring;
Renewed shall be blade that was broken,
The crownless again shall be king.

— *J. R. R. Tolkien,* The Lord of the Rings

Renewal, Not Return

Bad news for some of you: a true "return" to the old ways, to classical, traditional home life, is not possible. That ship has sailed to the gray havens.

So what does winning this great culture war look like? Here's what it doesn't look like: millions of suburban families decamping to the woods and living off the land. If we all did that, the woods would be pretty crowded. I prefer to never go near a live chicken, and you can't make me.

Fortunately, you can embrace the domestic extremist lifestyle any-where. The beauty of the simple, almost imperceptible (to the outside world) changes you'll make is that they work in any environment, and in any type of household. The real "return" simply happens in your mind.

We can't go back in time—and we don't have to. You may not know this, but the female body is also a *time machine*. It is a slightly myste-rious portal between the beginnings of humanity and the most distant reaches of the future. It is a door between the heavenly realm of preex-istence and the world of the real. When the body produces a life, it is bringing a primordial act of creation into the present—and with it, a chance to start anew.

All you have to do is remember and reawaken these ancient memo-ries. Your ancestors long to see themselves echoed in the face of a child born hundreds, even thousands, of years after they breathed their last.

Let your descendants come! You are going to be a revolutionary. A radical. You are going to have to live with wild abandon, with reckless disregard for hidebound, mainstream rules.

Because the Current Way is not working. Everyone is unhappy, joyless, and stressed. It's time to try a new way. An old way, actually. It's the only way left!

My deepest wish is that some of those who read this will join me in taking back our modern nightmare of a culture—and our country—by becoming ever-so-slightly more domestic. Start small. Take baby steps. But hurry; we don't have much time.

What's coming our way is not going to be pleasant. I am not looking forward to the newfangled and exciting future our elites have planned for us. Things like pod life. Chinese-style social credit. Cancellation and speech codes. Mass consensus that little kids can switch genders. More young women tricked into relinquishing their precious souls and bodies to the Sex Industrial Complex. Older women robbed of the chance to raise children as they're herded instead onto a career path that leads them away from family formation.

More men and boys emasculated, branded "toxic," feminized, and disarmed of both spiritual tools and physical weapons. Businesses and schools dumping meritocracy in favor of strict racial quotas for hiring and admission. Disfavored ethnic groups made to bend the knee in the name of "equity" and "privilege."

And meanwhile, Big Tech, Big Pharma, and Big Corp are everywhere, always, watching and listening, swamping us with messages, mandates, guidelines, targeted ads, and nefarious psychological influences. Short-sighted and cruel economic policies are eating away at regular people as the elites get richer. Fentanyl overdoses are now the leading cause of death among Americans ages eighteen to forty-five.[1] Political oppression and persecution are rising—which you will soon find out if you make the mistake of having an opinion not ordained by the mainstream.

And everywhere, fertility rates are in freefall. Atomization, loneliness, childlessness, and psychic emptiness are epidemic.

Don't like it? Want to resist? Speak out? Good—that will make you easier to catch.

Your survival in this unpleasant dystopia will depend on specific, real-world actions you start taking today. Nihilism is not productive. The future is not yet written; with a little luck, we can turn this thing around. Not just survive, but bloom and grow for many vibrant generations to come, in our still-beloved, still-vibrant country.

Becoming a domestic extremist is your last best hope. That's why this book is aimed squarely at the people I am counting on to take the lead on this: American women. You've been playing at being girlbosses for years, and what has it gotten you? Now it's your real time to shine, ladies. If enough of you can shake the cold metal bit of modernity out of your mouths, break free from the feminist barn you didn't even realize you were trapped in, and run free, there is hope for all humanity.

It's time for all of us, men and women, to reject the bleak indoctrination we have all been breathing in like oxygen since birth.

Not all of you will figure out how to save yourselves. Some of you are not yet prepared to do what needs to be done. Fine, not everyone has to.

But families who can forge their own little cultures, who can fill their homes and their children with love and virtue and something stronger than any pleasures the internet can offer are unstoppable. Families like this are kryptonite to the ruling class.

With enough babies, your family will be far too big to fit in a pod anyway. The pod will reject *you*.

Victory via the Nuclear Option

Interesting term, "nuclear family." If you split a nuclear family up into its atomized pieces, it can set off a devastating chain reaction. The fallout spreads to everyone around it. But an *intact* nuclear family is a weapon with secret powers. It remains the most potent defense you can build against the Forces of Darkness.

Build your own adorable nuclear family and become radioactive to the Regime. It gives you untold superpowers, including long-lasting immunity from modern trends, media lies, and cultural rot. You will need as many superpowers as you can conjure to fight the supervillains arrayed against us. They fear the nuclear family, and they should, because they have no lasting defense against it. If you can get to the final level of the game without falling into the devious traps they placed in your path, you defeat the final boss. Congratulations.

If more people play and win, eventually it is Game Over for the bad guys.

If just a small fraction of young adults can be redirected from their current path and talked into becoming more domestic, it will spell the end for what ails us.

Your best protection is to invest all your youthful energy into building a family culture that is outside of, and in many cases opposed to, mainstream culture. Becoming more domestic means rediscovering much-maligned but tried-and-true traditions that have kept humanity going: marriage between a monogamous mating pair, a father and a mother together raising a child, multiple siblings, and childcare largely performed by family members instead of paid strangers.

It means resurrecting and renewing "archaic" values like chastity, modesty, honor, and loyalty. Imagine if every American under thirty decided to become a little more modest, maybe even dabble in chastity, and take a break from porn. Imagine if men reclaimed *chivalry* as a code. What would this country look like? I guarantee you it couldn't look any worse than it does now! Would more people be a little happier? They couldn't be any unhappier, right?

What will your daily life look like after you reassert your God-given authority over your domestic affairs, personal and private? What untold benefits could you reap from resisting the vapid, short-term temptations offered by our decadent culture? What would it be like to *choose* to live a life that gives you the best possible odds for leaving behind children and grandchildren who don't hate you or each other?

This is the road that is open to you—all you have to do is take the first step. It's not going to be hard for most of you to adopt this lifestyle. There's no special equipment or advanced degrees required. There's no math. Anyone can become a domestic extremist. If I can do it, trust me—so can you.

It's past time to reclaim our families and our female identities from the clutches of the cultural overlords.

We must do our best to become *more domestic than they could ever imagine.*

We will cling bitterly to our families, our men, our homes, our children, and our own identities.

We will refuse to believe the Big Lies of feminism.

We will reclaim our children, and what we teach them.

We will assert ownership and agency over our own lives.

We will crush their so-called culture—simply by exiting it.

Folks, we've got to do the work.

Even if means doing women's work.

Now begone, before we drop a house full of children on you!

CHAPTER 23

Saving the Planet—One Family at a Time

A Modest Proposal

*One cannot divine or forecast the conditions that will
make happiness; one only stumbles upon them by
chance, in a lucky hour, at the world's end, somewhere,
and·holds fast to the days.*

— Willa Cather

The Cost of Living (as a Domestic Extremist)

Having an adorable family and the ability to survive on one income so your wife can choose to stay home is a flex, as the kids say. Everyone wants to afford a place with a yard where the kids can frolic in the sprinklers and you can grill on Sunday. Women who choose to stay home with their babies use no fossil fuels since they don't commute to work. Their carbon footprint is toddler-sized.

We used to call this the American Dream: the ability to raise a family the way you want to. This is all but impossible now; economically out of reach for all but the highest earners or those willing to sacrifice not just luxuries, but basic necessities. Exhorting young women to quit their jobs and have five kids is easy for me to say—I won't be there to help pay for groceries or put gas in the minivan.

Consider that our modern economy was only recently reconfigured around a two-parent income. It's funneling you straight into a trap designed to separate mothers from their children often and early. It yanks your babies out of your arms and tosses them into the nearest infant prison. The economic reality of daily life is organized around mothers getting back to work as fast as possible. Otherwise, GDP might go down. Heaven forfend!

Resisting the double-income-plus-daycare lifestyle is almost impossible unless you are self-sufficient in some other way. This conundrum reminds me of the scene in *Poltergeist* when the portal to hell opens up in the children's bedroom, and they cling desperately to their headboard as everything in the room is sucked into its gaping vortex.

What is to be done? Tucker Carlson and Blake Masters have spoken eloquently about this double-income dilemma. Former domestic extremist Elizabeth Warren even wrote a whole book about it called *The Two-Income Trap* before she ditched common sense and went full native.

Jokes aside, it's a painful obstacle that prevents many from achieving their dreams of a domestically extreme life. Food, rent, or kids—you can only choose two.

Instead of wasting billions of dollars on improved Metaverse VR goggles, drones for delivering dog food, and shady bioweapons labs in unstable foreign nations, why can't we target some resources to young married couples who want bigger families?

You want to call it a tax break? Fine. Think of it instead as a Domestic Extremist Genius Grant to worthy, family-minded married couples. Complete an application, make your case, receive your funds, and stay home with your newborn.

Given the numbers of thieves and lowlifes among our citizenry, we would need a robust anti-fraud process, but we'll work out those details later. If we really care about saving the country and encouraging people to stay home with their youngest kids, we are going to have to declare a state of emergency. This is a national crisis, and it's time for action.

We don't need more daycare subsidies or "quality affordable child-care," as Nancy Pelosi laughably calls it. The federal government spends $26 billion a year on childcare and early childhood programs.[1] Meanwhile, most babies are already born with high-quality affordable childcare built right in—otherwise known as "their mother."

Here's how it might work. Let's say you are married and want to have a third child. You can't stand the thought of returning straight to work after this one, you can barely afford your current daycare, and you want to be able to nurse your baby for longer than maternity leave will allow. But you and your spouse don't make enough money to survive on a single income. You're going to have to move in with your parents or to a much smaller home to make it happen.

I once faced this dilemma myself. Getting myself out of my office job so I could stay home with my last baby required an enormous reordering of our lives. My husband needed to find a new job, and it all had to happen fast. My go-back-to-work date was swiftly approaching. My coworkers at the office were preparing for my triumphant return after a couple months off. I knew there was no way I'd leave my newborn with a stranger, but with a large family in a very expensive city, my income helped keep the household afloat.

I prayed for assistance. Mostly to Saint Joseph, begging him to carry me through this crisis.

Help arrived shortly after, in the form of a new job for my husband. By the skin of our teeth, we squeaked through the bottleneck. I gleefully informed my company that I was quitting for good, giving up my platinum perks for something better—the unrivaled joy of cuddling and nursing my last newborn for as long as I wanted. They'd have to kill me to get her away from me. Actually, they wouldn't have to—the stress of being away from her would have killed me.

I thought about my female colleagues who had returned to work after six weeks, their tiny newborns enrolled "in school" for nine hours a day, and I shuddered.

We were lucky that we were relatively established in careers and had other options. If we had been young and just starting a family, it would have been impossible.

Obey the Babies

It's time for America to start doing what the babies want for once. What do babies want? Their needs are simple and ancient. You know what they want—you wanted all the same things once. They want to be conceived. They want to be permitted to be born. They want to be loved by both their natural parents. They want to be breastfed and kept close to their mother for as long as possible. They want siblings. They want to spend their days at home, not shuttled to a strip mall storefront baby prison that smells like vomit and Lysol. They want their mother's arms and their father's hugs.

It's not a lot to ask. They simply want what every baby ever born has wanted!

The Domestic Extremist Genius Grant could act as a desperately needed release valve to the incredible pressure young families are under. It's a good deal. A smart trade.

Parents get: enough money to raise their own baby and conserve their energy so they can have a few more.

America gets: happier families, calmer children, lower rates of female despair, a more robust culture, more future taxpayers, and a population no longer in irreversible collapse.

What form would this money take? I'm not an economist, so I'm just spitballing here, but how about a stipend for the third child, an exemption from all income taxes for the first year or so, 100 percent tax-deductible baby gear and supplies—and zero percent interest on a first home. I don't know! You smart guys can figure that out, but all I know is, if we have enough money to send hundreds of billions of dollars of weapons to Ukraine and the Taliban, maybe we can help some American families grow.

Next time you see a baby, look into his eyes. He is telling you that he agrees with me.

Or maybe he's just making a weird face while he poops.

Coda

To those who think becoming domestically extreme is out of reach economically: Do not reject it as a luxury lifestyle. You don't have that luxury. The global economy, barring total zombie apocalypse or the sun exploding, will continue cranking right along. People will be born, live, work, and die. You go to war with the ovaries you've got.

There is no time like your present to start your future. You can start *this very second*, the moment you put down this book. Don't let other people dictate when you're allowed to seek a better, more fulfilling way of life; not even me.

I have faith in you—together, we can do this.

Now go and let your heart lead you to the hidden path that's always been there, just waiting for you to find it.

Death closes all: but something ere the end,
Some work of noble note, may yet be done,
Not unbecoming men that strove with Gods.
The lights begin to twinkle from the rocks:

Acknowledgements

The awkward truth about writing a book about the importance of family is that, in order to write said book, you are constantly forced to shoo said family out of your writing room, lock the door, and drag heavy furniture in front of it. So first, let me thank my children for (mostly) letting me attempt a project this big. Bringing you guys into the world is the only truly worthwhile thing I've ever done or ever will.

This book started as an idea I had a long time ago, but I probably never would have gotten around to writing it if Tony Daniel had not slid into my DMs on Twitter. Thank you, Tony, my wise and wonderful Regnery editor, for talking me into this. (My children, however, would like a word.) Thank you also to the inimitable Harry Crocker for his warmth and faith in me. Invictus maneo!

Props also to Mark Hemingway (and his excellent taste) for giving Tony the idea for a Peachy book. I'm much obliged to you, sir. (My children, however, would like a word.)

Let it be known that Peachy Keenan could never have blossomed into the internet nano-celebrity she is today without the discerning gentlemen at The American Mind. Ryan Williams, Matthew Peterson, James Poulos, Spencer Klavan, David Bahr, and Seth Barron: you are, as my mother would say, mensches of the highest order.

Shout out to the brilliant and very patient Mike Jackson of Beck & Stone for taking my idea for the cover and designing it so wonderfully. I'm eternally grateful.

To my American Mind readers and my followers on Twitter: Your support, encouragement, DMs, and kind words truly mean the world to me. Thank you for Supporting Womyn's Voices™—or at least, this woman's voice.

I'd also like to thank the Based Queens out there who are Doing the Work: writing, tweeting, podcasting, and doing what they can to take our culture back from the fetid feminist swamp, especially the fabulous Noelle Mering, Helen Roy, Inez Stepman, Bridget Phetasy, Mary Harrington, Louise Perry, and Alex Kaschuta, among others. Buy their books, read their essays, and listen to their words. They are helping lead us out of the fell darkness.

To my friends in real life and in various Fed-proof digital encrypted chats (you know who you are, and probably so do the Feds): thank you for your jokes, your edifying fellowship, and for creating an oasis of sanity in a universe gone mad.

I also want to acknowledge some amazing mothers I am privileged to know—my fellow OG domestic extremists. You won't find them on Twitter or TV. Instead, the Real Trad Wives of America are doing the heavy lifting to keep civilization from total collapse—by simply and quietly raising lovely families. M.D., N.T., E.G., M.C., L.B., N.M., M.B., M.P., C.H., E.A., C.R., H.G., K.T., A.L., L.B., M.G., G.T., M.G., A.Z., B.F., and so many others: I am grateful every day for your friendship and your example. If our clueless overlords knew how powerful you were, they would be sore afraid. May Our Lady's mantle always protect you and thank you for (mostly) having different initials.

I could never have accomplished a project like this without the examples of my magnificent mother and my marvelous mother-in-law, archetypal boomers who rejected second-wave feminism and chose to do selfish things like "stay home" to "raise kids," much to the dismay of their bra-burning peers. With a couple dozen grandchildren between the two of them, their lives are proof of concept that kids are good, and more kids are even better.

Thank you to my siblings, who tolerate their sister's ~~rants~~ musings and are excellent parents themselves. Our relationship today is proof that there is nothing like having brothers and sisters, and you're going to need as many as you can get. A special thanks to my eagle-eyed sister for tirelessly reading and copyediting everything I send her!

To my haters, past, present, and future: I can't quite thank you, but I forgive you and I pray daily for your eternal souls not to burn in hell.

Of course, I wouldn't be the domestic extremist I am today without my husband, a man who looks excellent in a tuxedo and happens to be a wonderful cook *and* a certified newborn swaddling expert. My real life began the fateful night we met. He talked me into taking this wild ride with him, and I'm glad I said yes, to all of it. He is the real peach behind Peachy.

I wrote this book mostly on the weekends, which is where, you know, moms keep all their "free time." These are the brief fractions of a second between basketball practice, baseball practice, ballet, gymnastics, music lessons, Boy Scouts, play rehearsal, haircuts, doctor's appointments, dentist appointments, Sunday Mass, Target trips, birthday parties, and fifty thousand other tasks that somehow must get done. I truly believe I only made it to the end of this monumental undertaking (and didn't end up at the undertakers) thanks to the intercession of Saint Francis de Sales, patron saint of writers, Saint Joseph, patron saint of families, and Saint Agatha, patron saint of women in danger. Pray for them, and please, pray for me.

And finally, thank *you*, dear reader, for getting this far. An unread book is the sound of one hand clapping. I truly hope you enjoyed it.

The culture is lit and I had a ball. I guess I'm signing off after all.

— PEACHY KEENAN, *somewhere in California, spring 2023*

P.S. If any of you care to drop me a note, you can reach me on Twitter @keenanpeachy.

Notes

Why This Book

Epigraph: Ernst Jünger's *The Forest Passage*.

1. Danedri Herbert, "Justice Dept. Threatens to Sic FBI on Parents as Domestic Terrorists," The Sentinel, October 11, 2021, https://sentinelksmo.org/justice-dept -threatens-to-sic-fbi-on-parents-as-domestic-terrorists.
2. Lauren Chen (@TheLaurenChen), "These people belong in jail. This is a hill I'm willing to die on," Twitter, July 2, 2022, 9:25 p.m., https://twitter.com /TheLaurenChen/status/1543405646049058816.

Introduction

Epigraphs: Voltaire and Aristotle.

1. Janet Adamy, "Births in U.S. Drop to Levels Not Seen Since 1979," *Wall Street Journal*, May 5, 2021, https://www.wsj.com/articles/births-in-u-s-drop-to-levels-not -seen-since-1979-11620187260.
2. Jon Miltimore, "Black Lives Matter's Goal to 'Disrupt' the Nuclear Family Fulfills a Marxist Aim That Goes Back a Century and a Half," FEE Stories, September 24, 2020, https://fee.org/articles/black-lives-matter-s-goal-to-disrupt-the-nuclear-family -fits-a-marxist-aim-that-goes-back-a-century-and-a-half.
3. James Poulos, *Human, Forever: The Digital Politics of Spiritual War* (Canonic, 2021).
4. Jacob Siegel, "The Red-Pill Prince," *Tablet*, March 20, 2022, https://www.tabletmag .com/sections/news/articles/red-pill-prince-curtis-yarvin.
5. *Tucker Carlson Tonight*, August 1, 2022, accessed via https://www.dailymotion .com/video/x8ctd1e.

Chapter 1: Your Fleeting Fertility

Epigraphs: Max Fischer in *Rushmore* and Elon Musk.

1. Jill Filipovic, "Women Are Having Fewer Babies because They Have More Choices," *New York Times*, June 27, 2021, https://www.nytimes.com/2021/06/27/opinion /falling-birthrate-women-babies.html.
2. Bryan Walsh, "Future Perfect," *Vox*, January 1, 2022, https://link.vox.com/view/6 08adc1091954c3cef028496fmq9p.2bn/6241f153.
3. "U.S. Pet Ownership Statistics," American Veterinary Medical Association, 2018, https://www.avma.org/resources-tools/reports-statistics/us-pet-ownership- statistics.

4. United Nations, "World Population Prospects 2022," Department of Economic and Social Affairs, https://population.un.org/wpp/Maps.
5. James Gallagher, "Fertility Rate: 'Jaw-Dropping' Global Crash in Children Being Born," BBC News, July 15, 2020, https://www.bbc.com/news/health-53409521.
6. Emil Vollset et al., "Fertility, Mortality, Migration, and Population Scenarios for 195 Countries and Territories from 2017 to 2100: A Forecasting Analysis for the Global Burden of Disease Study," *Lancet* 396 (July 14, 2020), https://doi.org/10.1016/S0140-6736(20)30677-2.
7. Luke Rogers, "Covid-19, Declining Birth Rates, and International Migration Resulted in Historically Small Population Gains," United States Census Bureau, December 21, 2021, https://www.census.gov/library/stories/2021/12/us-population-grew-in-2021-slowest-rate-since-founding-of-the-nation.html.
8. Katherine Schaeffer, "Striking Findings from 2021," Pew Research, December 17, 2021, https://www.pewresearch.org/fact-tank/2021/12/17/striking-findings-from-2021.
9. "Farmer Bill," *Land Report*, January 11, 2021, https://landreport.com/2021/01/farmer-bill.
10. Claire O'Neill, "IVF Success Rates by Age in 2022—United States Data," Fertility Space, n.d., https://fertilityspace.io/blog/ivf-success-rates-by-age-in-2021-united-states-data.
11. "The Growing Popularity of Egg Freezing," Quartz, February 8, 2022, https://qz.com/2122021/preserving-fertility-the-growing-popularity-of-egg-freezing.
12. Karen Gilchrist, "Egg Freezing, IVF, and Surrogacy: Fertility Benefits Have Evolved to Become the Ultimate Workplace Perk," MSN, March 14, 2022, www.msn.com/en-us/money/markets/egg-freezing-ivf-and-surrogacy-fertility-benefits-have-evolved-to-become-the-ultimate-workplace-perk/ar-AAV1AKP.
13. Ibid.
14. Ibid.
15. "What Is Chekhov's Gun? Definitions, Tips and Examples," ReedsyBlog, May 28, 2018, https://blog.reedsy.com/chekhovs-gun.

Chapter 2: Your Role

Epigraphs: BAP's *Bronze Age Mindset* and G. K. Chesterton.

1. Tim Teeman, "Top Trans Officer Bree Fram on the Military, Marriage, and Joining Space Force," Daily Beast, August 20, 2021, https://www.thedailybeast.com/top-trans-officer-bree-fram-on-the-military-marriage-and-joining-space-force.
2. A curette is a thin metal surgical tool used to scrape the contents of the uterus during an abortion.
3. Benedict Carey and Robert Gebeloff, "Many People Taking Antidepressants Discover They Cannot Quit," *New York Times*, April 7, 2018, https://www.nytimes.com/2018/04/07/health/antidepressants-withdrawal-prozac-cymbalta.html.
4. Kurt Zindulka, "Majority of Women Remain Childless at Thirty for First Time Ever in Britain," Breitbart, January 28, 2022, https://www.breitbart.com/europe/2022/01/28/majority-of-women-remain-childless-at-thirty-for-first-time-in-britain.
5. Mary Harrington, "Reactionary Feminism," *First Things*, June 2021, https://www.firstthings.com/article/2021/06/reactionary-feminism.

Chapter 3: Your Gender

Epigraphs: *The Big Lebowski* and Matt Walsh's 2022 documentary, *What Is a Woman?*.

1. Ryan Smith, "Adele's 'I Love Being a Woman' BRIT Awards Speech Sparks Transphobia Debate," *Newsweek*, February 9, 2022, https://www.newsweek.com/adeles-i-love-being-woman-brit-awards-speech-sparks-transphobia-debate-1677505.
2. Cheryl Cooky, "Lia Thomas' NCAA Championship Performance Gives Women Sports a Crucial Opportunity," NBC News, March 21, 2022, https://www.nbcnews.com/think/opinion/we-should-be-celebrating-lia-thomas-we-did-jackie-robinson-ncna1292521.
3. "Eric Vilain," UCLA Institute for Society and Genetics, https://socgen.ucla.edu/eric-vilain.
4. "Gender Questions Surround Track and Field Star," NPR, September 14, 2009, https://www.npr.org/templates/story/story.php?storyId=112810116.
5. Abigail Shrier, "The Transgender Threat to Women's Sports," *Newsweek*, October 20, 2020, https://www.newsweek.com/transgender-threat-womens-sports-opinion-1540418.
6. Ibid.
7. Audrey Conklin, "Petit Family Murderer Says He Is Transgender, Taking Hormone Pills," Daily Caller, October 30, 2019, https://dailycaller.com/2019/10/30/petit-family-murderer-transgender.
8. "Half of All Transgender Prisoners Are Sex Offenders or Dangerous Category A Inmates," Fair Play for Women, November 9, 2017, https://fairplayforwomen.com/transgender-prisoners.

Chapter 4: Your Virtues

Epigraph: Marilyn Monroe.

1. Bridget Phetasy, "I Regret Being a Slut," *Beyond Parody with Bridget Phetasy* (Substack), August 17, 2022, https://bridgetphetasy.substack.com/p/slut-regret.
2. Alan, "Antes e depois do feminismo: 37 exemplos de como o feminismo destrói mulheres por dentro e por fora," Liberalismo da Zoeira, August 5, 2018, https://liberalismodazoeira.com/antes-e-depois-do-feminismo-37-exemplos-de-como-o-feminismo-destroi-mulheres-por-dentro-e-por-fora.
3. Alyssa Rosenberg, "'WAP' Is Completely Filthy. We Could Use a Lot More Pop Culture Like It," *Washington Post*, August 18, 2020, https://www.washingtonpost.com/opinions/2020/08/18/wap-is-completely-filthy-we-could-use-lot-more-pop-culture-like-it.
4. Margaret Harper McCarthy, "Camille Paglia's 'Sexual Realism,'" Public Discourse, August 16, 2018, https://www.thepublicdiscourse.com/2018/08/39367.
5. Anonymous, "How to Hide a Promiscuous Past from Your New Man," AFRU, https://afru.com/hide-a-promiscuous-past/.
6. "Asexual Spectrum—from Ace to Z," Asexuals.net, n.d., https://www.asexuals.net/asexual-spectrum.
7. Magdalene Taylor, "The 'Breeding Kink,' Explained," Giddy, May 7, 2021, https://getmegiddy.com/breeding-kink-explained.
8. Jaimee Bell, "What Is a Breeding Fetish?" Sofia Gray, July 31, 2020, https://sofiagray.com/blog/what-is-a-breeding-fetish.

9.   Marissa Newby, "Internalized Misogyny in Breeding and Impregnation Kink," 4W, September 8, 2021, https://4w.pub/internalized-misogyny-in-breeding-and -impregnation-kink.

Chapter 5: Men

Epigraphs: C. S. Lewis's *The Abolition of Man* and Camille Paglia.
1.   Scottie Andrew, "A Memorial to Firefighters Killed in 9/11 Was Vandalized in a New York Village," CNN, July 10, 2020, https://www.cnn.com/2020/07/10/us/9-11 -memorial-new-york-damaged-trnd/index.html.
2.   Robert Brodsky, "Thomas Jefferson Statue at Hofstra Relocated to College Museum," *Newsday*, July 23, 2020, https://www.newsday.com/long-island /education/thomas-jefferson-statue-hofstra-c17560.
3.   Carrie Gress, "Second-Wave Feminists Pushed the Sexual Revolution to End America, and It's Working," Ethics & Public Policy Center, April 19, 2022, https:// eppc.org/publication/second-wave-feminists-pushed-the-sexual-revolution-to-end -america-and-its-working.
4.   Katherine Schaeffer, "Striking Findings from 2021," Pew Research, December 17, 2021, https://www.pewresearch.org/fact-tank/2021/12/17/striking-findings-from -2021.
5.   Justin Wolfers, "More Woman Than Men Are Going to College. That May Change the Economy," *New York Times*, November 23, 2021, https://www.nytimes.com /2021/11/23/business/dealbook/women-college-economy.html.
6.   "Make vs. Female Incarceration Rates," Fair Punishment, May 11, 2022, https:// fairpunishment.org/male-vs-female-incarceration-rates.
7.   Wolfers, "More Women Than Men Are Going to College."
8.   Paul Hemez and Chanell Washington, "Number of Children Living Only with Their Mothers Has Doubled in Past 50 Years," United States Census Bureau, April 12, 2021, https://www.census.gov/library/stories/2021/04/number-of-children-living -only-with-their-mothers-has-doubled-in-past-50-years.html.
9.   Zenitha Prince, "Census Bureau: Higher Percentage of Black Children Live with Single Mothers," *Afro News*, December 31, 2016, https://afro.com/census-bureau -higher-percentage-black-children-live-single-mothers.
10. Vanessa Brown, "US Woman Serving 10 Years in Jail for Her Role in Mother's Murder Does Exclusive Interview with Dr. Phil," News.com (Australia), November 24, 2017, https://www.news.com.au/lifestyle/real-life/news-life/us-woman-serving -10-years-jail-for-her-role-in-mothers-murder-does-exclusive-interview-with-dr-phil /news-story/4b77caaedba514d40281b74e14c59578.
11. Tony Silva and Tina Fetner, "Men's Feminist Identification and Reported Use of Prescription Erectile Dysfunction Medication," *Journal of Sex Research* (February 1, 2022), https://doi.org/10.1080/00224499.2022.2029810.
12. Pascal-Emmanuel Gobry, "A Science-Based Case for Ending the Porn Epidemic," Ethics & Public Policy Center, December 15, 2019, https://eppc.org/publication /a-science-based-case-for-ending-the-porn-epidemic.
13. See the NoFap website, https://www.nofap.com.

Chapter 6: A Soul Mate

Epigraphs: *101 Dalmatians* (1961) and Mark Twain.

1. Krista K. Westrick-Payne, "Marriage Rate in the U.S.: Geographic Variation, 2020," Bowling Green State University, 2022, https://www.bgsu.edu/ncfmr/resources/data /family-profiles/westrick-payne-marriage-rate-US-geographic-variation-2020-fp-22 -07.html.

2. Richard Fry and Kim Parker, "Rising Share of U.S. Adults Are Living without a Spouse or Partner," Pew Research Center, October 5, 2021, https://www.pewresearch .org/social-trends/2021/10/05/rising-share-of-u-s-adults-are-living-without-a-spouse -or-partner.

3. "Why Women File 80 Percent of Divorces," Divorce Source, January 20, 2016, https://www.divorcesource.com/blog/why-women-file-80-percent-of-divorces.

4. Diana Bruk, "Marriage Experts Explain Why Women Initiate Divorce More Than Men," Best Life, February 5, 2020, https://bestlifeonline.com/women-initiate-divorce -more-than-men.

5. Honor Jones, "How I Demolished My Life," *The Atlantic*, December 28, 2021, https://www.theatlantic.com/family/archive/2021/12/divorce-parenting/621054.

Chapter 7: Your Unborn Children

Epigraph: Saint Teresa of Calcutta (Mother Teresa).

1. Planned Parenthood, "Planned Parenthood of Greater New York Announces Intent to Remove Margaret Sanger's Name from NYC Health Center," news release, July 21, 2020, https://www.plannedparenthood.org/planned-parenthood-greater-new -york/about/news/planned-parenthood-of-greater-new-york-announces-intent-to -remove-margaret-sangers-name-from-nyc-health-center.

2. See, for example, the results of a search for "Planned Parenthood" at losangeles.net: https://www.losangeles.net/planned-parenthood-locations?page=1.

3. Camille Studer, "Legalization of Abortion: How Women's Strength Overturned Argentina," Azickia, March 10, 2021, https://azickia.org/legalization-of-abortion -how-womens-strength-overturned-argentina?lang=en.

4. Sam Dorman, "Unsealed Docs Show Planned Parenthood Charged $25G for Body Parts, Blood Samples within Months," Fox News, April 16, 2020, https://www .foxnews.com/politics/unsealed-invoices-planned-parenthood-daleiden-25k.

5. Life Institute, "Down Syndrome and Abortion—The Facts," Life Institute, https:// thelifeinstitute.net/info/down-syndrome-and-abortion-the-facts.

6. Amy Richards as told to Amy Barrett, "LIVES; When One Is Enough," *New York Times*, July 18, 2004, https://www.nytimes.com/2004/07/18/magazine/lives-when -one-is-enough.html.

7. Chrissy Clark, "Actress Busy Phillips Gave Thanks to Her Abortion for Her Professional Success," The Federalist, March 5, 2020, https://thefederalist.com/2020 /03/05/busy-phillips-gave-bizarre-rant-thanking-her-abortion-for-her-professional -success.

8. New York State Force on Life and the Law, *Thinking of Becoming an Egg Donor? Get the Facts before You Decide!* (New York: State of New York Health Department), https://www.health.ny.gov/publications/1127.pdf

9. Leah Campbell as told to Andrea Stanley, "Donating My Eggs Destroyed My Chance of Having Kids," Redbook, April 28, 2017, https://www.redbookmag.com/life /a49922/egg-donation-endometriosis.

10. Chris Bodenner, "Uneasy about the Ethics of Egg Donation," *Atlantic*, January 17, 2017, https://www.theatlantic.com/health/archive/2017/01/uncomfortable-with-the -ethics-of-donor-eggs/622610.

11. "Egg Donation—Donors—FAQ," A Perfect Match, 2017, https://www .aperfectmatch.com/Egg-Donation-Program/For-Donors/faq.html.

Chapter 8: Your Maternal Instinct

Epigraph: Agatha Christie.

1. Chelsea Conaboy, "Maternal Instinct Is a Myth That Men Created," *New York Times*, August 26, 2022, https://www.nytimes.com/2022/08/26/opinion/sunday /maternal-instinct-myth.html.

2. Ibid.

3. Merritt Tierce, "The Abortion I Didn't Have," *New York Times*, December 2, 2021, https://www.nytimes.com/2021/12/02/magazine/abortion-parent-mother- child.html.

4. Ibid.

5. Ibid.

6. Erica Komisar, *Being There: Why Prioritizing Motherhood in the First Three Years Matters* (New York: Tarcher Perigee, 2017).

7. Ibid.

8. Tierce, "The Abortion I Didn't Have."

Chapter 9: Your Real Job

Epigraphs: G. K. Chesterton and Klaus Schwab.

1. "Attorney General Merrick B. Garland Statement on Supreme Court Ruling in Dobbs v. Jackson Women's Health Organization," U.S. Department of Justice, news release no. 22-663, June 24, 2022, https://www.justice.gov/opa/pr/attorney-general-merrick -b-garland-statement-supreme-court-ruling-dobbs-v-jackson-women-s.

2. Katharina Buchholz, "Only 15 Percent of CEOs at Fortune 500 Companies Are Female," Statista, March 8, 2022, https://www.statista.com/chart/13995/female-ceos -in-fortune-500-companies.

3. Darina L., "Shocking Male vs Female CEO Statistics 2022," Leftronic, January 23, 2022, https://leftronic.com/blog/ceo-statistics.

4. Sheryl Sandberg, *Lean In: Women, Work, and the Will to Lead* (New York: Alfred A. Knopf, 2022), reprint edition.

5. "About Us," Catalyst.org, 2023, https://www.catalyst.org/mission.

6. "Workshops," Catalyst.org, 2023, https://www.catalyst.org/workshops.

7. "MARC by Catalyst," Catalyst.org, 2022, https://www.catalyst.org/marc.

8. Oriana Pawlyk, "Defense Bill Sets Up New Maternity Uniform Loan Program for Pregnant Troops," Military.com, December 10, 2020, https://www.military.com /daily-news/2020/12/10/defense-bill-sets-new-maternity-uniform-loan-program -pregnant-troops.html.

9. Mary to the angel of the Lord, Luke 1:37–38.

10. Thomas Barrabi, "Meta Investigated Sheryl Sandberg for Using Corporate Resources to Plan Wedding," *New York Post*, June 3, 2022, https://nypost.com/2022/06/03 /meta-investigated-sheryl-sandberg-for-using-corporate-resources-to-plan-wedding -report.

11. Ibid.

Chapter 10: Your Parental Authority

Epigraphs: Adam Swift and Melissa Harris-Perry.

1. Libs of TikTok (@libsoftiktok), "Seen in a New Jersey School," Twitter, June 21, 2022, 12:41 p.m., https://twitter.com/libsoftiktok/status/1539287405408157707.
2. Jan Jekielek, "Paul Rossi: How My Private School Tried to Force Me to Indoctrinate My Students," *Epoch Times*, March 24, 2022, https://www.theepochtimes.com/paul -rossi-how-my-private-school-tried-to-force-me-to-indoctrinate-my-students _4358267.html.
3. Paul Rossi, "I Refuse to Stand by While My Students Are Being Indoctrinated," Catholic Education Resource Center, April 2021, https://www.catholiceducation .org/en/education/philosophy-of-education/i-refuse-to-stand-by-while-my-students -are-being-indoctrinated.html.
4. Sarah Jones, "How to Manufacture a Moral Panic," *New York*, July 11, 2021, https://nymag.com/intelligencer/2021/07/christopher-rufo-and-the-critical-race -theory-moral-panic.html.
5. Benjamin Wallace-Wells, "How a Conservative Activist Invented Conflict over Critical Race Theory," *New Yorker*, June 18, 2021, https://www.newyorker.com /news/annals-of-inquiry/how-a-conservative-activist-invented-the-conflict-over -critical-race-theory.
6. Christopher F. Rufo, "Embracing Critical Race Theory, Teacher's Union Says They— Not Parents—Control What Kids Learn," *New York Post*, July 5, 2021, https:// nypost.com/2021/07/05/embracing-critical-theory-teachers-union-says-they-control -what-kids-learn.
7. Martin Bürger, "New Sex Ed Teaches New Jersey Minors about Sodomy and How to Consent to It," Lifesite News, June 8, 2020, https://www.lifesitenews.com/news /new-sex-ed-teaches-new-jersey-minors-about-sodomy-and-how-to-consent-to-it.
8. Tiara Mack (@MackDistrict6), "Really excited for the house sex ed bill hearing later today. Teaching comprehensive, queer inclusive, pleasure based sex was a highlight of my time teaching," Twitter, February 2, 2022, 10:47 a.m., https://twitter.com /MackDistrict6/status/1488901829886885892?s=20&t=pukjHXBHdIHp _Bkhw9nt3Q.
9. New Discourses, "Groomer Schools 1: The Long Cultural Marxist History of Sex Education," YouTube, November 19, 2021, https://www.youtube.com/ watch?v=tDEP0JGW3c8&ab_channel=NewDiscourses.
10. Paul Bois, "Disney CEO Bob Chapek Issues Groveling Apology to Company LGBTQ Activists," Breitbart, April 8, 2022, https://www.breitbart.com/entertainment/2022 /04/08/disney-ceo-bob-chapek-issues-groveling-apology-to-company-lgbtq- activists.
11. Elle Purnell, "Disney Executives Admit: Of Course We're Grooming Your Children," The Federalist, March 30, 2022, https://thefederalist.com/2022/03/30/disney -executives-admit-of-course-were-grooming-your-children.
12. Paul Bond, "Nearly Forty Percent of U.S. Gen Zs, 30 Percent of Young Christians Identify as LGBTQ, Poll Shows," *Newsweek*, October 20, 2021, https://www .newsweek.com/nearly-40-percent-us-gen-zs-30-percent-christians-identify-lgbtq -poll-shows-1641085.

13. "Children See Pornography as Young as Seven, New Report Finds," BBFC, September 26, 2019, https://www.bbfc.co.uk/about-us/news/children-see -pornography-as-young-as-seven-new-report-finds.

Chapter 11: Your Happiness

Epigraph: Proverbs 17:22.
1.   Betsey Stevenson and Justin Wolfers, "Paradox of Declining Female Happiness— December 2008 Revisions (draft)," Yale University Law School, October 16, 2008, https://law.yale.edu/sites/default/files/documents/pdf/Intellectual_Life/Stevenson _ParadoxDecliningFemaleHappiness_Dec08.pdf.
2.   Ibid.
3.   Alicia Lasek, "Older Women Account for Highest Rates of Rising Antidepressant Use: CDC," McKnight's Long-Term Care News, September 8, 2020, https://www .mcknights.com/news/clinical-news/older-women-account-for-highest-rates-of-rising -antidepressant-use-cdc.
4.   Sandy Cohen, "Suicide Rate Highest among Teens and Young Adults," UCLA Health, March 15, 2022, https://connect.uclahealth.org/2022/03/15/suicide-rate -highest-among-teens-and-young-adults.
5.   Song lyrics from the Billie Eilish song "xanny."
6.   Rainey Horwitz, "The Dalkon Shield," *Embryo Project Encyclopedia*, January 10, 2018, https://embryo.asu.edu/pages/dalkon-shield.
7.   Brooke Sjoberg, "'This Is So Unbelievably Common': Women on TikTok Are Talking about Their Experiences with Birth Control Side Effects," Daily Dot, May 7, 2022, https://www.dailydot.com/irl/birth-control-side-effects.
8.   From the reader comments on Kristin M. Lesney, "MY IUD Nightmare," Our Ordinary Life, March 2010, https://www.ourordinarylife.com/2010/03/my-iud- nightmare-mirena-iud-side-effects.

Chapter 12: A Domestic Extremist's Origin Story

Epigraph: G. K. Chesterton.
1.   Stu Cvrk, "Conquest's Second Law of Politics in America," RedState, December 29, 2020, https://redstate.com/stu-in-sd/2020/12/29/conquests-second-law-of-politics -in-america-n301120.
2.   Henry David Thoreau, *Walden*.
3.   These are references to the 1998 movie *The Big Lebowski*, which you should watch. I use many other references to this movie, one of my ur-texts, throughout the book; my fellow Achievers will find them all.
4.   Timothy H. J. Nerozzi, "Stacey Abrams Says 'No Such Thing' as 6-Week Fetal Heartbeat: 'Manufactured Sound,'" Fox News, September 22, 2022, https://www .foxnews.com/politics/stacey-abrams-says-no-such-thing-6-week-fetal-heartbeat -claims-manufactured-sound.

Chapter 13: Become an Anti-Feminist

Epigraphs: Proverbs 11:22 and Coco Chanel.
1.   Helen Lewis, "To Learn about the Far Right, Start with the Manosphere," *The Atlantic*, August 7, 2019, https://www.theatlantic.com/international/archive/ 2019/08/anti-feminism-gateway-far-right/595642.

2.   "The manosphere is a collection of websites, blogs, and online forums promoting (to varying degrees) masculinity, misogyny, and opposition to feminism." See "Manosphere," Wikipedia, n.d., https://en.wikipedia.org/wiki/Manosphere.

3.   Francesca Bacardi, "Christina Aguilera Sports Bedazzled Strap-On during LA Pride Performance," PageSix, June 13, 2022, https://pagesix.com/2022/06/13/christina -aguilera-wears-strap-on-during-la-pride-performance.

4.   Hilary Brueck, "Depression among Gen Z Is Skyrocketing—a Troubling Mental Health Trend That Could Affect the Rest of Their Lives," Business Insider, March 21, 2019, https://www.businessinsider.com/depression-rates-by-age-young-people -2019-3?op=1.

5.   Jenet Erickson, James L. McQuivey, and Brad Wilcox, "Perspective: What Does It Mean to Be 'Very Feminine' in America Today?" *Deseret News*, March 29, 2022, https://www.deseret.com/2022/3/28/22991318/perspective-in-praise-of-the-new -femininity-masculinity-gender-womens-history-month.

6.   Ibid.

Chapter 14: Explore Promiscuous Monogamy

Epigraphs: Mae West and *The Big Lebowski*.

1.   Louise Perry, *The Case against the Sexual Revolution* (Medford, Massachusetts: Polity Press, 2022), 79.

2.   Ibid., 111.

3.   McKenna Meyers, "Fatherless Daughters: How Growing Up without a Dad Affects Women," We Have Kids, March 7, 2022, https://wehavekids.com/family -relationships/When-Daddy-Dont-Love-Their-Daughters-What-Happens-to-Women -Whose-Fathers-Werent-There-for-Them.

4.   Eloise Hendy, "We've Spent 10 Years on Tinder—Will We Spend Eternity?" Yahoo!, August 18, 2022, https://www.yahoo.com/now/ve-spent-10-years-tinder-053000640 .html.

5.   Emily Witt, "A Hookup App for the Emotionally Mature," *New Yorker*, June 11, 2022, https://www.newyorker.com/culture/annals-of-inquiry/feeld-dating- app-sex.

6.   Tanyel Mustafa, "10 Years of Tinder: How Has the App Changed Dating, Sex and the Pursuit of Love?" *Metro*, August 18, 2022, https://metro.co.uk/2022/08/18/10 -years-of-tinder-how-has-the-app-changed-dating-sex-and-love-17118060.

7.   Louise Perry, "I'm 30. The Sexual Revolution Shackled My Generation," Common Sense, August 20, 2022, https://www.commonsense.news/p/im-30-the-sexual -revolution-shackled.

8.   "What's the Average Age of a Child's First Exposure to Porn?" Fight the New Drug, April 21, 2022, https://fightthenewdrug.org/real-average-age-of-first-exposure.

9.   "Principles of Harm Reduction," National Harm Reduction Coalition, 2020, https:// harmreduction.org/about-us/principles-of-harm-reduction.

10. Katie Notopolous, "Caleb from West Elm Is Bad at Dating but Probably Didn't Deserve Being Pushed through the TikTok Meat Grinder," Buzzfeed News, January 21, 2022, https://www.buzzfeednews.com/article/katienotopoulos/caleb-from-west -elm-meme.

11. Christine Emba, "Straight People Need Better Rules for Sex," *New York Times*, April 7, 2022, https://www.nytimes.com/2022/04/07/opinion/sex-consent-dating-boundaries.html.

12. Nick Levine, "What Is 'Radical Monogamy'?" *Vice*, March 8, 2022, https://www.vice.com/en/article/m7vxxy/what-is-radical-monogamy.

Chapter 15: Cultivate a Marriage Mindset

Epigraph: Audrey Hepburn.

1. Lyrics from Lana Del Rey's 2013 song "Young and Beautiful."

2. Brad Wilcox and Lyman Stone, "Too Risky to Wed in Your 20s? Not If You Avoid Cohabiting First," *Wall Street Journal*, February 5, 2022, https://www.wsj.com/articles/too-risky-to-wed-in-your-20s-not-if-you-avoid-cohabiting-first-11644037261.

3. Ibid.

4. Melissa Mitas, "'I Love Lucy': The Last Words Desi Arnaz Said to Lucille Ball and the Special Day He Said Them," CheatSheet, October 6, 2020, https://www.cheatsheet.com/entertainment/i-love-lucy-the-last-words-desi-arnaz-said-to-lucille-ball-and-the-special-day-he-said-them.html.

5. Elizabeth Boskey, PhD, "What Does Demisexual Mean?" Verywell Health, August 1, 2022, https://www.verywellhealth.com/demisexual-5077647.

6. "allosexual," Dictionary.com, July 30, 2020, https://www.dictionary.com/e/gender-sexuality/allosexual.

7. Pamela Druckerman, "When I Let My Husband Have a Threesome," *Esquire*, June 16, 2015, https://www.esquire.com/lifestyle/sex/a35748/threesome-for-husband-personal-essay.

8. Ibid.

9. Ibid.

Chapter 16: Have More Than Two Kids

Epigraph: C. S. Lewis.

1. Baxter Dmitry, "WEF Caught Scrubbing 'You Will Own Nothing and Be Happy' Post from Internet," News Punch, June 9, 2022, https://newspunch.com/wef-caught-scrubbing-you-will-own-nothing-and-be-happy-post-from-internet.

2. "8 Predictions for the World in 2030," World Economic Forum via Internet Archive, February 6, 2017, https://archive.org/details/8-predictions-for-the-world-in-2030.

3. Alex Kaschuta (@kaschuta), "Thread of massive life changes since becoming a mom ..." (thread), Twitter, January 7, 2022, 4:20 p.m., https://twitter.com/kaschuta/status/1479563542747623425.

4. Emma Green, "A World without Children," *The Atlantic*, September 20, 2021, https://www.theatlantic.com/politics/archive/2021/09/millennials-babies-climate-change/620032.

5. Tom Scocca, "Your Real Biological Clock Is You're Going to Die," Hmm Daily, October 18, 2018, https://hmmdaily.com/2018/10/18/your-real-biological-clock-is-youre-going-to-die.

Chapter 17: Lean in—to Parenthood

Epigraph: *Raising Arizona.*
1. Katherine Schaeffer, "Striking Findings from 2021," Pew Research, December 17, 2021, https://www.pewresearch.org/fact-tank/2021/12/17/striking-findings-from -2021.
2. Lyrics from the song "Let It Go" in the movie *Frozen.*
3. Spencer Klavan, *How to Save the West: Ancient Wisdom for 5 Modern Crises* (Washington, D.C.: Regnery, 2023).

Chapter 18: Respect Domestic Life

Epigraphs: Saint Mother Teresa of Calcutta (Mother Teresa) and Titus 2:3–5.
1. Carrie Gress and Noelle Mering, *Theology of Home: Finding the Eternal in the Everyday* (Gastonia, North Carolina: TAN Books, 2019).
2. Amanda Prestigiacomo, "Feminist Jill Filipovic Trashes Stay-at-Home Moms: Unambitious, Bad Example for Kids," Daily Wire, March 11, 2021, https://www .dailywire.com/news/feminist-jill-filipovic-trashes-stay-at-home-moms-unambitious -bad-example-for-kids.
3. Joanne L. Bagshaw, *The Feminist Handbook: Practical Tools to Resist Sexism and Dismantle the Patriarchy* (Oakland, California: New Harbinger Publications, Inc., 2019).
4. Honor Jones, "How I Demolished My Life," *The Atlantic*, December 28, 2021, https://www.theatlantic.com/family/archive/2021/12/divorce-parenting/621054.

Chapter 19: Have Faith

Epigraphs: Saint Teresa of Calcutta (Mother Teresa) and Saint Augustine.
1. Noelle Mering, *Awake, Not Woke: A Christian Response to the Cult of Progressive Ideology* (Gastonia, North Carolina: TAN Books, 2021).
2. Kenneth Clark's 1969 BBC documentary *Civilisation*, Episode 1.
3. Quote from Woody Allen's 1986 movie *Hannah and Her Sisters.*
4. Alexander Solzhenitsyn, "Godlessness: The First Step to the Gulag," Templeton Prize lecture at London, May 10, 1983, https://orthochristian.com/47643.html.

Chapter 20: Reclaim Your Parental Authority

Epigraphs: Ernst Jünger's *The Forest Passage* and *Schoolhouse Rock.*
1. Eileen AJ Connelly, "Angeli Gomez Says Uvalde, Texas Cops Threatened Her for Speaking Out," *New York Post*, June 4, 2022, https://nypost.com/2022/06/04/angeli -gomez-says-she-was-threatened-by-uvalde-texas-cops.
2. Alex Hammer, "Michigan Middle School Hides Trans Status of Student from Her Parents as Counsellor Warns Teachers Only to Use Child's 'Birth Name' and Pronoun 'He' during Parent Teacher Conferences," *Daily Mail*, June 10, 2022, https://www .dailymail.co.uk/news/article-10904273/Michigan-public-middle-school-hides -transgender-status-student-parents.html.
3. Taylor Lorenz, "Meet the Woman behind Libs of TikTok, Secretly Fueling the Right's Outrage Machine," *Washington Post*, April 19, 2022, https://www.washingtonpost .com/technology/2022/04/19/libs-of-tiktok-right-wing-media/?itid=hp_politics.

4. Marjorie Hernandez, "California Mother Claims Teachers Manipulated Her Daughter to Change Her Gender Identity," *New York Post*, January 24, 2022, https:// nypost.com/2022/01/24/mother-sues-teachers-for-brainwashing-student-to-identify -as-transgender.

5. Mairead Elordi, "Washington State Tells Teachers to Hide Student Gender Transitions From Parents," Daily Wire, February 24, 2022, https://www.dailywire .com/news/washington-state-tells-teachers-to-hide-student-gender-transitions-from -parents.

6. Jeremiah Poff, "Loudoun Schools Told Teachers to Keep Gender Transitions Secret from Parents," *Washington Examiner*, April 5, 2022, https://www .washingtonexaminer.com/restoring-america/equality-not-elitism/loudoun-schools -told-teachers-to-keep-gender-transitions-secret-from-parents.

7. Anders Hagstrom, "Kansas Teacher Wins $95,000 after Parents Pushed Her to 'Deceive' Parents about Student's Gender Identity," Fox News, September 1, 2022, https://www.foxnews.com/us/kansas-teacher-wins-school-pushed-her-deceive -parents-students-gender-identity.

8. Bradford Richardson, "Religious Parents Lose Custody of Transgender Teen for Refusing Hormone Treatment," *Washington Times*, February 20, 2018, https://www .washingtontimes.com/news/2018/feb/20/religious-parents-lose-custody-transgender -teen.

9. Abigail Shrier, "When the State Comes for Your Kids," *City Journal,* June 8, 2021, https://www.city-journal.org/transgender-identifying-adolescents-threats-to-parental -rights.

10. Tori Richards, "Mother of Trans Teenager: Los Angeles County Killed My Daughter," *Washington Examiner*, March 22, 2022, https://www .washingtonexaminer.com/news/mother-of-transgender-teenager-los-angeles-county -killed-my-daughter.

11. "Gender Nation," Los Angeles Unified School District, https://achieve.lausd.net/Page /17935.

12. Monica Chen, "'Lawn Boy' Is Pedophilic. Here's Why. (Explicit)," The Spring Magazine, January 28, 2022, https://thespringmagazine.com/2022/01/28/lawn-boy -is-pedophilic-heres-why-explicit.

13. Maria Wheeler, "Parents Horrified by Controversial Book 'Gender Queer'—'It's Child Pornography,'" *Independent Chronicle*, October 30, 2021, https:// independentchronicle.com/parents-horrified-by-controversial-book-gender-queer-its -child-pornography.

14. Justin Epps, "Gender Queer: A Memoir Is Latest Graphic Novel Facing School Controversy," Screenrant, November 23, 2021, https://screenrant.com/gender-queer -memoir-graphic-novel-school-library-controversy.

15. Hannah Grossman, "Kentucky School Official Compares Parent to Hitler in 'Gender Queer' Book Clash," *New York Post*, August 24, 2022, https://nypost.com/2022 /08/24/kentucky-educrat-defends-pornography-book-alludes-hitler.

16. Penny Starr, "85,000 Moms for Liberty Take on School Boards across the U.S: Our Mission Is to Save America by Empowering Parents," Breitbart, April 23, 2022, https://www.breitbart.com/politics/2022/04/23/85000-moms-for-liberty-take-on -school-boards-across-the-u-s-our-mission-is-to-save-america-by-empowering -parents.

17. Mark Moore, "Youngkin's Victory in Virginia Seen as Win for 'Parental Rights' in Education," *New York Post*, November 3, 2021, https://nypost.com/2021/11/03/glenn-youngkin-win-seen-as-victory-for-virginia-school-parents.

18. Rick Moran, "Virginia Parents Announce 'Not a Domestic Terrorist' March in Washington," PJ Media, October 17, 2021, https://pjmedia.com/news-and-politics/rick-moran/2021/10/17/virginia-parents-announce-not-domestic-terrorists-march-in-washington-n1524549.

19. "Study Shows Kids Who Are Homeschooled Could Miss out on Opportunity to be a Gay Communist," Babylon Bee, June 13, 2022, https://babylonbee.com/news/study-shows-kids-who-are-homeschooled-could-miss-out-on-opportunity-to-be-a-gay-communist.

20. Anonymous, "Teachers Unions," Open Secret, 2022, https://www.opensecrets.org/industries/indus.php?ind=L1300.

21. Website of the Institute for Catholic Liberal Education: https://catholicliberaleducation.org.

22. Hillsdale's K–12 program: https://www.k12.hillsdale.edu.

23. Recommended colleges through the Cardinal Newman Society: https://www.cardinalnewmansociety.org/college.

24. Steve Warren, "VA Judge Finds Transgender Teen Guilty of Sexual Assault in Loudoun County High School Girl's Bathroom Case," CBN News, October 26, 2021, https://www1.cbn.com/cbnnews/us/2021/october/va-judge-finds-transgender-teen-guilty-of-sexual-assault-in-loudoun-county-high-school-girls-bathroom-case.

25. Website of the Homeschool Legal Defense Association: https://www.hslda.org.

26. Cathy Duffy Reviews website: https://www.cathyduffyreviews.com.

27. Hamish Bowles, "Playtime with Harry Styles," *Vogue*, November 13, 2020, https://www.vogue.com/article/harry-styles-cover-december-2020; Jeremy O. Harris, "Lil Nas X Is in the Right Place at the Right Time," *GQ*, November 15, 2021, https://www.gq.com/story/lil-nas-x-musician-of-the-year-2021; Maura Hohman, "Madonna's Son David Banda Wears Sporty Red Dress during Night out with Mom," MSN, May 30, 2022, https://www.msn.com/en-us/music/celebrity/madonnas-son-david-banda-wears-sporty-red-dress-during-night-out-with-mom; Jelena Aska, "Boys in Dresses: 20 Celeb Parents Who Threw Gender Norms out the Window," Moms, January 22, 2019, https://www.moms.com/boys-in-dresses-20-celeb-parents-who-threw-gender-norms-out-the-window; Alex Gurley, "Jamie Lee Curtis' Daughter Ruby Made Her Red Carpet Debut after Publicly Coming Out as Transgender," Buzzfeed, October 13, 2022, https://www.buzzfeed.com/alexgurley/jamie-lee-curtis-ruby-red-carpet-halloween-ends.

28. Bonnie Phillips, "Poll: 21% of Generation Z Self-Identify as LGBTQ+," Connecticut Health Team, February 21, 2022, http://c-hit.org/2022/02/21/poll-21-of-generation-z-self-identify-as-lgbtq.

29. "Gender Dysphoria and ASD," Autism Research Institute, Spring 2016, https://www.autism.org/gender-dysphoria-autism.

30. Victor Kiprop, "How Many Animals Are There in the World?" WorldAtlas, March 20, 2018, https://www.worldatlas.com/articles/how-many-animals-are-there-in-the-world.html.

31. "Child Welfare," Youth.gov, n.d., via https://youth.gov/youth-topics/lgbtq-youth/child-welfare.

Chapter 21: Live Happily Ever After
Epigraph: Saint Joan of Arc.

Chapter 22: The Nuclear Option
Epigraph: J. R. R. Tolkien's *Lord of the Rings*.
1. Audrey Conklin, "Fentanyl Overdoses Become No. 1 Cause of Death among US Adults, Ages 18–45: 'A National Emergency,'" Fox News, December 16, 2021, https://www.foxnews.com/us/fentanyl-overdoses-leading-cause-death-adults.

Chapter 23: Saving the Planet—One Family at a Time
Epigraph: Willa Cather.
1. Grover J. "Russ" Whitehurst, "Why the Federal Government Should Subsidize Childcare and How to Pay for It," Brookings Institute, March 9, 2017, https://www.brookings.edu/research/why-the-federal-government-should-subsidize-childcare-and-how-to-pay-for-it.
2. Alfred, Lord Tennyson, *Ulysses*.

Index